Fundamentalism at Home and Abroad

Analysis and Pastoral Responses

Gerald A. Arbuckle, SM

M
G

A Michael Glazier Book

LITURGICAL PRESS
Collegeville, Minnesota

www.litpress.org

A Michael Glazier Book published by Liturgical Press

Cover design by Monica Bokinskie. Cover image courtesy of Thinkstock.

Library of Congress Cataloging-in-Publication Data

Names: Arbuckle, Gerald A., author.
Title: Fundamentalism at home and abroad : analysis and pastoral responses /
    Gerald A. Arbuckle, SM.
Description: Collegeville, Minnesota : Liturgical Press, 2017. | "A Michael
    Glazier book." | Includes bibliographical references and index. |
    Description based on print version record and CIP data provided by
    publisher; resource not viewed.
Identifiers: LCCN 2016052529 (print) | LCCN 2017010513 (ebook) |
    ISBN 9780814684498 (ebook) | ISBN 9780814684245
Subjects: LCSH: Violence—Religious aspects—Catholic Church. |
    Fundamentalism. | Religious fundamentalism. | Catholic Church—
    Doctrines.
Classification: LCC BX1795.V56 (ebook) | LCC BX1795.V56 A725 2017 (print)
    | DDC 200.9/051—dc23
LC record available at https://lccn.loc.gov/2016052529

For

Pope Francis—

A challenger of fundamentalism

By the Same Author

The Chatham Islands in Perspective: A Socio-Economic Review
(Wellington: Hicks Smith, 1971)

Strategies for Growth in Religious Life (Alba House / St Pauls Publications, 1987)

Out of Chaos: Refounding Religious Congregations
(Paulist Press / Geoffrey Chapman, 1988) (USA Catholic Press Award)

Earthing the Gospel: An Inculturation Handbook for Pastoral Workers
(Geoffrey Chapman / Orbis Books / St Pauls Publications, 1990)
(USA Catholic Press Award)

Grieving for Change: A Spirituality for Refounding Gospel Communities
(Geoffrey Chapman / St Pauls Publications, 1991)

Refounding the Church: Dissent for Leadership
(Geoffrey Chapman / Orbis Books / St Pauls Publications, 1993)
(USA Catholic Press Award)

From Chaos to Mission: Refounding Religious Life Formation
(Geoffrey Chapman / Liturgical Press, 1996)

Healthcare Ministry: Refounding the Mission in Tumultuous Times
(Liturgical Press, 2000) (USA Catholic Press Award)

Dealing with Bullies: A Gospel Response to the Social Disease of Adult Bullying
(St Pauls Publications, 2003)

Confronting the Demon: A Gospel Response to Adult Bullying
(Liturgical Press, 2003)

Violence, Society, and the Church: A Cultural Approach (Liturgical Press, 2004)

Crafting Catholic Identity in Postmodern Australia
(Catholic Health Australia, 2007)

A 'Preferential Option for the Poor':
Application to Catholic Health and Aged Care Ministries in Australia
(Catholic Health Australia, 2008)

Laughing with God: Humor, Culture, and Transformation (Liturgical Press, 2008)

Culture, Inculturation, and Theologians: A Postmodern Critique
(Liturgical Press, 2010)

Catholic Identity or Identities? Refounding Ministries in Chaotic Times
(Liturgical Press, 2013) (USA Association of Catholic Publishers Award, 2014)

Humanizing Healthcare Reforms (Jessica Kingsley, 2013)

The Francis Factor and the People of God: New Life for the Church
(Orbis Books, 2015)

Intentional Faith Communities in Catholic Education: Challenge and Response
(St Pauls Publications, 2016)

Contents

Acknowledgments

This book is a sequel to *Violence, Society, and the Church: A Cultural Approach* (Liturgical Press, 2004) in which I briefly referred to fundamentalist movements. Since then I have spoken to many people about fundamentalism in our modern world and their comments have been of significant help in shaping this book. In particular, I wish to thank Hans Christoffersen, editorial director at Liturgical Press, Anthony Maher, Brian Cummings, SM, and Jan Snijders, SM, but I alone am responsible for the book's shortcomings. My thanks to Robert Ellsberg, Orbis Books, for permission to use and adapt material from chapter 6 of my book *The Francis Factor and the People of God* (2015). The community of Campion Hall, Oxford University, once more provided a hospitable atmosphere in which to plan and commence the research for this book.

Introduction

Fundamentalism is a sickness that is in all religions. . . . Religious fundamentalism is not religious, because it lacks God. It is idolatry, like idolatry of money.[1]

—Pope Francis

A person who thinks only about building walls, wherever they may be, and not building bridges, is not Christian. This is not the gospel.[2]

—Pope Francis

Fundamentalism in its multiple different expressions is a global reality. It is today vigorously alive at home and abroad and Pope Francis is right: "Fundamentalism is a sickness that is in all religions." Fundamentalists are people who are outraged when they see the world around them abandoning the religious values they hold dear. They are fighting back in the cause of what they consider truth. They are reacting to threats to their identity in militant ways, whether in the use of words and ideas or ballots or, in extreme cases, bullets and bombs. The responses to these threats are simplistic and those who question them are branded intolerantly as enemies of the truth.

[1] Pope Francis, comments to journalists on the plane returning from Africa, November 30, 2015. www.lifesitenews.com/news/pope-francis-attacks-funda mentalist-catholics-dismisses-condom-ban-as-unimp (accessed March 26, 2016).

[2] Pope Francis reacting to presidential candidate Donald Trump's declaration that a wall must be built to keep Mexicans from entering the United States. ww.edition.cnn.com/2016/02/18/politics/pope-francis-trump-christian-wall (accessed July 28, 2016).

This book is intended to assist people in all walks of life who are increasingly puzzled and concerned about contemporary fundamentalist attitudes and movements and who wish to understand their nature: why they arise and how they themselves can constructively respond to them.

The disturbing fact is that every individual and culture is capable of fundamentalist attitudes and actions. Christ once used an incident to help his disciples understand how they themselves had unconsciously become trapped in fundamentalist thinking. The disciple John said to Jesus, "Teacher, we saw someone casting out demons in your name, and we tried to stop him because he was not following us" (Mark 9:38). John, like a good fundamentalist, thought that only the disciples could have such noble power, but Jesus is quick to respond: "Do not stop him; for no one who does a deed of power in my name will be able soon afterward to speak evil of me. Whoever is not against us is for us" (Mark 9:39-40).

Fundamentalism: Response to Cultural Trauma

Fundamentalist movements are most active and culturally apparent whenever there are periods in which radical political, social, or economic changes cause cultural trauma in a nation as a whole or in smaller institutions or communities.[3] These changes threaten to destroy cherished personal and cultural identities and esteemed moral values. Widespread feelings of bewilderment and frustration result. People then desperately search for quick explanations of what is happening and ways out of their overwhelming confusion. The atmosphere is ripe for the unsophisticated solutions offered by fundamentalist populist and charismatic leaders.

For most people fundamentalism in the modern world has become synonymous with a radical form of Islam. Islamic fundamentalism has supplanted communism as the ghost haunting the Western consciousness—a ghost that looms ever larger following the terrorist

---

[3] See Nancy T. Ammerman, "North American Protestant Fundamentalism," in *Fundamentalisms Observed*, ed. Martin E. Marty and R. Scott Appleby (Chicago: University of Chicago Press, 1991), 56.

attacks on New York and Washington, DC, on September 11, 2001;[4] the recent appalling terrorist assaults in London, Paris, Brussels, Orlando, Istanbul, Baghdad, Dhaka, Nice, and Saint-Etienne-du-Rouvray; and the ostensible incapacity of the Western powers to destroy the shadowy, furtive, and murderous al-Qaeda network and the public butchering cruelty of the Islamic State (ISIS). In the Middle East, Islamic extremists are slaughtering fellow Muslims and persecuting, even murdering, Christians and other minorities. The West, however, has yet to realize that the military response may provide interim solutions to terrorism but in the long term they intensify religious anger and inspire more fanaticism. We first need to understand the multifaceted political, economic, and social causes of Islamic fundamentalism.

Yet Islamic fundamentalist movements have received a disproportionate amount of media attention in recent times due to the physically violent nature of their actions.[5] This is unfortunate because fundamentalism in many shapes and forms is very much present in our Western societies though most often less observably physically violent. Yes, fundamentalist economic, political, nationalistic, religious movements are aplenty in the West. Right-wing, populist, anti-immigrant movements are on the rise in Europe, the United States, Australia, and elsewhere. We in the West have to stop thinking of ourselves as "angelic and that Islam is the Devil incarnate."[6] After all, the Western world has significantly contributed to the rise of Islamic fundamentalism.

Fundamentalism and Religion

Religion has resurfaced as a global social force in the rise of fundamentalist movements. Since religion is an important basis of moral certainty, people frequently and passionately turn to it as a motivating

---

[4] See Stuart Sim, *Fundamentalist World: The New Dark Age of Dogma* (Cambridge: Icon Books, 2004), 3–12.

[5] See David C. Rapoport, "Comparing Militant Fundamentalist Movements," in *Fundamentalisms and the State*, ed. Martin E. Marty and R. Scott Appleby (Chicago: University of Chicago Press, 1993), 445–46.

[6] Chris Barker, *Cultural Studies: Theory and Practice* (London: Sage, 2012), 274.

force in shaping identity, values, and movements. Religion has commonly been defined as "the belief in Spiritual Beings,"[7] but we must broaden our understanding of religion.[8] Thomas Luckmann defines religion *functionally* as "the capacity of the human organism to transcend its biological nature through the construction of objective, morally binding and all-embracing universes of meaning."[9] Thus religion offers people a means of interpreting the world in which they live. Understood in this sense, people can change any belief into a religion.[10] "For where your treasure is, there your heart is also" (Matt 6:21). For example, people can become so attached to free market economics, that is, markets unrestrained by government interference, or to nationalism that they turn them into religions. They become idolatrous, a substitute for God, as Pope Francis has said. In a number of countries, where traditional institutional religions are weakly present, civil religions powerfully influence the development and maintenance of fundamentalist groupings, as we can see, for example, in the United States (see chapter 3).

The Wisdom of "Not-Knowing"

Fundamentalists have an exaggerated and haunting desire for absolute certainties in areas of life where this may not be immediately possible. Pope Francis warns Christians against this fundamentalist thinking: "If the Christian . . . [wants] everything clear and safe, they will find nothing. . . . Those who today always look for disciplinarian solutions, those who long for an exaggerated doctrinal 'security,' those who stubbornly try to recover a past that no longer exists—they

---

[7] Edward B. Tylor, "Notes on the Modern Survival of Ancient Amulets against the Evil Eye," *Journal of the Royal Anthropological Institute of Great Britain and Ireland*, no. 19 (1890): 54.

[8] See Andre Droogers, "Defining Religion: A Social Science Approach," in *The Oxford Handbook of the Sociology of Religion*, ed. Peter B. Clarke (New York: Oxford University Press, 2011), 263–79.

[9] Thomas Luckmann, cited by Arthur L. Greil and Lynn Davidman, "Religion and Identity," in *Sociology and Religion*, ed. James A. Beckford and N. J. Demerath (London: Sage, 2007), 554.

[10] See Bhikhu Parekh, *A New Politics of Identity: Political Principles for an Interdependent World* (Basingstoke: Palgrave Macmillan, 2008), 140.

have a static and inward-directed view of things." [11] In fact, in the mystery of God's plan, the way to true wisdom is also through submitting to the darkness of "not-knowing." For example, let us reflect on the story of Job. His secure world suddenly disintegrated when he lost everything: wealth, health, and family. He confesses the chaos and his inability to understand the reasons for his afflictions: "so I am allotted months of emptiness, and nights of misery are apportioned to me" (Job 7:3). He refuses to accept the simplistic answers his friends give for his afflictions. Yet while sitting in the gloom of the "not-knowing," Job discovers an energizing hope beyond human imagination: "For I know that my Redeemer lives, and that at last he will stand upon the earth" (Job 19:25).

Likewise, Jesus in his agony in Gethsemane acknowledges his own "not-knowing" in the midst of an incredible darkness of soul. What is the Father asking of him? Why do his chosen disciples not understand his agony of darkness and offer him consolation? Jesus rests in the chaos of desolation and discovers newness and confidence in response to his prayer: "The hour has come. . . . Get up, let us be going. See, my betrayer is at hand" (Mark 14:41-42). Not surprisingly, therefore, the advice of the fourteenth-century author of *The Cloud of Unknowing* remains just as relevant for today's Christian when we are tempted to find simplistic solutions to the world's present turmoils: "So set yourself to rest in this darkness as long as you can, always crying out after him whom you love. For if you are to experience him or to see him at all, insofar as it is possible here, it must be in this cloud." [12]

Structure and Overview

There are six chapters in this book. Chapter 1, "Defining Fundamentalism in Our Contemporary World," offers several definitions of fundamentalism and describes the various characteristics of

[11] Pope Francis, www.americamagazine.org/pope-interview (accessed October 1, 2013).

[12] Anonymous, *The Cloud of Unknowing*, ed. James Walsh (New York: Paulist Press, 1981), 121.

fundamentalist movements; examples of different types of fundamentalism are reviewed and explained. Chapter 2, "Understanding the Cultures of Fundamentalism," evaluates the critical role of mythologies in the development of identities in fundamentalist movements. For example, although the two major branches of Islam, Sunni and Shia, accept the Prophet Muhammad as the founder of Islam, they developed different founding mythologies that significantly affect how they relate to each other, often in a conflicted manner. Thus, second-generation Muslim immigrants to Western countries frequently find themselves in a mythological no-man's-land, making them susceptible to the voices of radical leaders.

The third chapter, "From Cultural Trauma to Fundamentalism: The Role of Religion," explains how cultural crises and their resulting trauma can be catalysts for the rise of fundamentalist movements. When people feel they do not control their lives or share in the benefits of globalization, they strike out, often in fundamentalist ways. The power of religion as a motivating and justifying force in these movements is analyzed with examples from different parts of the world: Japan, Iran, Australia, and the United States. One section of the chapter is devoted to the history and role of civil religion in fundamentalist groups in the United States.

Chapter 4, "Catholic Fundamentalism: An Analysis," highlights the factors that led to the cultural trauma following Vatican II. Once the secure mythology of any culture is questioned or undermined, cultural trauma with all its de-energizing and confusing emotions commonly results. The culture of the Catholic Church is no exception, as Pope Francis has pointed out: "We Catholics have some [fundamentalists]—and not some, many—who believe in the absolute truth and go ahead dirtying the other with calumny, with disinformation, and doing evil."[13] Particular Catholic fundamentalist movements are listed and examined.

Chapter 5, "Islamic Fundamentalism: Responding to Cultural Trauma," offers an overview of the historical rise of schisms within the Islamic faith. Contemporary Islamic fundamentalist movements like Wahhabism, Muslim Brotherhood, Al-Qaeda, Taliban, and ISIS are examined in their political and social contexts. There is also a

---

[13] Pope Francis (November 30, 2015).

focus on the recent development of the suicide-martyrdom phenomenon among Islamic fundamentalists. Chapter 6, "Fundamentalism: Pastoral Responses," explains various ways we can respond constructively and pastorally to fundamentalism at home and abroad.

Anthropological Lens

Pope Francis frequently reminds us that as evangelizers we must be aware of the complexities of contemporary cultures. We need, he writes, the professional insights of social scientists.[14] Hence, while I draw on the multidisciplinary research of many authors, this book looks at fundamentalism through the particular lens of cultural anthropology. No previous knowledge of this academic discipline is required. The major mission and contribution of anthropology has long been, and continues to be, to enhance our awareness of the power and reality of culture in people's lives. Fundamentalist movements are cultures and the study of cultures is the special task of cultural anthropology. The unique task of anthropologists is to unearth what is hidden from the consciousness of people about how they culturally interact with one another.[15] Sociologists mainly concentrate on the present, while anthropologists recognize that an understanding of the past is necessary to better grasp what is happening in the present: "Remember the days of old, consider the years long past; ask your father, and he will inform you; your elders, and they will tell you" (Deut 32:7).

To be an anthropologist one needs to be "humbly curious, ready to question, criticize, explore, and challenge ideas, the status quo, to look at the world with fresh eyes and think about the classification systems and cultural patterns that we take for granted."[16] Cultural anthropology has been called by anthropologist Raymond Firth "an inquisitive, challenging, uncomfortable discipline, questioning established positions . . . peering into underlying interests, if not

---

[14] See Pope Francis, Encyclical *The Joy of the Gospel* (*Evangelii Gaudium*) (Strathfield, Australia: St. Pauls, 2013), par. 40.

[15] See Gerald A. Arbuckle, *Earthing the Gospel: An Inculturation Handbook for Pastoral Workers* (Maryknoll, NY: Orbis Books, 1990), 1.

[16] Gillian Tett, *The Silo Effect* (London: Little Brown, 2015), 48.

destroying fictions and empty phrases . . . at least exposing them."[17] Anthropologists are preoccupied with the gap between rhetoric and reality; they "can never take anything entirely at face value, but are compelled to constantly ask: *why.*"[18] Hopefully readers may find that the following pages testify to the accuracy of this description.

[17] Raymond Firth, "Engagement and Detachment: Reflections on Applying Social Anthropology to Social Affairs," *Human Organization* 40 (1981): 200. Anthropologist Richard T. Antoun writes that anthropologists should aim for empathy rather than sympathy in their research, that is, to feel with the people they are studying but all the time trying to avoid "judging their 'truth' or 'falsity,'" but this "does not imply that one has to surrender one's own beliefs, but it does imply that one has to appreciate other perspectives." *Understanding Fundamentalism: Christian, Islamic, and Jewish Movements* (Lanham: Rowman and Littlefield, 2008), vii.

[18] Tett, *The Silo Effect*, 251, 50.

Chapter 1

Defining Fundamentalism in Our Contemporary World

[Fundamentalists fear that their identity is threatened in a world
that is] stifling, chaotic and dangerously out of control.[1]

—Oliver McTernan

Fundamentalism has become a religion of rage.[2]

—Karen Armstrong

Key Points

- Change in the meaning of "fundamentalism"
- Definitions of contemporary fundamentalism
- General characteristics of fundamentalist movements
- Types of fundamentalist movements
- The aims and strategies of contemporary terrorism

---

[1] Oliver McTernan, *Violence in God's Name: Religion in an Age of Conflict* (London: Darton, Longman and Todd, 2003), 35.

[2] Karen Armstrong, *The Battle for God: Fundamentalism in Judaism, Christianity and Islam* (London: HarperCollins, 2001), 216.

Since the word "fundamentalism" evokes strong global and local emotional reactions the purpose of this introductory chapter is simply to summarize the ways in which significant authors define the term. We will see that despite the differences in the definitions there are nonetheless a number of strikingly similar emphases, which will be explained. Subsequent chapters, for example, those that describe Catholic and Islamic fundamentalist movements, build on the clarifications and insights of this foundational chapter.

The word "fundamentalist" was first used in 1920 to describe supporters of *The Fundamentalists*, a version of essential beliefs published and distributed by two devout Christian brothers, Lyman and Milton Stewart, who were also Californian oil millionaires.[3] Protestant theologians were deeply concerned that liberalism would undermine religious faith, so they detailed five principals, or "fundamentals" of faith, that must be adhered to: "1. the inerrancy of Scripture, 2. the Virgin Birth of Christ, 3. his substitutionary atonement, 4. his bodily resurrection, and 5. the authenticity of his miracles."[4] For adherents, the Scriptures were held to be literally true, "the absolute transcript of God's mind."[5] Those who accepted these principles were called fundamentalists.

The term "fundamentalist" did not originally have a pejorative connotation, but this has radically changed. It now has a disparaging quality. It has been extended to define people who adhere to fundamentalism, that is, an historically recurring negative tendency particularly within Judeo-Christian-Muslim traditions, which occurs as an authoritarian religious reaction particularly to the fears of anomie or chaos evoked by postmodernism and globalization. But the term has also become the metaphor of choice to describe radical forms of nationalism and other forms of ideological expression, for example, market economics. Fundamentalism today, however, "is not a single monolithic phenomenon or movement,"[6] and individuals will have

---

[3] See George Marsden, *Fundamentalism and American Culture: The Shaping of Twentieth Century Evangelicalism, 1870–1925* (New York: Oxford University Press, 1980), 118–19.

[4] Ibid., 117.

[5] James M. Gray, cited by Marsden, *Fundamentalism and American Culture*, 122.

[6] Jack D. Eller, *Introducing Anthropology of Religion*, 2nd ed. (London: Routledge, 2015), 285.

different levels of commitment to the goals of a particular movement.[7] Moreover, because no one definition satisfies all authors, it is preferable to list a number of definitions. Readers will notice that while the authors stress some common themes they also differ in their emphasis on specific points.

> [Fundamentalists fear their identity is threatened in a world that is] stifling, chaotic and dangerously out of control.[8]

> An aggressive and marginalized religious movement which, in reaction to the perceived threat of modernity seeks to return its home religion and nation to traditional orthodox principles, values, and texts through the co-option of the central executive and legislative power of both the religion itself and the modern national state.[9]

> [Fundamentalisms] are embattled forms of spirituality, which have emerged as a response to a perceived crisis. They are engaged in a conflict with enemies whose secularist policies and beliefs seem inimical to religion itself.[10]

> Movements of religiously inspired reaction to aspects of global processes of modernization and secularization . . . the struggle to assert or reassert the norms and beliefs of "traditional religion" in the public order.[11]

> [Fundamentalism is] a specifiable pattern of religious militancy by which self-styled true believers attempt to arrest the erosion of religious identity, fortify the borders of the religious community, and create viable alternatives to secular structures and processes.[12]

---

[7] See Rhys H. Williams, "Movements Dynamics and Social Change: Transforming Fundamentalist Ideology and Organizations," in *Accounting for Fundamentalisms*, ed. Martin E. Marty and R. Scott Appleby (Chicago: University of Chicago Press, 1994), 824.

[8] McTernan, *Violence in God's Name*, 35.

[9] Patrick Arnold, "The Rise of Catholic Fundamentalism," *America* (April 11, 1987): 298.

[10] Armstrong, *The Battle for God*, xi.

[11] Martin Marty and R. Scott Appleby, eds., *Fundamentalisms and the State* (Chicago: University of Chicago Press, 1993), 2, 5.

[12] R. Scott Appleby, *The Ambivalence of the Sacred: Religion, Violence, and Reconciliation* (Oxford: Rowman and Littlefield, 2000), 86.

[Fundamentalism is] a proclamation of reclaimed authority over a sacred tradition which is to be reinstated as an antidote for a society perceived to have strayed from its cultural moorings.[13]

[Fundamentalism argues] that society has become degenerate because it has lost its moral moorings, that this is caused by the corrosive climate of secularism and scepticism brought about by globalization and rationalist influences, and that it can only be regenerated by reconstituting it on religious foundations.[14]

[Fundamentalisms] are radical revisions of the past provoked by changes that threaten the continuity of the tradition. . . . The goal of resistance is to re-create the excitement and commitment of the original believing community.[15]

Fundamentalism is best understood as both a religious response to the marginalization of religion and an accompanying pattern of religious activism with certain specifiable characteristics.[16]

Fundamentalism . . . is a distinct phenomenon whose various components hang together well enough to give it a clear identity. It arises in a society with a deep and pervasive sense of disorientation and degeneration, and consists in using the institutions of the state to reconstitute it on a religious basis.[17]

Broadly understood, fundamentalism includes a literalized doctrine, religious or political, enclosed upon itself by the immutable words of the holy books. The doctrine is rendered both sacred in the name of a past of perfect harmony that never was, and the center of a quest for collective revitalization . . . a reaction to the fear of chaos.[18]

James Hunter calls fundamentalism a form of "organized anger" and says that all fundamentalist groups "share the deep and worri-

[13] Anson Shupe, "Religious Fundamentalism," in *The Oxford Handbook of The Sociology of Religion*, ed. Peter B. Clarke (Oxford: Oxford University Press, 2009), 481.

[14] Bhikhu Parekh, *A New Politics of Identity: Political Principles for an Interdependent World* (London: Palgrave Macmillan, 2008), 142.

[15] Steve Bruce, *Fundamentalism* (Cambridge: Polity, 2000), 14.

[16] Appleby, *The Ambivalence of the Sacred*, 101.

[17] Bhikhu Parekh, *A New Politics of Identity: Political Principles for an Interdependent World* (London: Palgrave Macmillan, 2008), 148.

[18] Robert Jay Lifton, *The Protean Self: Human Resilience in an Age of Fragmentation* (New York: BasicBooks, 1993), 10–11.

some sense that history has gone awry,"[19] the consequence of modernity and postmodernity. Perhaps a more relevant word than anger is rage. Richard Antoun also emphasizes the emotional aspect of fundamentalism: it is "an orientation to the world, both cognitive and affective. The affective, or emotional, orientation indicates outrage and protest against (and also fear of) change and against a certain ideological orientation, the orientation of modernism."[20]

Al-Qaeda and Rage

Islamic fundamentalism is ultimately motivated by outrage at the past and present impact of Western political and military domination, as well as cultural and economic dominance, which has come as the consequence of Western imperialism.[21] The present head of al-Qaeda, Ayman al-Zawahiri (see chapter 5), following the appalling London bombings of July 7, 2005, has said, "You made rivers of blood in our countries, so we blew up volcanoes of rage in yours."[22]

Fundamentalist movements are *for* something, that is they are concerned to advocate what are perceived to be crucial elements of their belief, "the worldview *and the truth* for practitioners."[23] Evangelicals insist that the Bible must be taken literally: it is a totally truthful manuscript and the source of knowledge for daily living, and Christians who deny this have been seduced by secular values. Islam makes similar claims for the Koran just as Marxists rely on the texts of Marx and Lenin; and Scientologists focus uncritically on the writings of their founder L. Ron Hubbard.[24] Fundamentalism is also *against* something, that is, fundamentalists believe they are fighting

---

[19] James Hunter, cited in *The Fundamentalist Phenomenon*, ed. Norman J. Cohen (Grand Rapids, MI: Eerdmans, 1990), 46.

[20] Richard T. Antoun, *Understanding Fundamentalism: Christian, Islamic, and Jewish Movements* (Walnut Creek, CA: AltaMira Press, 2001), 3.

[21] See ibid., 18.

[22] Ayman al-Zawahiri, cited by John Kelsay, *Arguing the Just War in Islam* (London: Harvard University Press, 2007), 204.

[23] Jack D. Eller, *Introducting Anthropology*, 281.

[24] See Lawrence Wright, *Going Clear: Scientology, Hollywood, and the Prison of Belief* (New York: Knopf, 2012).

in the cause of what they consider truth. Fundamentalists react to threats to their identity in aggressive ways, whether in the use of words and ideas or ballots or, in extreme incidents, bullets and bombs.[25]

Fundamentalist Movements: General Qualities

In light of these various descriptions of fundamentalism we are now able to list and briefly explain the qualities that are commonly found in fundamentalist movements. Since not all movements give the same degree of emphasis to individual qualities, subsequent chapters will further explain the significance of these characteristics.[26]

Religion: The Driving Force

There is a global religious resurgence and it is very significantly influencing the rise of contemporary fundamentalism.[27] For example, devotees of the Islamic religious rebirth vehemently demand that Islamic law and morality be forcefully followed. Without doubt, fundamentalists of all kinds are passionately committed to their religious beliefs. In fact, the ardent concern to preserve their religious heritage is *the* driving force motivating fundamentalists. The dramatic development of present-day, religiously inspired fundamentalist movements, however, indicate stressful changes in culture and society. In times of cultural trauma religion "in particular becomes the core set of values around which resentments cluster. Nationalism becomes a frequent accessory after the fact."[28] Judith Nagata correctly

---

[25] Fundamentalism is not the same as conservatism. The latter fulfils a necessary and constructive purpose because it is concerned with preserving a community's historical legacy, especially in times of cultural change. It encourages a cautious approach to change in order to preserve important values for society. See Patrick Arnold, *America* (April 11, 1987).

[26] Malise Ruthven speaks of "family resemblances" in fundamentalist movements despite their differences. *Fundamentalism: A Very Short Introduction* (Oxford: Oxford University Press, 2007), 6.

[27] See Monica D. Toft, Daniel Philpott, and Timothy S. Shah, *God's Century: Resurgent Religion and Global Politics* (New York: Norton, 2009), 1–19.

[28] Shupe, "Religious Fundamentalism," 487.

noted, however, that fundamentalism, which originally referred to institutional religion but is now a "metaphor of choice" being applied "to an everwidening range of ideas and behaviors,"[29] including nationalism, ethnicity, language, politics, and even the market and environment. Thus, as will be clarified in chapter 3, it is necessary to broaden the traditional notion of religion. For example, nationalism, dogmatic commitment to a particular type of economics or politics—these can become functionally religions for their adherents.

Crisis of Identity

Fundamentalists achieve power in times of actual or perceived cultural trauma: "The sense of danger may be keyed to oppressive and threatening social, economic, or political conditions, but the ensuing crisis is perceived as a *crisis of identity* by those who fear extinction as a people or absorption into an overarching syncretistic culture to such a degree that their distinctiveness is undermined in the rush to homogeneity."[30] They see "themselves as lacking, or barely hanging on to, cultural hegemony, underdogs in a constantly threatening secularist world that wishes them at worst destroyed and at best rendered irrelevant."[31] They feel their identity is under siege.

Decontextualized Scripture

Indian sociologist, T. K. Oommem, defined fundamentalism as "text without context."[32] This means that religious writings, which were always composed "in a particular historical, cultural context, are decontextualized and held to be applicable without consideration

---

[29] Judith Nagata, "Beyond Theology: Toward an Anthropology of 'Fundamentalism,'" *American Anthropologist* 103, no. 2 (2001): 481. See also Stuart Sim, *Fundamentalist World: The New Dark Age of Dogma* (Cambridge: Icon Books, 2004), 12.

[30] Martin Marty and R. Scott Appleby, "Conclusion: An Interim Report on a Hypothetical Family," in *Fundamentalisms Observed*, ed. Martin E. Marty and R. Scott Appleby (Chicago: University of Chicago Press, 1991), 822–23.

[31] Ibid., 486.

[32] Cited by Kevin J. Christiano, William H. Swatos, and Peter Kivisto, *Sociology of Religion: Contemporary Developments* (Walnut Creek, CA: Altamira Press, 2002), 249.

to local circumstances; all other competing texts are rejected as having any corresponding claim to truth."[33] Fundamentalists, unlike the average conservative believers aiming to retain the whole of tradition, choose instead only those texts and events in history that support their belief of a "divine" command to act in a prejudiced manner.[34]

That is, fundamentalists actively cling to a particular faith that defines it in an absolutist and literalist fashion.[35] They choose particular statements from the sacred texts of their religion or tradition to legitimate their actions[36] and ignore other important points; they "treat the religious tradition as a resource to be retrieved selectively, and applied situationally, in competition with secularism."[37] Islamic fundamentalists selectively choose and interpret passages from the Koran to legitimate their violent actions (see chapter 5). Among Catholic fundamentalists there is also a highly selective approach to what fundamentalists think pertains to the Church's teaching (see chapter 4). Statements on ecclesiastical authority, private sexuality, or incidental issues are obsessively emphasized, but the papal or episcopal pronouncements on social questions are ignored or considered matters for debate only. After the publication of St. John Paul II's encyclical letter *Sollicitudo Rei Socialis* in 1987, and in the 1986 Catholic Bishops' (USA) Pastoral Letter on the US economy, which criticized liberal capitalism and Marxist collectivism, fundamentalists like Richard Neuhaus and Michael Novak denounced these documents for containing, they asserted, a swing toward, or acceptance of, leftist/Marxist thinking. These critics believe that the capitalist system must be defended as the only authentic method to protect the freedom of the people.[38]

[33] Christiano, Swatos, and Kivisto, *Sociology of Religion*, 250.

[34] See McTernan, *Violence in God's Name*, 34.

[35] See John O. Voll, "Fundamentalism," in *The Oxford Encyclopedia of the Modern Islamic World Vol. II*, ed. John L. Esposito (New York: Oxford University Press, 1995), 32–34.

[36] See Parekh, *A New Politics of Identity*, 149.

[37] Appleby, *The Ambivalence of the Sacred*, 90.

[38] See Gregory Baum, "Neo-Conservative Critics of the Churches," in *Neo-Conservatism: Social and Religious Phenomenon*, ed. Gregory Baum (New York: Seabury Press, 1981), 43–50. See also Gerald A. Arbuckle, *Violence, Society, and the Church: A Cultural Approach* (Collegeville, MN: Liturgical Press, 2004), 208–9.

Simplistic Solutions

Fundamentalism is a reaction to uncertainty, to the "excess of openness and choice" that accompanies modern life; it is a way of setting boundaries, an 'anti-hermeneutic' "[39] that claims to end uncertainty by definitively terminating all arguments over interpretation. Their interpretation of the problems of the world and their solutions admit of no ambiguity. For example, Donald Trump, when seeking the presidential nomination, repeatedly gave simplistic solutions to complex political and economic problems facing the United States. His naïve responses reassured his audiences that he could quickly resolve their anxieties. Trump scoffed at anyone who dared to question him. How different Trump's behavior has been from that Abraham Lincoln! At President Lincoln's Second Inauguration in 1865, and as victory for the Union was close at hand, he refused in his short speech to be trapped in the current Evangelical fundamentalist discourse. Many of his listeners wanted him to declare that God was surely on the side of the Union. They believed that weighty political issues could be simplistically construed into good or evil: the Union is good and the Confederates are evil. Lincoln, recognizing the complexity of the tragic civil war, did not agree: "let us judge not that we be not judged."[40]

Symbolic Identities

Fundamentalists are boundary-setters. They are adept in symbolically marking themselves off from others by distinctive dress, customs, and conduct,[41] for example, earlocks, which are locks of hair worn in front of each ear by Hasidic and Yemenite Jewish males in accordance with the biblical prohibition against clipping the hair at the temples (Lev 19:27), and beards for orthodox Muslims. The symbols indicate rigid purity/impurity divisions between insiders and outsiders (see chapter 2).

[39] Nagata, "Beyond Theology," 481.

[40] Abraham Lincoln, cited by David Goldfield, *America Aflame: How the Civil War Created a Nation* (New York: Bloomsbury Press, 2011), 357.

[41] See Martin E. Marty and R. Scott Appleby, "Introduction," in *Fundamentalisms and the State: Remaking Polities, Economics, and Militance,* ed. Martin E. Martin and R. Scott Appleby (Chicago: University of Chicago Press, 1993), 4.

Militant Intolerance of Dissent

The fundamentalist pattern of militancy starts as a reaction to what is thought to be the infiltration of the religious community by secular or religious outsiders.[42] Fundamentalists believe their task is to make history accord with the orthodox principles of their traditional or civic religion. They are absolutely and intolerably certain they are right, demanding submission to "a totalitarian mindset which brooks of no opposition . . . an uncritical adherence to the creed."[43]

Their ideological intolerance of dissent[44] is expressed in various forms of physical, verbal, or political violence. For example, verbal violence is particularly evident in the Donald Trump campaign; his supporters feel so deeply threatened by dissenting voices that they encourage Trump to speak harshly of his opponents.[45] Violence "is the tool of consolidation in the name of reinstating a sacred regime. . . . It has become a highly probable, not just optional, strategy of choice."[46] George Marsden concludes that fundamentalist militancy typically happens when supporters of a formerly dominant religious culture feel endangered by cultural changes in society.[47] Not all fundamentalist movements are violent, but because they are intolerant of dissent, they have the potential to be violent. Terrorism is the worst form of violence; terrorists feel the need to express their violence through killing to "prove" their authentic commitment to the values they stand for.[48] We see this tragically evident today among the followers of al-Qaeda and ISIS.

Political Aims

Fundamentalists seek to dominate the central executive and legislative power either through democratic processes, for example, the Tea Party in the United States, *or* recourse to extreme violence, for

---

[42] See Appleby, *The Ambivalence of the Sacred*, 87.

[43] Sim, *Fundamentalist World*, 12.

[44] See discussion by Henry Olsen and Dante J. Scala, *The Four Faces of the Republican Party* (London: Palgrave Macmillan, 2016), 22–28.

[45] Ibid., 134–42.

[46] Sim, *Fundamentalist World*, 486.

[47] See Marsden, *Fundamentalism*, 240–41.

[48] See Stuart W. Twemlow, Frank C. Sacco, and George Hough, "A Socio-Psychoanalytic Perspective on Group Dynamics, Cults and Terrorism," *Socio-Analysis* 5 (2003): 57–78.

example, the Islamic revolution in Iran and the United States' intervention in Nicaragua in the 1980s. The US-backed coup in Chile in 1973 that resulted in the ascent of General Augusto Pinochet is also an example of intervening in the political process.[49] In Afghanistan, as in many other parts of the Islamic world, Islamists believe that "a truly Islamic society could be established only through an 'Islamic State,' which presupposes a revolution . . . to implement Sharia."[50] Fundamentalists frequently refuse to separate politics and religion; thus they seek political power to confront, capture, and use the state. They reject the authority of interpretive tradition, but nonetheless read sacred text in light of political objectives, seeking in the process to challenge and reconstruct the planet. Fundamentalist movements tend to draw their following from professional and working classes, although disproportionate numbers tend to come from among the young, educated, un-, or underemployed males.[51]

Conspiracy-Oriented

It is not unusual for fundamentalists to develop paranoid fantasies about the dangers their movements face. They see enemies where there are no enemies. For example, when Sunni fundamentalists occupied the sacred Kabah in Mecca, Khomeini in Iran denounced the sacrilege and blamed Israel and the United States.[52] Following Vatican II, Catholic fundamentalists alleged that a number of high-ranking bishops were closet Freemasons committed to destroying the Catholic Church.[53] Timothy McVeigh, the convicted bomber of the Oklahoma City federal building, firmly believed that the government was conspiring to undermine people's liberty.[54] Islamic fundamentalists commonly scapegoat activities, individuals, or groups of

---

[49] See Noam Chomsky, *September 11* (Crows Nest, NSW: Allen and Unwin, 2001), 23–26, 43–54, and *Who Rules the World* (London: Hamish Hamilton, 2016), 75. Pinochet proceeded to execute some three thousand people. See Kenneth Roth, "A Case Against America," *The New York Review of Books* (June 9, 2016): 4.

[50] Oliver Roy, "Has Islamism a Future in Afghanistan?" in *Fundamentalism Reborn? Afghanistan and the Taliban*, ed. William Maley (London: Hurst, 2001), 199.

[51] See Appleby, *The Ambivalence of the Sacred*, 87–88.

[52] See Armstrong, *The Battle for God*, 322.

[53] See William D. Dinges, "Roman Catholic Traditionalism in the United States," in *Fundamentalists Observed*, ed. Marty and Appleby, 89–91.

[54] See Appleby, *The Ambivalence of the Sacred*, 167–68.

people for the breakdown of so-called orthodoxy, for example, card playing, video machines, Hollywood, and feminists demanding equality. Modernity and postmodernity in their many forms are the "Great Satan." In a reaction to the modernization and secularization that the mullahs believe have corrupted the purity of Islam, Ayatollah Khomeini outlawed as "satanic" modern and postmodern activities that symbolized corruption in Iran.

The Trump technique involved confiding in angry followers that they are victims of a plot to be resolved through Trump's leadership. In his narrative, conspiring foreign governments have outsmarted a self-interested political elite in Washington that preys on the generosity of Americans. He enlivened a long tradition of conspiracy thinking in America like, for example, the anti-Catholic, racist Know-Nothing Party in the mid-nineteenth century.[55] Similarly, in 1849 a fundamentalist anti-Catholic new group, the Order of the Star-Spangled Banner, was formed in New York to promote nativist candidates for elected positions. Among other things, they wanted to restrict the political rights of foreigners and their sons unless they had been educated in American schools. One order editor wrote, "We can have no peace in this country until the Catholics are exterminated."[56]

Nostalgia for a Utopian Past

Nostalgia for an unreal utopian past is often a powerful factor in fundamentalist movements. People from "America to Austria" yearn for "a return to some hazily-remembered golden era before globalisation, offering jobs for life, upward mobility, and shared traditional values."[57] For Americans the golden era is the mid-twentieth century. For Republicans, this meant a world of secure marriages, deference for authority, and economic innovation; for Democrats, it was a period in history when a young person could leave school and go immediately into well-paid employment, assured of a pension and healthcare benefits. Forgotten in this nostalgia is that America and the world at large lived in fear of a nuclear disaster and a vast number of citizens

---

[55] See *The Economist* (July 25, 2016): 31; see also David Goldfield, *America Aflame: How the Civil War Created a Nation* (New York: Bloomsbury Press, 2011), 90.

[56] Quoted by Goldfield, *America Aflame*, 90.

[57] *The Economist* (July 16, 2016): 31.

lacked civil rights.[58] For older Catholic fundamentalists there is nostalgia for the security and power structures of the 1950s, and many vocations to religious life and the priesthood. Overlooked in this pre–Vatican II period is *inter alia* the inward-looking nature of the church's theology, its neglect of its calling of mission to a world in flux.

Skilled Use of the Media

Ironically fundamentalists often combine a commitment to a selectively imagined utopian past with a ready ability to use modern technology to propagate their beliefs. Fundamentalists, while rejecting modernity and postmodernity, can engage the most sophisticated Western methods of communication and force to spread their message, for example, the "Islamic State (i.e., ISIS) has been able to consolidate its ideological catchment with unprecedented stealth and efficiency. . . . By clever use of social media and digital film making it has eclipsed the counterweight mainstream media to broadcast its bloody deeds, its triumphs and its caliphate."[59] Following the tragic bombing in Brussels on March 22, 2016, ISIS effectively seized control of the world's media to circulate their admission of responsibility.[60]

Millenarian

Some fundamentalist movements are millenarian, for example, Islamic State followers expect the imminent and miraculous transformation of this world by supernatural means. Millenarianism is also an integral part of Western history. The Jewish religion centers on the hope of a future golden age and, of course, Christianity has reinforced this expectation with its teaching about Christ's second coming. The Christian hope of the age of perfect justice and love has

[58] See ibid., 66; Yuval Levin, *The Fractured Republic: Renewing America's Social Contract in the Age of Individualism* (New York: Basic Books, 2016).

[59] Abdel Bari Atwan, *Islamic State: The Digital Caliphate* (London: Saqi Books, 2015), 212.

[60] See Charlie Winter, "ISIS is Using the Media Against Itself," www.theatlantic.com/international/archive/2016/03/isis-propaganda-brussels/47 (accessed March 3, 2016).

over the centuries undergone many fundamentalist aberrations, especially in times of profound cultural and political trauma.[61] Marx and Lenin evolved the most powerful such aberration in recent centuries, with its emphasis on the utopian age of the classless society. Some Christians are called premillennialists, which means they believe the Day of Judgement will divide the saved from the damned *before* the expected thousand-year reign of the righteous; likewise it is common for Islamic fundamentalists to believe that the destruction of the world, the Armageddon, will precede the Day of Judgement. Others are postmillennialists, they believe Judgement Day will follow the millennium. In times of economic or social crisis the more pessimistic premillennialist view tends to prevail.

Great Britain: Brexit

A small but significant group of evangelical Protestants rejoiced when Britain voted to leave the European Union. For them the European Union was the evil empire of Babylon. They quoted from the Revelation to John: "Then I heard another voice from heaven saying: 'Come out of her, my people, so that you do not take part in her sins, and so that my do not share in her plagues' " (18:4). For them the Union represented the Antichrist, an "imposter whose appearance is a harbinger of the final battle before all earthly things come to an end."[62]

Most millenarian movements are also messianic. That is, salvation is to be directed by a human agent of the divine and the followers must commit themselves totally to this person and their teachings. For example, the Rastafarian fundamentalist movement, which was possibly the fastest-growing millenarian sect of the 1970s and 1980s, is a mixture of African and Christian concepts, drawing support from

---

[61] See Norman Cohn, *The Pursuit of the Millennium: Revolutionary Millenarians and Mystical Anarchists of the Middle Ages* (New York: Oxford University Press, 1974); Malcolm Bull, ed., *Apocalypse Theory* (Oxford: Blackwell, 1995).

[62] "For Hard-line Protestants, Leaving Europe is a Matter of Eschatology," www.economist.com/blogs/erasmus/2016/06/ulster-evangelicals-brexit (accessed July 5, 2016).

dispossessed blacks yearning for a sense of self-pride and identity.[63] Its followers dream of a black messiah who will lead them back to Africa and a fullness of identity. It first appeared among people who are poor in Jamaica in the early 1930s and spread among black people in Britain, parts of Europe, Australasia, and North America. Many campaigning politicians also messianically promise their followers the return to an utopian past.

Sects and Cults [64]

Fundamentalists tend to form themselves into sects and/or cults (see chapter 2). They believe that people in an established religious or political group have lost their original truth and zeal, so their task is to purify the group. If resistance is too great, fundamentalists may form a schismatic assembly. Fundamentalism in the Western world has generally tended to be confined to the middle class, whereas in India and Israel its mix of nationalism and religion has attracted people from all sections of society. In Islamic countries fundamentalism has appeared as the mouthpiece for the oppressed and marginalized and as the scourge of the decadent and materialist West.[65] Bruce Lawrence points out that contemporary Islamic fundamentalists sects represent "a delayed reaction to the psychological hegemony of European rule." Hence, they have tended to arise in the majority of Muslim countries only "after they had become independent nation-states, that is, in most instances, after World War II."[66]

Charismatic Leaders

A typical fundamentalist leader is a populist, homophobic, charismatic, authoritarian man who likes to bully.[67] The charismatic leader

[63] See Gary D. Bouma and Rod Ling, "Religious Diversity," in *The Oxford Handbook of the Sociology of Religion*, ed. Clarke, 511.

[64] The distinction between a sect and a cult is explained in chapter 2.

[65] See Walter Laqueur, *The New Terrorism: Fanaticism and the Arms of Mass Destruction* (London: Phoenix Press, 2001), 154.

[66] Bruce B. Lawrence, *Defenders of God: The Fundamentalist Revolt Against the Modern Age* (San Francisco: Harper and Row, 1989), 100–101.

[67] See Marty and Appleby, "Conclusion," in *Fundamentalisms Observed*, 830. Mark Juergensmeyer notes that "Virtually all radical religious movements of the

is considered to be a prophet who must be faithfully obeyed *without question* for the common good, like, for example, Winston Churchill during World War II, or Hitler, Stalin, and the Ayatollah Khomeini. Followers see in their leaders all the qualities for which they yearn.[68] The fundamentalist leader browbeats followers into submission without permitting dialogue like a schoolyard bully.[69] Further, most fundamentalists need a trustworthy person to interpret sacred texts and traditions in view of his or her political aims. Moreover, fundamentalist movements generally have a low level of political institutionalisation in which the resulting vacuum is filled by a cult of personality. For example, in communist systems cults of personality usually emerge when the party is weakly institutionalised: Mao Zedong in China, Ho Chi Minh in Vietnam, and Kim Il-Sung in North Korea.[70] Personality cults are also found in the Muslim world, with the most obvious example being the Ayatollah Khomeini in Iran.[71]

America: McCarthyism

During the late 1940s and early 1950s the identity of the American nation was under severe threat. People had become fearful of communism, thanks to the Soviet Union's acquisition of the atomic bomb, the Communist Party's ascendancy in China, the outbreak of the Korean war with the supporting involvement of China and Russia, while the alleged Soviet spy Alger Hiss had been convicted of perjury. "Midwesterners, long suspicious of the East Coast's foreign-policy class, and Catholics, bitter over Moscow's domination of their co-religionists in Eastern Europe, were particularly receptive to claims that Washing-

---

final decades of the twentieth century have had a homophobic twist." *The Terror in the Mind of God: The Global Rise of Religious Violence* (Berkeley: University of California Press, 2001), 202. The pattern is the same in contemporary Islamic fundamentalist movements.

[68] See Archie Brown, *The Myth of the Strong Leader: Political Leadership in the Modern Age* (London: Bodley Head, 2014), 6–7.

[69] See Gerald A. Arbuckle, *Confronting the Demon: A Gospel Response to Adult Bullying* (Collegeville, MN: Liturgical Press, 2003), 17–38.

[70] See Graeme Gill, "Personality Cult, Political Culture and Party Structure," *Studies in Comparative Communism* 17, no. 2 (1984): 111–21.

[71] See William Maley, "Interpreting the Taliban," *Fundamentalism Reborn?*, 18.

ton had sold out America to the Soviet Union."[72] This provided an apt environment for the rise of the charismatic and demagogic anti-communist Republican senator Joseph McCarthy (1908–1957). On February 9, 1950, in an address to the Women's club of Wheeling, West Virginia, he claimed without proof that 205 members of the Communist Party were working in the State Department, Washington, DC: "I have in my hand a list of 205 that were known to the secretary of state as being members of the Communist Party and are still making and shaping the policy of the State Department." This began a national political witch-hunt that lasted almost five years during which many innocent people suffered as scapegoats. He described a war between "two diametrically opposed ideologies . . . our Christian world and the atheistic Communist world" in which "our only powerful potential enemy has sent men to invade our shores . . . because of the traitorous actions of those who have been treated so well by this nation."[73]

It is true that there already existed a fear of domestic subversion cultivated by the FBI Director, J. Edgar Hoover, and the established House of Representatives Un-American Activities Committee (HUAC). But McCarthy's "skill' was his charismatic and bullying ability to take advantage of the existing low morale of the American people and ruthlessly hound mainly innocent citizens.[74] Six and a half million Americans were checked for loyalty. Hundreds lost their jobs and thousands more their reputations during the anti-communist witch-hunt. Accused officials benefited from neither judge nor jury—they were without legal recourse.[75] Finally the Senate voted in late 1954 to censure him for conduct unbecoming a senator.

[72] Peter Beinart, "The New McCarthyism of Donald Trump," *The Atlantic*, www .the atlantic.com/politics/archives/2015/07/donald-trump-joseph-mccarthy /399056/ (accessed March 3, 2016).

[73] Joseph McCarthy, "Address at Wheeling" (February 9, 1950), www.history matters.gmu.edu/d/6456 (accessed January 1, 2016).

[74] For a critical analysis McCarthyism, see Ted Morgan, *Reds: McCarthyism in Twentieth-Century America* (New York: Random House, 2003); and Mark S. Massa, *Catholics and American Culture* (New York: Crossroad, 1999), 57–81, 226–27.

[75] See Terry H. Anderson, *The Movement and The Sixties* (New York: Oxford University Press, 1995), 3–20.

China: The Cultural Revolution

Mao Zedong, Chairman of the Communist Party of China, initiated this socio-political movement in 1966 and sought to end it three years later. He alleged that bourgeois elements had subverted the government and society at large with the aim of restoring capitalism. Millions of people died in the Cultural Revolution. One of his motives was a "utopian one. He appeared to believe that people power, no matter how bloody, could turn China into a socialist paradise."[76]

Neocapitalism[77]

Economic rationalism (or market capitalism, market economics, neoclassical capitalism, market liberalism) as a quasi-religious faith has become a powerful mythology in the emerging New Right political culture. Its proponents, like Margaret Thatcher and Ronald Reagan, permit no dissent. Profit is the sole measure of value and the economic profession serves as its priesthood.[78] It exalts unabashed greed, conspicuous consumption, and the widespread abandonment of civic virtue. It is based on the premise that anti-environmentalism, sustained economic growth, free markets, and economic globalization will benefit all. Neocapitalism wants lower taxation and reduced government spending and privatized government services.[79] Businesses employ this mythology to oppose taxes, regulations, and other government measures that constrain their activities, while they simultaneously lobby for government hand-outs as they did, for example, during the financial crisis. Social and religious conservatives are reassured by its absolutism and emphasis on individual autonomy.[80] Contained in the fundamentalist mythology of the economic rationalist culture (its operational wing is called the "new managerialism") is the Social Darwinist

[76] *The Economist* (May 14, 2016): 69; see also Frank Dikotter, *The Cultural Revolution: A People's History 1962-1976* (London: Bloomsbury, 2016).

[77] See Arbuckle, *Violence, Society*, 170–71.

[78] See David C. Korten, *When Corporations Rule the World* (London: Earthscan, 1996), 103.

[79] Ibid.

[80] See www.longviewinstitute.org/projects/marketfundamentalism (accessed March 1, 2016).

assumption that the poor are poor through their own fault and that welfare services worsen poverty so they must be reduced. Economic rationalists also aim to change public institutions into pseudo-businesses,[81] for example healthcare is considered an economic commodity and must be subject to the principles of supply and demand of the marketplace. They tragically have, as Pope Francis says, "a blind confidence in technical changes."[82]

The dramatic rise of for-profit hospitals in the United States and Australia in recent years is an example of this economic ideology: financial return to shareholders, not the quality of services to patients, is the primary aim of healthcare services. The planners of healthcare reforms in many countries such as Britain, Australia, and New Zealand, are now more commonly economists or accountants, not people with a background in healthcare delivery.[83] Pope Francis describes the impact that economic rationalists have on the environment: They "doggedly uphold the myth of progress and tell us that ecological problems will solve themselves simply with the application of new technology and without any need for ethical considerations or deep change."[84] Economic fundamentalists have conspiracy theories too, for example, they believe that people like President Obama who advocate government assistance for those without private insurance are conspiring to undermine effective economic rationalist policies. Like other fundamentalists, economic rationalists distrust history.[85] As John Saul comments in the 1995 Canadian Massey Lectures, "we have come to so forget our own history that we are now compliantly acting in a suicidal manner, believing that economics can lead—where in the past it has

[81] See Cris Shore and Susan Wright, "Coercive Accountability," in *Audit Cultures*, ed. Marilyn Strathern (London: Routledge, 2000), 63–85.

[82] Pope Francis, Encyclical *On Care for Our Common Home* (Laudato si') (London: St Pauls Publications, 2015), par.14.

[83] See Michael Pusey, *Economic Rationalism in Canberra: A Nation Building State Changes Its Mind* (Cambridge: Cambridge University Press, 1992), 59–75; and Robert Blank, *New Zealand Health Policy: A Comparative Study* (Auckland: Oxford University Press, 1994), 134; Gerald A. Arbuckle, *Humanizing Healthcare Reforms* (London: Jessica Kingsley, 2013), 90–101.

[84] Pope Francis, *On Care*, par. 60.

[85] For a critique of market economics see David Harvey, *A Brief History of Neoliberalism* (New York: Oxford University Press, 2005), 152–206.

always failed to do so. . . . We have fallen in love with an old ideology that has never paid off in the past."[86]

"Siloism" in Healthcare

"Siloism" is a fundamentalist attitude to be found in some organizations that occurs when departments or groups of people refuse to share information with other departments or groups.[87] The medical profession is very divided, with minimal corporate identity and little feeling of belonging to the healthcare systems they serve, like, for example, the National Health Service in Britain. Different specialities have their own colleges: in Britain there are the Royal College of General Practitioners and the Royal College of Physicians. These subcultures are "medical silos,"[88] that is, groups of specialists who keep to themselves, are overly sensitive to the importance of hierarchical status, and discourage the sharing of information with other professional silos that they distrust.[89] This is fundamentalism: their jealously guarded individualism is inimical to the development of team-work[90] across the silo barriers, between themselves and nurses, and between themselves and managers. Because of this individualism, the degree of mutual support among medical clinicians is poor. Little wonder that many experience high levels of unaddressed stress and "seem to deny the effect of stress and fatigue on performance,"[91] further discouraging them from openly acknowledging and discussing their medical errors with their colleagues. For this reason, the Garling Report into the acute care services of the public hospitals in New South Wales, Australia, concluded that a "new model of teamwork will be

[86] John R. Saul, *The Unconscious Civilization* (Toronto: Penguin, 1997), 123.

[87] See Gillian Tett, *The Silo Effect* (London: Little Brown, 2015); Arbuckle, *Humanizing*, 112.

[88] See Peter Garling, *Final Report of Inquiry: Acute Care Services in NSW Public Hospitals– Overview* (Sydney: NSW Government, 2008), 4.

[89] See Henry Mintzberg, *Managing* (Harlow: Pearson, 2009), 169–70.

[90] See J. Bryan Sexton, Eric J. Thomas, and Robert L. Helmreich, "Error, Stress, and Teamwork in Medicine and Aviation: Cross Sectional Surveys," *British Medical Journal* 320 (March 18, 2000): 745–49.

[91] Ibid., 745.

required to replace the old individual and independent 'silos' of professional care."[92]

Types of Fundamentalism

Separatists

Some fundamentalist groups, for example, Mennonites, Amish, and Hutterites in the United States, Hijra wa Takfir in Egypt, and Hasidic Jews in Israel and the United States, aim to separate from the wider society to greater or lesser degrees for fear that their traditions will be undermined. The Amish people, whose religious roots go back to the Anabaptists, must obey the regulations of their church, the rules that embrace most aspects of daily life, including dress styles and bans or restrictions on the use of power-line electricity, telephones, automobiles. In their lifestyle and religion they see themselves as the authentic heirs of Christianity. The Amish, however, "have lived with industrialized America for centuries, [and] they have moderated its influence on their personal lives, their families, their communities, and their values."[93]

Activists

As noted above, active fundamentalists seek to infiltrate and use the executive and legislative power of a political authority either through democratic processes or recourse to extreme violence. Two types of activists, therefore, can be identified: democratic and violent fundamentalists.

"Democratic" Fundamentalists[94]

"Democratic" fundamentalists, for example, the Moral Majority or Tea Party in the United States, are prepared to work through democratic political and legislative processes to achieve their goals. However, many American fundamentalists who romanticize their

---

[92] See Garland, *Overview*, 4.
[93] See John A. Hostetler, *Amish Society*, 4th ed. (Johns Hopkins Press, 1993), 3.
[94] See Arbuckle, *Violence, Society*, 197–98.

republic's democratically minded founders often vigorously support foreign wars and even terrorism in order to impose or protect American values of democracy, for example, the American covert and overt interventions in Nicaragua, Guatemala, and El Salvador.

In the United States, fundamentalist Evangelicals were traditionally seen as "anti-political soul-savers who waited for the second coming of Christ, wanted to live decent lives and be left alone except when they would convert others."[95] This dramatically changed in 1979 when Evangelical fundamentalist Jerry Falwell recognized that "in spite of everything we are going to turn the nation back to God . . . the national crisis [is] growing quickly out of hand."[96] The cultural traumas that catalysed Falwell and his followers into action during the 1960s and 1970s were:

1. The Expressive Revolution in the 1960s radically challenged traditional American values, and the conventional understanding of family and society: the rise of feminists, "hippies," anti-institutional behaviour of students in universities, anti-war activists, secular humanism,[97] even gays and atheists.[98]

2. In 1962 the US Supreme Court declared school-sponsored prayer unconstitutional. Public outrage was immediate and widespread. For millions of Americans, the Court had "kicked God out of the schools" to use a phrase common at the time.[99]

3. The US Supreme Court decision in 1973 to legalize abortion rights.

4. The struggle over the Equal Rights Amendment beginning in the late 1970s.

5. The military defeat in Vietnam.

---

[95] Martin E. Marty, "The New Christian Right," *The Tablet* (April 23, 1988): 462. The theme of fundamentalism in the United States is more fully explained in chapter 3.

[96] Jerry Falwell, *Strength for the Journey* (New York: Simon and Schuster, 1987), 358.

[97] Timothy L. Haye, a virulent anti-Catholic evangelical preacher and writer, detailed these issues in his book, *The Battle for the Mind: A Subtle Warfare* (Old Tappan, NJ: Fleming H. Revell, 1980).

[98] See Eller, *Introducting Anthropology*, 289.

[99] See Steven K. Green, *The Bible, the School, and the Constitution: The Clash that Shaped Modern Church-State Doctrine* (New York: Oxford University Press, 2012).

As political theorist William E. Connolly writes, these events helped to consolidate the Southern Baptist Church during the 1960s "through a common feeling of betrayal and resentment."[100] Falwell believed that "the moral degeneration of America had gone so far as to demand an active response."[101] Organized political action was seen as the only way to achieve the traditional aims of fundamentalist Evangelicals. Thus Falwell formed the Moral Majority dominated by traditional Protestant fundamentalists, but at the same time the movement attracted Protestants of all kinds, Jews, and Roman Catholics. Its platform was sharply focused: pro-life, pro-traditional family/morality, pro-American, pro-national defense, and pro-Israel. Falwell believed that God entered actively in history. Events such as the AIDS scourge were God's judgement against America's sexual immorality, and that America's choice as a Christian nation, and indeed its very existence as a Christian nation, depended on Christian political activism.

> Christians such as these understand history as a struggle between Christ and anti-Christ, through which the latter seeks the erosion of American sovereignty particularly through international financial regimes, leading to a violent struggle in which they will be called upon to bear witness and from whose horrible devastation they will be delivered. America's power, they contend, depends on the Christianization of the nation-state.[102]

Other fundamentalist movements followed. Christian Reconstructionism, a radical Calvinist Presbyterian movement, aimed to institute a religious society and religious government in the United States: it advocated "ultra-conservative economic theory and calls for a theocracy that would include a reinstitution of Old Testament civil

---

[100] William E. Connolly, *The Ethos of Pluralization* (Minneapolis: University of Minnesota Press, 1995), 110.

[101] Steve Bruce, *The Rise and Fall of the New Christian Right: Conservative Protestant Politics in America 1978–1988* (Oxford: Clarendon Press, 1990), 17.

[102] Roger Friedland, "The Constitution of Religious Political Violence: Institution, Culture, and Power," in *The Oxford Handbook of Cultural Sociology*, ed. Jeffrey C. Alexander, Ronald N. Jacobs, and Philip Smith (New York: Oxford University Press, 2012), 451.

law."[103] One of the founders of the movement, Rousas J. Rushdoony (1916–2001), declared: "The law is therefore the law for Christian man and Christian society. Nothing is more deadly or more derelict than the notion that the Christian is at liberty with respect to the kind of law he can have."[104] By "law," Rushdoony meant the ancient Hebrew law. Reconstructionists, despite their radical economic and theological roots, helped to develop early critiques of secular humanism that deeply influenced the emergence of the Christian Right.[105] At the same time, the New Right,[106] emerged in the political scene as an ideological political movement with distinctive values, a strong emphasis on maintaining the American way of life and America as the world's capitalist superpower, and with clear-cut answers to contemporary social and economic challenges. The Moral Majority supported the New Right, giving it religious legitimation; the revitalized conservative ideology was pronounced to be God's will for America. It became a religious and patriotic duty to support laissez-faire market capitalism and decreasing aid to the poor.

Senator Barry Goldwater, an early leader of the New Right, confidently declared that "extremism in defense of liberty is no vice."[107] The presidencies of Ronald Reagan and George H. W. Bush were deeply influenced by this political philosophy, for example, in their secret weapon sales to Iran and their undeclared war on the Nicaraguan government. President Bush, when he pardoned officials for their involvement in these activities, claimed that they had been inspired by patriotism that made their deeds pure.[108] Niccolo

---

[103] See Marsden, *Fundamentalism and American Culture*, 248. Reconstructionists demanded that women return to their ancient inferior status; the banning of any religion that refuses to accept Mosaic law; the criminalization of abortion, punishable by death. The movement has almost ceased to exist.

[104] Rousas J. Rushdoony, *The Institutes of Biblical Law* (Nutley, NJ: Craig Press, 1973), 8–9. The movement has declined.

[105] See Marsden, *Fundamentalism and American Culture*, 248.

[106] See Bruce, *The Rise and Fall*, 25–49; Pippa Norris, *Radical Right: Voters and Parties in the Electoral Market* (New York: Cambridge University Press, 2005), 72–73.

[107] Barry Goldwater, cited by Theodore White, *The Making of the President 1964* (Toronto: Signet Books, 1965), 261.

[108] See S. L. Sutherland, "Retrospection and Democracy," in *Cruelty and Deception: The Controversy over Dirty Hands in Politics*, ed. Paul Rynard and David P. Shugarman (Orchard Park: Broadway Press, 2000), 218–20.

Machiavelli, the fifteenth-century political philosopher, would have agreed with this political fundamentalism: "You should adopt whole-heartedly the policy most likely to save your homeland's life and preserve her liberty."[109]

Violent Fundamentalists[110]

Violence can range from manipulating facts and truth to physical assault on people and property. Fundamentalists who commit them-selves to physical violence believe they are living in exceptional times that threaten their beliefs, and this permits them to suspend normal requirements of their religion, such as respect for human rights.

Christian Identity Movement[111]

The Christian Identity Movement is a loose association of diverse groups including: Anglo-Israelites, white supremacists, John Birch Society, some militia movements, and the Ku Klux Klan.[112] Its membership claims that Caucasian people are the spiritual and literal descendants of the ten lost tribes of ancient Israel; for some members blacks and Jews are the greatest threats to white Christian civilization.[113] These virulent racist groups, which are prone to physical violence, have in common the belief that the end of the world is to be preceded by a cleansing war, during which all non-whites will be killed. Predictions differ about the signs of Christ's second coming and Armageddon. They include race war or a Jewish-supported United Nations takeover of the United States. Many followers advocate physical struggle against what they describe as the forces of evil, for example, Timothy McVeigh, the convicted bomber of the

---

[109] Niccollo Machiavelli, *Selected Political Writings*, ed. David Wooton (Indianapolis: Hackett, 1994), 215.

[110] See Arbuckle, *Violence, Society*, 198–200.

[111] See Juergensmeyer, *Terror in the Mind*, 30–35.

[112] See Keller, *Introducing Anthropology*, 291–92.

[113] See Nancy T. Ammerman, "North American Protestant Fundamentalism," in *Fundamentalisms Observed*, ed. Marty and Appleby, 35.

> Oklahoma City federal building in 1995, was influenced by
> Christianity Identity thinking.[114]

Toward the end of his life, Ayatollah Khomeini explained why
Islamic fundamentalists are able to use terrorism even though this is
normally against Shia beliefs. He claimed that since the very survival
of the Islamic Republic of Iran was threatened, parts of the Islamic
law were to be bypassed in favor of the supreme jurist's (i.e.,
Khomeini's) decisions.[115] In this way he justified the establishment
of state terrorism in Iran and his support of Islamic terrorists in other
parts of the world. Likewise, the fundamentalist Taliban in Afghanistan, and "pro-lifers" who kill abortionists or blow-up medical buildings, all claim that exceptional times demand ruthless responses.
White supremacists in the United States, who destroy property and
kill, assert that the laws of the land no longer apply to them, for
governments are corrupt and evil. God is calling them to be his special
prophets and all previous laws are suspended.

Fundamentalist sects, impassioned by desires for apocalyptic redemption, either turn their violence on themselves, for example,
when nine hundred died in a mass suicide-murder spree in Jonestown,
Guyana, in 1978; or they turn their violence on the innocent. The
examples of the latter are many: Aum Shinriko in his subway attack
in Tokyo in 1995,[116] the terrorist bomb attack in downtown Oklahoma
City in the same year by Timothy McVeigh and Terry Nichols, and
the terrorist assaults in New York and Washington, DC, and the 2016
terrorist offensives in London, Paris, and Brussels.

Terrorism is "criminal behavior designed primarily to generate
fear in the community, or a substantial segment of it, for political
purposes."[117] In addition to the political purpose the motivation of
terrorist organizations may be nationalist (e.g., Basque Nationalism,

[114] See Juergensmeyer, *Terror in the Mind*, 31. Religious terrorists are obsessed
with an apocalyptic vision and claim that they are fighting in the final battle
against evil: "a cosmic conflict, which allows for no compromise as [they] are
dealing with demonic forces, and which permits [them] to dispense with everyday moral norms." McTernan, *Violence in God's Name*, 34.

[115] See Appleby, *The Ambivalence of the Sacred*, 89.

[116] Ibid., 104.

[117] Chalmers Johnson, *Revolutionary Change* (Stanford: Stanford University
Press, 1982), 154.

the Irish Republican Army), ideological (e.g., the Red Brigade in Italy in the 1970s and early 1980s), or religious (e.g., the Taliban, Hamas, Hezbollah—the Lebanese Shia movement). All of these movements have one thing in common, namely, to create enough fear in the population to force governments to make desired political changes.[118] Terrorists see themselves as the victims for they fear that their identity is endangered in a world that is "stifling, chaotic and dangerously out of control."[119] Terrorist movements have existed for centuries sometimes involving thousands of members, but in recent times, there has been a radical change in their character. Now, given the increasing availability of sophisticated technology, a small group or individuals, difficult to infiltrate or detect, can terrorize thousands and even millions of people.[120]

Political terrorists aim at instrumental and primary targets. For example, in the case of the attacks on the World Trade Center in New York and the Pentagon, the primary target was the people of the United States, while the instrumental target was the people trapped in the planes and buildings. Today terrorism has become a ritual filled with powerful symbolism for local and global audiences. It has at least three strategic objectives:

1. To gain publicity for the terrorists' cause;

2. To show that a government cannot protect the people;

3. To force the government to overreact by turning the situation into a military one with the aim of so restricting a population's freedom so that people will eventually turn against their government and impel it to submit to the terrorists' demands.[121]

With the availability of weapons of mass destruction and advanced technology, terrorists can now imagine a further aim, namely to paralyze and undermine a nation's economic infra-structure, even the global economy itself. The dramatic terrorist attacks in the United

---

[118] See Bruce Hoffman, *Inside Terrorism* (New York: Colombia University Press, 1998), 43.

[119] Juergensmeyer, *Terror in the Mind*, 190.

[120] See Laqueur, *The New Terrorism*, 4–6; Jason Burke, *The New Threat: The Past, Present, and Future of Islamic Militancy* (New York: The New Press, 2015), 25–16, 233–34.

[121] See Johnson, *Revolutionary Change*, 156–68.

States, France, England, Belgium and elsewhere illustrate that this aim is now a real possibility.

Summary Points

- We are seeing something akin to a global epidemic of fundamentalism both religious and political.[122]

- All individuals, cultures, and religions have a capacity for fundamentalism.

- Fundamentalism is a form of organized institutional or civic religious anger in reaction to secularization, political changes, and globalization; it often intimidates or coerces people to achieve its ends.

- There are two broad categories of fundamentalist movements: separatist—they aim to separate from the wider society; activist—they seek to co-opt the executive and legislative power either through democratic processes or recourse to extreme violence.

- Violent fundamentalists, for example, Islamic extremists, use terrorism for their purposes. They claim that the killing of innocent people is justified because there is no other way to protect their sacred heritage, which they believe is in danger of annihilation.

Discussion Questions

1. What points in this chapter do you feel relate to your experience? Why?

2. Pope Francis writes, "Where profits alone count, there can be no thinking about the rhythms of nature, its phases of decay and regeneration, or the complexity of ecosystems which may be gravely upset by human intervention."[123] What form of funda-

---

[122] See Lifton, *The Protean Self*, 11, 160–89.
[123] Pope Francis, *On Care*, par. 139.

mentalism do you think he is speaking about? Do you identify signs of it in your country?

3. Many millions of innocent people are being displaced through violent fundamentalist movements, becoming unskilled migrants and refugees. What can you do to make these injustices better known in your community?

4. Often fundamentalist movements are generated because Christians have not welcomed the stranger into their midst. What are you, your school, and/or parish doing to make strangers welcome?

Chapter 2

Understanding the Cultures of Fundamentalism: The Power of Mythology

Fundamentalisms are . . . not only cultural but *cultures* or *potential cultures*. And . . . fundamentalisms are doing what must be done: they are offering not only a model *of* the world but a model *for* the world, one in which "ethos" and "worldview" match.[1]

—Jack D. Eller

The myth is a drama which begins as a historical event and takes on its special character as a way of orienting people to reality . . . whereas empirical language refers to objective facts, *myth refers to the quintessence of human experience, the meaning and significance of human life.* The whole person speaks to *us*, not just to the brain.[2]

—Rollo May

Key Points

- The necessity of ultimate meaning

- How myths can be used to distort history

- Myth and identity crisis in home-grown terrorists

[1] Jack D. Eller, *Introducing Anthropology of Religion*, 2nd ed. (Abingdon: Routledge, 2015), 285. Italics in original.
[2] Rollo May, *The Cry for Myth* (New York: Delta, 1991), 26. Italics in original.

- Relationship between ethnicity and fundamentalism
- Fundamentalist rituals for establishing boundaries of identity
- Various types of fundamentalism

Sayyid Qutb (1906–1966) was an Egyptian writer, educator, and religious leader. His writings about Islam, and especially his call for a violent revolution to establish an Islamic state and society, has significantly influenced the contemporary Islamic resurgence movements. Karen Armstrong, an expert on the development and persistence of fundamentalism, writes "Qutb saw history mythically. He did not approach the Prophet's life like a modern, scientific historian. . . . [He] knew there were other ways of arriving at the truth of what had really happened." [3] Armstrong correctly argues that in the Western world we fail to grasp the dynamics of fundamentalist movements, inspired by Qutb and others, simply because we no longer appreciate the fact that there are two ways of achieving truth: through *mythos* (myth) and *logos* (word).

It has often been assumed that our ancestors thought, spoke, and achieved knowledge in two important ways: through mythos and logos, the former being by far the more common. Logos is the rational, pragmatic, objective, and scientific knowledge that permits people to function in the world. This "is rationalistic language. This is specific and empirical, and eventuates in logic."[4] Since the Enlightenment it is commonly and falsely thought that Westerners no longer need mythos because it is assumed that everything that exists can be logically and scientifically measured. If it cannot be measured it does not exist. Indeed measurement has become a pandemic activity in modern science and human affairs. Since myths cannot be measured, the truths they contain do not exist.

Given the widespread mythological resurgence of nationalism, religion, and fundamentalism this claim that the world is becoming increasingly secular, that is, that Westerners do not need mythos, has

---

[3] Karen Armstrong, *The Battle for God: Fundamentalism in Judaism, Christianity and Islam* (London: HarperCollins, 2001), 241.
[4] May, *The Cry*, 26.

proved a dangerous fallacy.[5] "Religion . . . has re-emerged with a vengeance as a global social force—with fundamentalism as the most vengeful."[6] Myths are at the heart of every culture. They are the glue that binds people together giving them a sense of identity and purpose. Myths are as indispensable in our contemporary world as in the past. They drive everyone not just fundamentalists. Without myths we are unable to know what things are, what to do with them, and how to relate to them; they are the source of meaning in our lives. Myth seeks to articulate what cannot be stated in simple logical language. That is, myth "does not attempt to be 'factual' or rational, and so it cannot be demonstrated or verified."[7] Logos, with its emphasis on rational thinking alone, cannot possibly address issues of ultimate meaning.[8] But myths answer the issues of ultimate meaning; they respond to the need we and fundamentalists have for the sense of purpose in our lives. As May writes, "Whereas empirical language refers to objective facts, *myth refers to the quintessence of human experience, the meaning and significance of human life.* The whole person speaks to *us*, not just to our brain."[9]

This chapter examines the nature and power of culture in shaping fundamentalism in a series of axioms.

Axiom 1

Culture is a "silent language"; we are rarely conscious of its powerful emotional and cognitive content.

People are inescapably shaped by the culture in which they live. On one occasion three friends, an Englishman and two Nigerians, were walking down the Strand, which is an intensely bus and noisy street in the heart of London. The two Nigerians were trying to con-

---

[5] See John Micklethwait and Adrian Wooldridge, *God is Back: How the Global Rise of Faith is Changing the World* (London: Penguin, 2009); see also Monica D. Toft, Daniel Philpott, and Timothy S. Shah, *God's Century: Resurgent Religion and Global Politics* (New York: Norton, 2011).

[6] Eller, *Introducing Anthropology*, 280.

[7] Ibid., 79.

[8] See Armstrong, *The Battle for God*, 365.

[9] May, *The Cry*, 26.

verse with the Englishman, but though the latter could see their lips moving, he could hear little of what they were saying. He shouted above the traffic noise that it would be possible to carry on a conversation only when they were in a quieter side street. Then someone dropped a coin on the sidewalk and the Englishman immediately bent down to pick it up, for he alone of the three had heard the coin hit the concrete.

Why did the Englishman alone hear the coin fall, but he was unable to follow the conversation of his companions because of the traffic sounds? The answer is simple. The Englishman, from early childhood, had become accustomed to hear the "all important" sound of coins clicking together or into money boxes, but not so his Nigerian friends. They had been trained to hear quite different sounds. Culture has such power that it dramatically influences what we feel, see, hear, and smell. Its power enters into every fiber of our being without us ever being fully conscious of its influence.[10]

Culture is truly a "silent language."[11] It is so soundless that we do not know we are encased in culture until suddenly we become aware that it no longer exists! I recall my first visit to Rome as a student in 1958. I decided to take a walk in the late afternoon but very quickly became lost in the streets. I could not read the Italian signs and I feared to cross the streets in the midst of terrifying traffic. I asked for help but no one could speak English! I began to panic as darkness descended. This simple incident taught me that without the comforting presence of my familiar culture I am surely lost! Culture, therefore, can be defined as:

> A pattern of meanings, encased in a network of symbols, myths, narratives and rituals, created by individuals and subdivisions, as they struggle to achieve their identities in the midst of the competitive pressures of power and limited resources in a rapidly globalizing and fragmenting postmodern world, and instructing its adherents about what is considered to be the correct and orderly way to feel, think, and behave.[12]

[10] See Gerald A. Arbuckle, *Earthing the Gospel: An Inculturation Handbook for Pastoral Workers* (Maryknoll, NY: Orbis Books, 1990), 26.

[11] See Edward Hall, *The Silent Language* (New York: Doubleday, 1959).

[12] Gerald A. Arbuckle, *Culture, Inculturation, and Theologians: A Postmodern Critique* (Collegeville, MN: Liturgical Press, 2010), 17.

This definition has several advantages. First, it stresses that cultures are not entities frozen in time without internal conflict and closed to outside forces, but processes in which people strive to discover meaning in an ever-changing and often threatening milieu of limited resources. Second, it emphasizes that culture shapes people's *emotional* responses to the world around them. It infuses the deepest recesses of our humanity, especially on the level of feeling. One day I had the terrifying experience of flying through severe turbulence across the Pacific. As we landed in my country New Zealand I saw in the distance an Air New Zealand plane with the well-known national symbol—a fern leaf—spread over its tail. Suddenly I felt relief. I was home secure and safe. This incident provides a further clue to the meaning of culture. The common definition of a culture is primarily "what people *do* around here," but this is too superficial. Rather culture is "what people *feel* about what they do." Culture is that which tugs at the heart! The New Zealand symbol tugged at my heart. I *felt* after the dangers of the flight that I belonged in a familiar and safe place. This comment by psychoanalyst Erich Fromm, therefore, is particularly incisive. The "fact that ideas have an emotional matrix" is "of the utmost importance" as this is "the key to the understanding . . . the spirit of a culture."[13]

The third value of the definition is its emphasis on power and the struggle to negotiate personal and institutional identities. Roland Barthes (1915–1980), focuses on the immense power to coerce of symbols and myths within popular culture. He shows how racism, sexism, and colonialism loiter behind seemingly innocent advertisements. The power of myth is to be found, he argues, in its potential to make an arbitrary system of values appear as a system of facts. Use this or that soap and you will be "pure."[14] For Michel Foucault (1926–1984) power is the pattern of texts, the specialized languages and networks of power relations operating in and defining a particular field. For him, power and knowledge are really the same thing and he is a master of revealing vested power interests. People who control specialized disciplines, for example, government officials and mass media moguls, hold extraordinary power in society, power that can

---

[13] Erich Fromm, *The Fear of Freedom* (London: Routledge and Kegan Paul, 1960), 240.

[14] See Roland Barthes, *Mythologies* (St. Albans: Paladin, 1973).

rarely be challenged by outsiders. Power insidiously permeates every aspect of a culture and is psychologically invasive and oppressive.[15] Followers of fundamentalist Donald Trump feel they lost power and a sense of belonging to uncaring, impersonal bureaucrats and politicians in Washington, DC (see chapter 3). Islamic fundamentalists feel that Islam has for centuries been dominated by Western colonial cultures, hence the need to struggle to regain power in order to achieve control in their own hands to shape authentic Islamic identities.

Axiom 2

Because we desperately fear chaos, culture provides us with a sense of felt order and predictability.

Note that the emphasis in the definition is on the way to feel, not just the way to think and behave. Culture is first how people feel collectively about important things in life. Notice also the words "correct" and "orderly." People want to feel secure and safe within an orderly environment because what we most fear as humans is chaos or disorder. Think about a simple fact of life: How easy is it for you to give up your favorite armchair to a visitor, for a day or a week? How comfortable are you when your daily routine is suddenly changed, even in little things? Confused? Ill at ease? Culture is about felt order and maintaining predictability. When things are out of order, we do not feel at peace until they are returned to what we feel to be their rightful place.

Sociologist Peter Berger calls culture *nomos* (i.e., "felt order" or "the predictable") because it protects us from what we most fear—the awesome insecurities of *anomy* (chaos, or the radical breakdown of felt order). Nomos, Berger writes, is "an area of meaning carved out of a vast mass of meaninglessness, a small clearing of lucidity in a formless, dark, almost ominous jungle."[16] Culture, in this sense, is a human

---

[15] See Michel Foucault, *The Order of Things: An Archaeology of the Human Sciences* (New York: Vintage, 1974); Arbuckle, *Culture, Inculturation*, 11–12.

[16] Peter Berger, *The Sacred Canopy: Elements of a Sociological Theory of Religion* (New York: Doubleday, 1969), 23.

creation that protects us from the fear-evoking dark abyss of disorder. Cultures have been also defined as "defences against anxieties" and "containers of anxieties."[17] Shirley P. Lowry concludes her study of myths with this assertion: "Most mythic systems agree on this basic point: What promotes cosmic order, harmony, and life is good, and what promotes chaos, disintegration, and death is evil."[18]

Fear of Terrorism/Fear of Chaos

It is true that more people die from falling in the bath than terrorism, argued President Obama. But terrorism is very different from accidental death or even from random murder. The public reacts to terrorism so strongly because they sense that their government cannot fulfill is basic duty, namely, to maintain order and to keep fear-evoking chaos at bay, that is, to keep the public safe from unknown enemies. The fear that terrorism provokes is not just a statistical delusion but also an inkling that people who know no limits are organizing a conspiracy against the state and the public.[19]

Axiom 3

The constituent elements of all cultures are symbols, myths, and rituals.

When I see a photograph of my mother, I experience her presence, not just as a thought but as a living and vital presence. Symbols are multivocal, that is, they accumulate layer upon layer of meanings over time. Thus, two people may use the word "church" and think they are communicating only to discover that they are not being understood, simply because the word evokes different feelings and meanings in different people. We can never be neutral in the presence of symbols; they cause us to react in positive *or* negative ways. In

---

[17] See Gareth Morgan, *Images of Organization* (Beverly Hill: Sage, 1986), 199–231.
[18] Shirley P. Lowry, *Familiar Mysteries: The Truth in Myth* (New York: Oxford University Press, 1982), 131.
[19] See *The Economist* (March 26, 2016): 12.

Iran prior to the revolution against the modernising legislation of the Shah, from exile, the Ayatollah Khomeini encouraged women to adopt the veil as a powerful symbol of their religious protest. As symbols relate primarily to the hearts of people, so rational or logical attacks on them do not necessarily destroy their importance.

Rejection of the Flag

In 2015, the New Zealand government suggested that the nation should adopt a new flag. However, the possibility of a flag with the traditional national fern leaf on an all-black background was immediately rejected because people *felt* it reminded them of the jihadist black flag used by ISIS members. Such is the power of a symbol.

A myth, contrary to its popular meaning, is a set of narrative symbols or a story that retells a truth so important to group and individual identities that it cannot be articulated in precise and technical or nonexpressive language. Myths are value-impregnated beliefs or stories that inspiringly bind a group of people together at the deepest level of their group life—beliefs that they live by and live for, even, in some instances, die for.[20] Myths articulate what is morally right and wrong. Without myths, people have no place in the universe. This helps to understand why I felt panicky when I lost my way in Rome. My unconsciously imbibed New Zealand myths were unable to offer me comforting ways to understand the unfamiliar Italian culture.

Ritual is the visible expression of myths. It is the gesture that articulates what people believe. Through ritual people give flesh to the values and goals expressed in myths.[21] For example, when a government decides to reduce financial aid to people who are poor because they believe their poverty is their own fault, this is a ritual that expresses the fundamentalist mythology of market economics. The

---

[20] See Robert M. MacIver, *The Web of Government* (London: Macmillan, 1947), 4.

[21] See Arbuckle, *Culture, Inculturation*, 81–97.

importance of ritual for fundamentalists will be discussed in more detail in axiom 9.

Axiom 4

Myths are a response to our innate need to make reality unambiguously simple.

Social reality is too complex and ambiguous for people to manage. Thus the innate yearning is to make reality simple and unambiguous and to create order where there is only chaos. We make, as anthropologist Mary Douglas explains, ambiguous perceptions conform to schematic mythological patterns and so discard dissonant observations. Whatever does not fit into orthodox classification systems and which violates or crosses symbolic borders, tends to be viewed as "polluting."[22] Myths exist in order to allow us to live in a world in which causes are simple and neatly defined.

Mythologies satisfy basic human needs by offering: (1) a *legitimating reason for existence*, that is, a need to find some satisfying reason for why things exist. Myths provide passionately held charters for living, models *for* how life is to be lived and the values that should underpin it. (2) A *simple, coherent or orderly cosmology*, that is, an explanation of where we fit in a comprehensible and safe world. This relieves anxieties. Fundamentalists particularly offer their followers a highly simplified and neatly ordered mythological response to anxieties about a chaotic world. Anthropologist Mircea Eliade writes that "myths describe the various and sometimes dramatic breakthroughs of [what is considered to be] the sacred into the world. . . . It is the sudden breakthrough of the sacred that really *establishes* the World and makes it what it is today."[23] (3) A *social/political organization*, that is, a framework which allows us to work together in some degree of harmony and thus avoid chaos. (4) An *inspirational vision*, that is, an overall view that inculcates a sense of shared pride and belonging to community. Donald Trump's presidential campaign call

---

[22] Axiom 7 explains this notion of polluting further.

[23] Mircea Eliade, *Myth and Reality*, trans. Willard R. Trask (Prospect Heights, IL: Waveland Press, 1998), 6.

to "Make America Great Again" touched followers who felt the American vision of sacred pride had been lost. Sociologist Peter Berger comments on this quality of inspiration that enlivens the heart, "It is through myths that men are lifted above their captivity in the ordinary, and attain powerful visions of the future, and become capable of collective actions to realize such visions. . . . By definition, myth transcends both pragmatic and theoretical rationality, while at the same time it strongly affects them."[24]

By mythically defining and structuring the world, human persons are able to grasp to some degree the regions beyond human control which influence well-being and destiny. No matter how committed we are to deepening our grasp of the meaning of myths, they still remain somewhat ambiguous and mysterious, because they attempt to express what can never be fully explained. The more we try the more we discover new and unexpected meanings in myths. All groups, including fundamentalists, will have founding myths that provide ultimate binding forces of identity and hope for the future. Founding myths are like beams in a house. They are not exposed to outside view, but they are the inner, essential structure that holds people together in a unique culture. For the United States, the founding myth is the new Israel, the new Promised Land where democracy will protect its citizens from the corrupting forces of monarchs and dictators. The narratives of American fundamentalists draw on this founding myth, while modifying it to suit their political, nationalist, or religious purposes.

Sunni and Shia Muslims: Different Founding Myths

The divide between Sunni and Shia dates to the death of the Prophet Muhammad; while these two sects share many fundamental beliefs and customs, they differ in doctrine, law, theology, and ritual practice. From Lebanon and Syria to Iraq and Pakistan, recent conflicts have emphasized the sectarian divide, tearing communities apart, simply because their founding mythologies are significantly different. The great majority of the

---

[24] Peter L. Berger, *Pyramids of Sacrifice: Political Ethics and Social Change* (Harmondsworth: Penguin, 1974), 32.

world's Muslims are Sunnis. The name "Sunni" is derived from "Ah al-Sunnah," or "People of the Tradition." The tradition refers to practices based on what the Prophet Muhammad said, did, agreed to, or condemned. All Muslims are guided by the Sunnah, but Sunnis emphasize its primacy. The Prophet Muhammad prior to his death in 632 made no arrangements for his succession. Some believed that a new leader should be chosen by consensus and they become known as Sunnis. Thus the succession passed to a trusted aide, Abu Bakr. Others asserted that only the prophet's descendants should be caliph, in particular, Ali, the prophet's cousin and son-in-law. Ali did eventually become the fourth caliph but after his assassination his sons, Hassan and Hussein, claimed the title. After the martyrdom of Hussein in 680 those who believed that Ali should have been the immediate successor of the Prophet became known as Shia or Shiites (a contraction of "Shiat Ali," meaning "followers of Ali"). In brief, "Where Sunnis have made the life of Muhammad a myth, Shiis have mythologized the lives of his descendants."[25] Sunni extremists frequently denounce Shia as heretics who should be killed (see chapter 5).[26]

Axiom 5

Myths can be residual.

A residual myth is one with little or no daily impact on a group's life, but at times can surface to become a powerful operative myth. We have only to think of the way residual myths of nationalism reappeared in parts of the Soviet Union once it broke apart. Or consider the contemporary resurgence of Scottish nationalism that had laid apparently dormant for three hundred years. The residual myth of fundamentalism is so powerful in the United States that it resurfaces whenever the nation experiences significant political, economic, or

[25] Armstrong, *The Battle for God*, 45.
[26] See www.bbc.com/news/world-middle-east-16047709 (accessed March 3, 2016).

social trauma (see chapter 3). Integral to the founding mythology of Australia was its policy to exclude people who did not have white skin. Though the policy has been officially rejected, nonetheless, from time to time the residual mythology re-emerges through a new narrative. Thus, in the late 1990s Pauline Hanson founded a fundamentalist political party with an anti-Asian and anti-Indigenous platform.[27] Slobodan Milosevic, the Serb leader, manipulated Serbian public opinion in his incendiary speech of June 28, 1989 by invoking a residual myth of humiliation when he recorded the defeat of Serbs by Muslims in 1389. The people responded with enthusiastic support.

Axiom 6

The aims of history and myths are different.

> The myth is a drama which begins as a historical event and takes on its special character as a way of orienting people to reality.[28]
>
> —Rollo May

The aims of myth and history differ; myth is concerned not so much with a succession of events as with the moral significance of these happenings.[29] A myth is a moral commentary on the beliefs, values, and rituals of a culture. Rollo May describes it this way, "The myth is a drama which begins as a historical event and takes on its special character as a way of orienting people to reality."[30] Thus Winston Churchill can be depicted in historical and mythological ways. As seen from the historical perspective, he is depicted as fitting

---

[27] See Catriona Elder, *Being Australian: Narratives of National Identity* (Sydney: Allen and Unwin, 2007), 10–13, 125. Hanson returned to the Australian parliament in 2016 with a significantly increased majority. She campaigned to stop further Muslim immigration and halt the intake of Muslim refugees; she wants surveillance cameras in all mosques and Islamic schools and a ban on the construction of new mosques.

[28] May, *The Cry*, 26.

[29] For a fuller explanation, see Gerald A. Arbuckle, *Violence, Society, and the Church: A Cultural Approach* (Collegeville, MN: Liturgical Press, 2004), 7–13.

[30] May, *The Cry*, 26.

into a definite time period, influencing and being influenced by events around him. If, however, he is evaluated as a person who exemplifies the virtues of courage and practical daring in the face of immense difficulties, then we are assessing him by the founding mythology of the English people. Ultimately, a story that develops into a myth can be true or false, historical or unhistorical, but what is important is not the myth itself but the purpose it serves in the life of an individual, a group, or a whole people.[31]

Myths, if poorly understood, can twist history because they are a complex mixture of remembering, forgetting, interpreting, and inventing. Some historical events may be systematically denied or forgotten. That is, myths may not correspond with historical facts. Churchill was an effective leader in World War II, but a disastrous leader as the First Lord of the Admiralty in the first World War, an historical point that is often forgotten in the mythology surrounding him today. Serbs may recall that Bosnian Muslims were Christians in the past, before their Ottoman subjugation, but overlook or deny that the Bosnians' conversion was real and serious; "or Jews may remember that they had a homeland and state in Palestine twenty-five hundred years ago but forget or deny that they lost it subsequently and that the land has been occupied by other groups since then."[32] Islamic fundamentalists distort history by misreading the founding story and sayings of the Prophet Muhammad (see chapter 5). Americans do violence to history if they "treat certain phrases—'one nation under God,' 'In God We Trust'—as sacred texts handed down [to them] from the nation's founding."[33] The phrase "under God" was only incorporated into the Pledge of Allegiance in 1954; the national motto "In God We Trust" was not approved by Congress until 1956. Author Kevin Kruse argues that corporate America supported these additions to American mythology to implant in the minds of people

---

[31] See Arbuckle, *Culture, Inculturation*, 10–11.

[32] Jack D. Eller, *From Culture to Ethnicity to Conflict: An Anthropological Perspective on International Ethnic Conflict* (Ann Arbor: University of Michigan Press, 1999), 40.

[33] Kevin M. Kruse, *One Nation Under God: How Corporate America Invented Christian America* (New York: Basic Books, 2015), 294.

that capitalism and free enterprise were blessed by heaven.[34] A group can also develop a myth that has little or no foundation in history but which is no less commanding or operational. For example, Hitler invented the myth that the German people were the authentic descendants of the Aryan race and therefore had the authority and the power to dominate Europe, including having the obligation to exterminate the weak.

Axiom 7

Groups see their culture as clean or pure, while other cultures are dirty or impure, and therefore dangerous— to be avoided, changed, or eliminated.

Through symbols, myths, and rituals cultures have an inbuilt tendency to create boundaries with potentially powerful feelings dividing "us" from "them"! This is the social disease of ethnocentrism. The English poet Rudyard Kipling describes ethnocentrism in this way, "All nice people like Us are We, and everyone else is They."[35] This us/they is the superior/inferior dynamic that haunts all fundamentalist groups. Anthropologist Mary Douglas' explanation helps to throw some further light on this dynamic.

Douglas focuses on a people's understanding of "purity" and "pollution."[36] Her language appears at first sight to be somewhat dramatic, but her insights are important to an understanding of fundamentalist cultures. Her concept of pollution does not refer to the intrinsic hygienic properties of things but rather to their symbolic

---

[34] See Kruse, *One Nation*, passim. Difficulties arise when the mythologies of different nations claim the same founding figure. Russia and post-Soviet Ukraine assert that Vladimir the Great, a prince who over one thousand years ago accepted Christian baptism for his disruptive tribes. To the Russians, that was the founding action of their statehood. On the other hand, Ukrainians claim they alone are the authentic descendants of Vladimir. This historical and mythological dispute underlies today's smouldering war. See *The Economist* (January 2, 2016): 60.

[35] Rudyard Kipling, *Debts and Credits* (London: Macmillan, 1926), 327–28.

[36] See Mary Douglas, *Purity and Danger: An Analysis of the Concepts of Pollution and Taboo* (London: Routledge and Kegan Paul, 1966).

qualities as "matter out of place."[37] For Douglas, when explaining her understanding of pollution, the object of our deepest anxieties is everyday dirt. It evokes an attitude, "ugh!" and demands a response, "clean-up!" An appreciation of what causes things to be called dirty or clean, Douglas argues, may uncover the deepest mysteries of the moral order itself, the reasons that some societies renew and reaffirm their fundamental collective feelings and beliefs, while others become entrapped in fundamentalism.[38]

The question is—why are some things considered dirty and other things clean? Why are shoes judged dirty when placed on the table, but clean when on the floor? It is the location that defines their dirtiness and its power to evoke a reaction. Ideas of dirt and feelings of being disgusted arise when things are outside their usual boundary system. Examples embrace how we consider our relation to hair, fingernails, and skin taken from the body, or pots and pans being placed in the bedroom away from the kitchen. As Douglas writes, "Dirt is the by-product of a systematic ordering and classification of matter, in so far as ordering involves rejecting inappropriate elements."[39] This means that what is thought to be dirty is relative. Douglas comments, "It's a relative idea. Shoes are not dirty in themselves, but it is dirty to place them on the dining-table . . . it is dirty to leave cooking utensils in the bedroom. . . . In short, our pollution behaviour is the reaction which condemns any object or idea to confuse or contradict cherished classifications."[40] It is not just a question of factual location that condemns something as dirty or clean. Shoes are not dirty just because they are on the table rather than on the floor, but because they *should* be on the floor, and *not* on the table. There is a moral quality to reality that renders the issue of classification, and misclassification, as a matter of right and wrong. When we say that shoes should not be on the floor we are not only stating a fact about "the mechanical appropriateness of nature, but a moral evaluation of that order."[41] Dread of pollution is like fear of immorality or sin.

[37] Ibid., 36.
[38] See Robert Wuthnow, et al., *Cultural Analysis* (London: Routledge and Kegan Paul, 1984), 85.
[39] Douglas, *Purity*, 48.
[40] Ibid.
[41] Wuthnow, *Cultural*, 87.

"Impure"

For radical Muslims, the Americans' hammering of Afghanistan and Iraq, and its indifference about Israel's pounding of the Palestinians, have made America the principal enemy, the "impure nation" and the "great defiler," the basic cause of the Arab world's tribulations. "In prayer halls from Java to London, [radical] Muslims recite the Qunut, an additional *raka'a*, or prostration, added during times of calamity, accompanied by the words 'May God destroy America.' "[42] On the other hand, Osama bin Laden at first said that jihad should be waged solely against impure non-Muslims but he soon supported jihad against what he saw as the corrupt, evil Muslim leaders in Arab countries who are polluting the pure teachings of Muhammad.

Every human society and organization subscribes, mostly *unconsciously*, to rules of purity and pollution in some form or other. A culture (or subculture) is a purity system, that is, it tells people what is pure and clean, or evil and therefore dangerous or polluting. The fear of pollution defines and protects the boundaries of a group. Pollution, as opposed to purity, interferes with the acceptable equilibrium, destroys or confuses desirable boundaries, and evokes destructive forces or conditions. As Douglas writes, "In short, our pollution behaviour is the reaction which condemns any object or idea likely to confuse or contradict cherished classifications."[43] Contemporary refugees trying to land in Australia or Europe are daring to break orderly boundaries and thus are creating among citizens a fear of being polluted. They are "them" and the self-righteous citizens are "we." When there are reactions of this kind it is not surprising that fundamentalist attitudes and movements develop among us.

Pollution, as opposed to purity, interferes with the acceptable equilibrium, destroys or confuses desirable boundaries, and evokes destructive forces or conditions. As Douglas writes, "In short, our pollution behavior is the reaction which condemns any object or idea

[42] *The Economist* (February 2, 2002): 41.
[43] Douglas, *Purity*, 36.

likely to confuse or contradict cherished classifications."[44] The potential for violence is unlimited. Islamic fundamentalists regard Western civilization as a polluting force to be kept at a distance and/or destroyed. Saudi Arabia is one of only nineteen countries in the world that criminalizes apostasy, the turning away from one religion to another; it is one of twelve countries where it is punishable by death. Apostasy is believed to be a polluting evil. Hitler, inspired by his fundamentalist ideology, considered that particular peoples—Jews, people with disabilities, gays, and gypsies—endangered the purity of the Aryan race and had to be eliminated. In possibly the most horrible expression of this logic of pollution, he cleansed the fatherland by turning "dirty" Jews into "clean" soap.[45]

Pharisees: Fundamentalists?

The Pharisees were a Jewish group at the time of Christ. In the New Testament the Pharisees are depicted in positive terms: they caution Jesus that Herod endangers his life (Luke 13:31); they invite him for meals (Luke 7:36-50; 14:1); Jesus admires their zeal (Matt 23:15) and their concern for perfection and purity (Matt 5:20); they shelter early Christians (Acts 5:34; 23: 6-9). However, some were undoubtedly fundamentalist because they despised the ignorant in the name of their own self-righteousness (Luke 18:8-14), and they ritually forbade all contact with sinners and publicans for fear of becoming ritually impure, thus confining God's love according to their own narrow viewpoint; some consider Jesus and his followers are so ritually impure and dangerous that they plot against his life (Matt 12:14). They also thought that they had some rights over God, because of their practice (Matt 20:1-15). Since they could not implement in practice this ideal, Jesus says, they act as hypocrites; they insist on mere external formalities but do not themselves observe the legal burdens which they impose on others, thus they are "white-

---

[44] Ibid., 36.

[45] See Alan Dundes, "A Study of German National Character Through Folklore," *Journal of Psychoanalytic Anthropology* 4 (1981): 265–364.

washed tombs" (Matt 23:27).[46] Sin was made purely external. Their fundamental weakness "was their refusal to admit that Judaism could reach any further development beyond themselves; they called a halt to the saving activity and power of God."[47]

Axiom 8

People struggle to create through narrative their personal and institutional identities in the midst of competing, coercive forces.

The myth, or story, carries the values of the society: by the myth the individual finds his sense of identity.[48]

—Rollo May

Myths are the stories that make our lives intelligible in the *past*, but the retelling of these stories in light of *present* needs are called narratives.[49] Myth and narrative are two sides of the one coin (see Figure 2.1). In narratives, myths from the past are applied to what concerns people today and in the process the myths are enlarged, altered, or even discarded.[50] As with myths, narratives are at the heart of cultures. The founding myth of modernity, for example, asserts that the individual is perfectible through his or her own efforts and that government must not interfere with this effort. This myth, the foundation of capitalism, was challenged in the period of the Great

[46] See Xavier Leon-Dufour, ed., *Dictionary of Biblical Theology* (London: Geoffrey Chapman, 1973), 428–29.

[47] John L. McKenzie, *The Dictionary of The Bible* (London: Geoffrey Chapman, 1965), 669. Raymond E. Brown, when explaining Matthew's inclusion of the Pharisees in the plot to arrest Jesus (Matt 26:4-5), notes that the evangelist is reflecting the anti-Jewish attitude of many ordinary converts at that time. Since the parallel verses in Mark and Luke make no mention of this, Brown concludes Matthew's version is but a caricature that reflected contemporary prejudices. See his book *The Death of the Messiah*, vol. 2 (New York: Doubleday, 1994), 1431.

[48] May, *The Cry*, 26.

[49] For a fuller explanation, see Arbuckle, *Culture, Inculturation*, 64–80.

[50] See ibid., 72.

Depression and again with the recent global economic downturn. Thus the myth of capitalism has had to be *somewhat* modified by the formation of a new narrative in the United States. Now we have a narrative that tells Americans that the federal government has a right to intervene at times directly in national monetary policies to protect the employment and health of people, even if this means reducing to some degree the freedom of the more wealthy. Politicians, however, still vigorously disagree about the extent to which this right can be exercised as explained below.

The Definition of Narrative

Narratives are about creating identity in the here and now, all the while drawing on myths of the past, though the myths may be changed or modified in the process without people being aware of what is happening; they are stories that recount in a variety of ritual ways, such as images, music, gestures but particularly language, a series of temporal events so that a meaningful succession is depicted, which is the plot; and they are found in all forms of human communication, so much so that human beings can be called "narrating animals."

Figure 2.1 Myths and narratives

Myths	Narratives
Stories that make sense of the past	Stories that apply myths to present context

Narratives of Fundamentalism

Fundamentalists create narratives that re-write the founding stories of their nation or the institution they belong to. For example, the Know Nothing political movement in the United States in the early 1850s was characterized by political xenophobia, anti-Catholic sentiment, and occasional violence against opposing groups. It was a reaction to anti-slavery advocates and the increasing presence of Catholic migrants from Ireland and Germany. Supporters felt that the founding mythology of the Constitution was being violated and they were determined to restore it to its original purity. Abraham Lincoln condemned them: "When Know-Nothings get control, [the founding document] will read 'all men are created equal, except Negroes, and foreigners, and Catholics.' "[51] The contemporary Tea Party movement is a further example of an American narrative fundamentalism. It again resurfaced in the Tea Party protests that occurred in 2009 against the government's bank bailouts and healthcare reform proposals. The party campaigns against government spending, is opposed to taxation increases, and presses for the reduction of the national debt. Adherents loudly and angrily assert that the country must return to an authentic interpretation of the Constitution which means in their narrative that the rights of the individual must have precedence in *all* important matters over the common good, a point rejected by the founders. Likewise Islamic fundamentalists develop a narrative drawing on the founding mythology of Islam under the Prophet Muhammad but in the process they radically change this mythology.

"Home-Grown Terrorists": Mythological Identity Vacuum

The phenomenon of locally born terrorists in Britain and elsewhere is difficult to explain. Poverty is a factor. Almost 70 percent of Muslim children in Britain are in poverty and depend on government support, and about 36 percent are unqualified for employment when they leave school. Likewise, in the suburbs of French cities like Paris poverty cripples the lives of immigrant families and unemployment is over 50 percent.[52] Poverty breeds widespread resentment. But poverty alone is not the cause of the radicalization of young people because it is increasingly noticeable that college and university students are among the young people who turn to terrorism. The fact is that those involved in terrorist plots have come from a wide range of ethnic, social, and educational backgrounds. The only thing they

---

[51] Abraham Lincoln, quoted by Orville V. Burton, *The Age of Lincoln* (New York: Hill and Wang, 2007), 65.

[52] See Lindsay Richards, "How to Explain the High Muslim Levels of Poverty?" http:csi.nuff.ox.ac.uk/?=270 (accessed June 8, 2016).

share is a common set of ideas and an unswerving willingness to act on them.[53]

One further common factor is that local Muslim terrorist tends most frequently to be a second-generation migrant.[54] Second-generation migrants in any country may experience considerable difficulties in adjustment. Often they must inhabit two cultural worlds at the same time: that of the school or workplace where they feel like aliens, and that of the home, where they are thought by their parents to be forgetful of the traditions of their ancestors. It is a dualism filled with tensions. The more parents insist on family traditions, the more their children feel alienated from the society they wish to adjust to, but which keeps refusing to accept them. Sometimes parents and their children are unable to communicate easily with each other, simply because they have no common language; parents have been too busy working to learn the local language well, and the young are too uninterested to learn the language of their parents.

Thus the young may live in a kind of cultural "no-man's land"; they are tempted to escape the tensions by joining gangs that are often anti-dominant society because there they find a much-needed sense of belonging.[55] Robert S. Leiken in his analysis of second-generation Muslim migrants in Europe agrees with this analysis and further clarifies the problem:

> The new country . . . offers him a de jure assimilation (France), a de facto segregation (Germany), or a multicultural identity (United Kingdom). . . . [But the] postmigrant Muslim extremist opts for an identity he chooses, not one he inherits. He adopts his own myth of return, to a golden age of Islamic intensity and purity. His anger finds a narrative that depicts his plight as Muslim oppression and channels that anger into jihad. The angry Muslim may riot or join a gang transformed into a terrorist only when he is armed with an ideology, a narrative, only when the Inside finds and embraces the Outside.[56]

[53] See Innes Bowen, *Medina in Birmingham, Najaf in Brent: Inside British Islam* (London: Hurst, 2014), 1.

[54] See Robert S. Leiken, *Europe's Angry Muslims: The Revolt of the Second Generation* (Oxford: Oxford University Press, 2012), 261–69.

[55] See Arbuckle, *Earthing the Gospel*, 175.

[56] Leiken, *Europe's Angry Muslims*, 266.

Bhikhu Parekh also emphasizes the power of religion to attract marginalized youth: "Freed from the ethnic, national and other ties, and turning to religion as the sole basis of their identity, young Muslims are available for mobilization by militant groups with a global agenda. These groups idealize and flatter them by describing them as the 'true elite' charged with the responsibility of standing up for the honour of the *umma* [the Muslim community]."[57]

Ethnicity and Fundamentalism

Ethnicity is the existence of culturally distinctive, self-conscious groups (ethnic groups) within a society, each claiming a unique identity based on a shared mythology and on social symbolic markers such as culture, language, religion, income, and physical characteristics, for example, skin pigmentation. Among the primary factors evoking the resurgence of ethnicity are discrimination, immigration, and the fundamental need people have to foster a sense of individual/group belonging and identity in the midst of a rapidly changing global world. The intensity of ethnic identity, or ethnicity, is generally dependent on the attitudes of the dominant or host group towards outsiders in its midst. If the outsiders approximate the culture of the host group, then their own ethnic identity may weaken, as is the case for Anglo-Saxon immigrants in Australia or the United States. Negative reactions to outsiders by the host society intensify the outsiders' ethnic internal bonding, as is the case among contemporary Mexican-Americans or Muslims in Western countries, but it can also lead to fundamentalist reactions on the part of members of the host society, for example, right-wing anti-immigrant movements in Europe. These points will now be further explained.

---

[57] Parekh, *The New Politics*, 125. See also Didier Leroy and Joost Hiltermann, "Why Belgium?" *NYR Daily*, www.nybooks.com/daily/2016/03/24/brussels -attacks-isis-wy-belgium/?utm (accessed March 29, 2016). Hugo Micheron, a researcher on French jihadists comments, "There are different routes into jihadism today, and I've seen several cases of radicalisation taking place within a couple of weeks." *The Economist* (July 23, 2016): 37.

Involuntary Ethnic Identities[58]

The ethnic identity of an oppressed group is called an involuntary, or ascribed, ethnicity; there is little or no escape from this negative labelling and oppression. In cases of ascribed ethnicity, the us/them dichotomy that is always present in ethnic relations is especially strong. The dominant group ("us"), often out of a sense of fear or of losing its position of power, pejoratively stereotypes the oppressed group ("them") and institutionalizes that oppression so that in key areas of life like employment, education, and social relationships, the oppressed are excluded from equality with the dominant group. To develop and legitimize this discrimination, the in-group frequently brands the out-group as racially or culturally inferior. This has happened to blacks in South Africa, Jews in Nazi Germany, and immigrants in parts of contemporary Europe. Involuntary ethnicity understandably breeds frustration and anger—a tragic atmosphere for the rise of fundamentalist movements. Members of the dominant host group commonly tend to isolate themselves geographically and socially to avoid unnecessary contact with the immigrant groups. The more affluent families of the in-group ensure that their children are educated, as far as possible, away from immigrant groups.

Anti-Muslim Prejudice Dictates Identities

Prejudice and discrimination against Muslims in Europe is fuelled by stereotyping and destructive views despite the fact that religions, as a social reality, are not monolithic. Because some Muslims are terrorists people incorrectly judge that collectively *all* Muslims must be terrorists.[59] In the language of anthropologist Mary Douglas, all Muslims are judged to be "dirty" and "polluting" the "clean" Western countries. Globally, anti-Muslim prejudice is growing in the wake of the attacks in London, Paris, and Brussels. Parekh comments, "Thanks to the widespread distrust of Muslims and the belief that they do not

[58] See Arbuckle, *Culture, Inculturation*, 104–18.
[59] See Amnesty International, *Choice and Prejudice: Discrimination against Muslims in Europe* (London: Amnesty International, 2012), passim.

wish to, and cannot, integrate, there is an extensive moral panic.[60] This has led to a growing spirit of intolerance and a nationalist backlash in almost every European country."[61] A study by the Pew Research Center in 2014 of seven European Union countries found that at least half of those surveyed in Italy and Greece had negative opinion of Muslims living in their country. In 2015, 40 percent held negative views of Muslims, the same level as in Britain.[62]

The anti-Muslim prejudice is being vigorously encouraged by right-wing politicians. For example: Donald Trump's vow to exclude Muslims and to have a wall built to separate Mexico from the United States; leaders from eastern Europe proclaim they will accept migrants from Syria only if they are Christian; Marine Le Pen, leader of the National Front, France, says, "Europe will no longer be Europe, it will turn into an Islamic republic. We are at a turning point, and if we don't protect our civilization it will disappear. I want to preserve our cultural and historic identity."[63] Geert Wilders, leader of the Party for Freedom, Holland, says, "Islam is the biggest threat, threatening our country and the entire Western world. We have too much mass immigration from Muslim countries and too many hate palaces (i.e., mosques). . . . Enough is enough."[64] Such intolerance encourages the disgruntled into sympathisers and radicals into bombers.[65]

---

[60] Moral panics are experiences of widespread anxiety or hysteria sparked off by apparently trivial events; social deviants must be named, bullied, and punished and then moral values will be restored to society. Moral panics divert society's attention away from more serious structural and social issues that cause violence. See Eirch Goode and Nachman Ben-Yehuda, *Moral Panics: The Social Construction of Deviance* (Oxford: Blackwell, 1994); Arbuckle, *Violence, Society*, 141–44.

[61] Parekh, *A New Politics of Identity*, 104.

[62] *The Guardian*, "Anti-Muslim Prejudice is 'Moving to the Mainstream,'" www.theguardian.com/world/2015/dec/05/far-right-muslim-cultural-civil-war (accessed March 29, 2016).

[63] Marine Le Pen, www.nytimes.com/2008/01/15/world/europe/15iht-debate.4.9237106.html (accessed March 29, 2016).

[64] Geert Wilders, cited by Amnesty International, *Choice and Prejudice*, 17.

[65] See *The Economist* (March 26, 2016): 12.

Voluntary Ethnic Identities

Unlike people who are discriminated against, people belonging to voluntary fundamentalist groups freely accept discrimination. Shortly after Afro-Americans in the United States began to demand respect for their history and origins, there developed what can be variously termed voluntary, symbolic, defensive backlash ethnicity among whites. Protests of self-righteous indignation from the white Americans still continue, especially when economic conditions worsen and the competition for employment intensifies. The following comments recorded in the United States aptly indicate this reaction: "Who are these black people? We are not racist. Affirmative action is racist because we are excluded. Why can't they be like us? We have worked hard for what we have got, and now these people are demanding from the government our hard-earned income. If they are poor, it is *their* fault."

As a consequence of this defensive pluralism there are demands for university programs in Irish, Jewish, and Polish studies. In France and Germany the nationalistic and often violent movements against foreign immigrants, especially those who belong to poor groups, are also examples of defensive fundamentalist ethnicity. The government is "being too kind with our resources" to these people, the protesters claim. The anti-immigrant movement and the One Nation Party that was established by Pauline Hanson in Australia are local examples. A Sydney taxi driver, when talking to me about New Zealand immigrants in Australia, complained that "these spongers are taking our jobs." Logical and rational arguments do little to counteract such expressions of defensive ethnicity. As explained earlier, people feel the need to blame someone, especially the powerless, for what they perceive to be a breakdown of the comfortable status quo.

Voluntary ethnicity means, therefore, that people like white middle-class Australians, in reaction to the growing identity demands of ethnic groups, may feel the need to redefine themselves more precisely by asserting their own ancestral self-worth and their right to maintain their power positions in society. The ethnicity of whites of European ancestry does not restrict their choice of a spouse, suburb, or friends or affect their access to employment and political opportunities. But the socioeconomic and political consequences of being Asian, Muslim, or Indigenous, are real and frequently hurtful and obstructive. These people are not generally free to choose their ethnic identity; its crippling boundaries are defined for them on the basis of their skin pigmentation, countries of origin, education or religion.

Ritual and Fundamentalism

Axiom 9

Ritual is the repetitive spontaneous or prescribed symbolic use of bodily movement and gesture to express and articulate meaning within a social context in which there is possible or real conflict and a need to resolve or hide it; boundary rituals in fundamentalist groups allow for no ambiguity. [66]

Ritual was briefly referred to in axiom 3. It needs to be more fully explained within the context of fundamentalism. Ritual is sometimes considered to be superficial, empty, and meaningless, a boring ceremony to be endured from time to time. On the contrary, ritual is among the most basic, frequent, and important of human actions. In fact, without ritual we cannot remain human for we would be unable to communicate with ourselves or with another.

Ritual is the means by which we seek and establish orderly roles and boundaries for ourselves and for society. It reassures us that we are in control in the midst of a chaotic world, as seen in something so ordinary as the traffic laws that give us a sense of safety when we drive.[67] Through ritual we give flesh to the values and goals expressed in myths. Take the simple act of shaking hands at the end of a school football or netball game between rival teams. The shaking of hands by opposing players is a ritual visibly expressing a founding myth of sport that despite the mutual aggression during play "it is still only a game."[68] Rituals aim to confirm common belonging or community, sometimes even when there are deep internal and inescapable

---

[66] See Robert Bocock, *Ritual in Industrial Society: A Sociological Analysis of Ritualism in Modern England* (London: George Allen and Unwin, 1974), 35–59; Arbuckle, *Culture, Inculturation*, 81–98.

[67] See Gerald A. Arbuckle, *Laughing with God: Humor, Culture, and Transformation* (Collegeville, MN: Liturgical Press, 2008), 46.

[68] It is increasingly common for members of opposing teams to semi-hug one another instead of shaking hands.

conflicts or divisions. Rituals seek to bring anxieties under control; they publicly proclaim who belongs and who does not. In fundamentalist groups rituals of belonging are rigidly set. There is no ambiguity; people are either in or out! For this reason boundary rituals are important to fundamentalists, who constantly police them to avoid any laxity of interpretation (see axiom 7).

Rituals can be "models for" or "models of." The purpose of "models for" rituals is to impose, reaffirm, and strengthen public conformity to the status quo. For example, sign posts reminding drivers to stop at certain intersections are "models for" rituals because public safety legally *demands* that people conform to the rules of the road in order to prevent deaths or injuries. Terrorist actions, such as the public beheading of hostages and others by ISIS, are "models for" rituals since they have a twofold purpose: to remind nonbelievers, first, that they "deserve" death for their infidelity; and second, that ISIS continues to have the global power to intimidate innocent victims. Similarly, the flying of the black ISIS flag. The use of the Latin language in the ritual of Mass by the breakaway Lefebvre fundamentalist movement clearly declares the identity of its members (see chapter 4). Models of rituals exist where consensus does not have to be imposed but needs to be reaffirmed or celebrated; the ritual transforms the attitudes of people. The ritual does not force values on people. For Americans the flag is a powerful symbol of national identity and its raising carries considerable ritual importance, especially in times of national tragedy or celebration.[69] We must never forget that rituals are saturated with symbolism; hence, we can never grasp the power of fundamentalist movements unless we are sensitive to this reality.

Types of Fundamentalist Cultures

Douglas has devised four models of culture that help to classify and explain the identity and behavior of different types of fundamentalist movements.[70] Douglas builds her typology on two variables: grid

---

[69] See Arbuckle, *Culture, Inculturation*, 81–98.

[70] For a deeper understanding of these models of Douglas, see Arbuckle, *Culture, Inculturation*, 42–48; for more references, see chapter 4, n. 69.

and group. "Group" refers to the strength of the boundary around a social group, while "grid" is concerned with the degree of hierarchy and social differentiation within it. Douglas argues that each position on the grid/group model has its own form of *cultural bias*, that is, it will tend to have a particular mythological worldview and set of values and a particular method of resolving differences.[71]

High Grid/Low Group Sects: bureaucracy	High Grid/High Group Sects: ISIS, Scientology
Low Grid/Low Group Cults: market fundamentalism	Low Grid/High Group Cults: New Age cults

Table 2.1: Types of Fundamentalist Cultures

Low Grid/High Group: Cults

A cult tends to be a more spontaneous, with slightly less rigid boundaries than sects, offering particular concrete benefits to its followers rather than the comprehensive worldviews and conceptions of salvation typical of sects. There are political cults in which a group of people attach themselves to a charismatic, populist leader, for example, Donald Trump; religious cults have followers of Indian gurus. Self-improvement or therapy cults are the New Agers.[72] Cults have a strong sense of collective identity, and are idealistic and at least *theoretically* egalitarian.

Low Grid/Low Group: Cults

Those societies that do not emphasize the common good tend to be individualistic and governed by relations of exchange. Market fundamentalism fits into this category, that is, the quasi-religious belief that unregulated markets will inevitably produce the best social and economic results (see chapter 1). As Stuart Sim commented in 2004,[73]

[71] See Philip Smith and Alexander Riley, *Cultural Theory: An Introduction* (Oxford: Blackwell, 2009), 78-80.
[72] See Arbuckle, *Violence, Society*, 192–95.
[73] Stuart Sim is professor of Critical Theory at the University of Sutherland, UK.

> Market fundamentalism can be considered the current economic paradigm. . . . [It is] certainly the model employed by the International Monetary Fund (IMF) and the World Bank in their dealings with the world's nation states. Its impact . . . [is] largely negative. . . . Market fundamentalism [is] in effect, the Protestant work ethic writ large. The links between Christian fundamentalism and market fundamentalism in America are very tantalising, with the Christian Right combining the two into a politically very powerful ideology.[74]

Global capitalism, as a fundamental cult, was on the precipice of disintegration in the early 2000s, and had to be rescued by national governments. Alan Greenspan, former Chairman of the Federal Reserve of the United States, has admitted the failure of his fundamentalist attitude: "[We] looked to the self-interest of lending institutions to protect shareholders' equity. . . . [But] I made a mistake in presuming that self-interest of banks and others was such that they were best capable of protecting their own shareholders."[75]

High Grid/High Group: Sects

A sect is a small, voluntary, exclusive religious, political or social grouping demanding total commitment from its followers and stressing its separateness from and rejection of society; examples of such sects are Scientology, the Unification Church (Moonies), and ISIS. Sects have a strong sense of collective identity, they are idealistic and generally male-dominated and authoritarian. Fundamentalist groups that are high-group and high-grid vigorously emphasize hierarchy, formal rules, and the maintenance of tradition. Boundaries are rigidly patrolled and dissent of any kind is not tolerated, as, for example, in the pre–Vatican II church.

---

[74] Stuart Sim, *Fundamentalist World: The New Dark Age of Dogma* (Cambridge: Icon Books, 2004), 102–3; see also Chris Lehmann, *The Money Cult: Capitalism, Christianity, and the Unmaking of the American Dream* (Brooklyn: Melville, 2016), passim.

[75] Alan Greenspan, quoted by Paul Mason, *Meltdown: The End of the Age of Greed* (London: Verso, 2009), 118; see also Pope Francis, Encyclical *On Care for Our Common Home* (*Laudato si'*) (London: St. Pauls, 2015), par.60.

High Grid/Low Group: Sects

This type, as in the previous model, has rigidly defined hierarchical governance structures, but differs from this model in that collective identity is weaker. Sociologist Max Weber highlighted the similarities between the mechanization of industry and the rapid spread of bureaucratic forms of organization. He saw that the bureaucratic form institutionalizes the process of administration in the same way as machines directs production. For him, bureaucracy is a "form of organization that emphasizes precision, speed, clarity, regularity, and efficiency achieved through the creation of a fixed division of tasks, hierarchical supervision, and detailed rules and regulations."[76] Having described the ideal type of bureaucracy, Weber warns against its potential to become fundamentalist and thus dominate people's lives.[77] To the bureaucrat, the world is a world of facts to be treated in accordance with pre-established rules: impersonally, without emotional or personal attachment to clients or fellow workers. When rules dominate, to the neglect of the common good, then we have a fundamentalist situation. In bureaucratic rationality the most important quality is *instrumental* reason, that is, *how* to do something rather than *why* to do it. The bureaucracy in its concern for the practical implementation of formal rules can become detached from the people it claims to serve. Integral to modernity is the possibility that rational means will displace morally sound ends. When that happens we have bureaucratic fundamentalism.

Summary Points

1. Myths, the social glue of every culture, have the power to lift people "above their captivity in the ordinary, and attain powerful visions of the future, and become capable of collective actions to realize such visions." Myths have the ability to transcend "both pragmatic and theoretical rationality, while at the same time it strongly affects them."[78]

---

[76] Gareth Morgan, *Images of Organization* (London: Sage, 1986), 24–25.

[77] See Arbuckle, *Violence, Society*, 108–111; see also Morgan, *Images of Organization*, 277–28.

[78] Berger, *Pyramids of Sacrifice*, 32.

2. Every fundamentalist movement has its own unique culture; its mythology provides its members with a powerful emotional sense of meaning, vision, and purpose in a chaotic and disturbing world.[79] The two major Islamic groups, Sunni and Shia, although they accept the Prophet Muhammad, have different founding mythologies that significantly conflict their attitudes and actions toward one another.

3. The aims of myth and history differ; myth is concerned not so much with a succession of events as with the moral significance of these happenings. Myths, if poorly understood, can twist history because it is a complex mixture of remembering, forgetting, interpreting, and inventing.

4. A powerful dynamic in the formation of fundamental groups is that cultures are inclined to see themselves as "clean" or "pure" and others as "dirty" or "impure," and therefore dangerous—to be avoided, changed, or eliminated.

5. Second-generation Muslim immigrants to Europe are often in a mythological no-man's-land, therefore, they are susceptible to the voices of radical leaders.

Discussion Questions

1. Can you identify any incident in your life, for example, sickness or culture shock, in which you experienced a feeling of chaos or a dramatic loss of meaning? What have you learned from this incident about the role of symbol, myth, and ritual in your life?

2. In light of the material in this chapter, how would you describe to a friend what fundamentalism means? Can you illustrate your explanation with examples?

3. Can you identify a minority group in your country? What adverse stereotypes does the dominant culture have of people who are members of this group? What did Jesus Christ do to challenge the negative stereotypes of minority groups in his time?

---

[79] See Robert Jay Lifton, *The Protean Self: Human Resilience in an Age of Fragmentation* (New York: Basic Books, 1993), 171–74.

4. Pope Francis writes, "The message [of the Gospel] that we proclaim always has a certain cultural dress, but we in the Church can sometimes fall into a needless hallowing of our own culture, and thus show more fanaticism than true evangelizing zeal."[80] What lessons are contained in this statement?

[80] Pope Francis, *The Joy of the Gospel* (*Evangelii Gaudium*) (Strathfield, Australia: St. Pauls Publications, 2013), par. 117.

Chapter 3

From Cultural Trauma to Fundamentalism: The Role of Religion

Fundamentalisms arise or come to prominence in times of crisis, actual or perceived.[1]

—Martin E. Marty and R. Scott Appleby

[Fundamentalisms] are embattled forms of spirituality, which have emerged as a response to a perceived crisis. They are engaged in a conflict with enemies whose secularist policies and beliefs seem inimical to religion itself.[2]

—Karen Armstrong

The sense of danger may be keyed to oppressive and threatening social, economic, or political conditions, but the ensuing crisis is perceived as a *crisis of identity* by those who fear extinction as a people.[3]

—Martin E. Marty and R. Scott Appleby

---

[1] Martin E. Marty and R. Scott Appleby, "Conclusion: An Interim Report on a Hypothetical Family," in *Fundamentalisms Observed*, ed. Martin E. Marty and R. Scott Appleby (Chicago: University of Chicago Press, 1991), 822. Italics in original.

[2] Karen Armstrong, *The Battle for God: Fundamentalism in Judaism, Christianity and Islam* (London: HarperCollins, 2000), xi.

[3] Marty and Appleby, *Fundamentalisms Observed*, 822–23.

Key Points

- Religion is integral to fundamentalist movements.

- Religion as mythology provides individuals with meaning and order.

- Civil religions increasingly serve the function of prescribing societal values.

- Narratives of refounding are not fundamentalist.

Too often research focuses exclusively on fundamentalist movements themselves while ignoring the external influences that foster them.[4] The Branch Davidian[5] incident in Waco, Texas, United States, in 1993, illustrates this point. Government agencies besieged the sect's compound for fifty-one days and eventually stormed the site causing the deaths of over eighty men, women, and children. A subsequent inquiry revealed an appalling ignorance of the internal dynamics of the sect on the part of the government agencies, including the possible consequences of an aggressive assault.[6]

The purpose of this chapter, therefore, is twofold: first, to focus on the ways in which cultural trauma in the wider society can act as a catalyst for the emergence of fundamentalist movements, and second, to examine religion's role in providing these movements with a mythology that imbues a sense of meaning and offers ways to cope in life. Fundamentalists are passionately committed to preserving their beliefs as they understand them. We will see that historically

---

[4] See David G. Bromley, "Violence and New Religious Movements," in *The Oxford Handbook of New Religious Movements*, ed. James R. Lewis (New York: Oxford University Press, 2004), 155; see also Arun Kundnani, *The Muslims are Coming: Islamophobia, Extremism, and the Domestic War on Terror* (London: Verso, 2014), 1–25.

[5] The Branch Davidians are a schismatic Seventh-Day Adventist sect formed in 1955.

[6] See John Hall, "Mass Suicide and the Branch Davidians," in *Cults, Religion and Violence*, ed. David G. Bromley and J. Gordon Melton (Cambridge: Cambridge University Press, 2002), 149–69; and Oliver McTernan, *Violence in God's Name: Religion in an Age of Conflict* (London: Darton, Longman and Todd, 2003), 38–39.

fundamentalism is most politically active and culturally apparent whenever there are periods of radical cultural upheaval that cause trauma in the nation as a whole or in smaller communities.[7] Because myths provide people with a set of experienced and cognitive meanings, as well as a sense of identity and order, a sudden change in mythic religious structures is generally a catastrophic experience. This becomes a catalyst for fundamentalist movements. Tumultuous cultural disruptions threaten or destroy cherished identities, esteemed moral values, and sense of belonging giving rise to feelings of anomie and bewilderment. People desperately search for explanations of what is happening and ways out of their overwhelming confusion. The atmosphere is ripe for the simplistic solutions offered by fundamentalists. Because "religion is an important source of moral certainty and is a pervasive force in most societies, their members turn to it, especially if they have tried and failed with secular alternatives."[8] Since the meaning of the word "religion" is highly contested we will first explain how it is to be culturally interpreted.[9]

Defining Religion

To the surprise of secularists religion has revived as a vital force in all parts of the world, including in the West. Religion in fact is an integral element of all contemporary fundamentalist movements, even in Western countries. Secularists have long held to what is termed "the secularization thesis,"[10] that is, "a process by which overarching and transcendent religious systems of old are confined in modern functionally differentiated societies to a subsystem alongside other subsystems, losing in this process their overarching claims

---

[7] See Nancy T. Ammerman, "North American Protestant Fundamentalism," in *Fundamentalism Observed*, ed. Martin E. Marty and R. Scott Appleby, 56.

[8] Bhikhu Parekh, *A New Politics of Identity: Political Principles for an Interdependent World* (Basingstoke: Palgrave Macmillan, 2008), 140.

[9] See Andre Droogers, "Defining Religion: A Social Science Approach," in *The Oxford Handbook of the Sociology of Religion*, ed. Peter B. Clarke (New York: Oxford University Press, 2011), 263–79.

[10] See Bryan S. Turner, *Religion and Modern Society: Citizenship, Secularisation and the State* (New York: Cambridge University Press, 2011), 28–29, 127–50.

over these other subsystems."[11] It is a theory devised in the nineteenth and twentieth centuries that claimed modern society is incompatible with religion and that religion would ultimately decline. Of course, the secularization thesis refers to traditional, institutionalized Christianity, whose numbers are declining in Western countries. The influence of religion over subsystems such as family, politics, education is increasingly being marginalized. Secularists, however, incorrectly conclude that "Christianity [is] the standard" in thinking about religion "and assume that all religions must be similar." But by classifying religion in this way "may ensure that we merely judge other bodies of belief in accordance with their perceived similarity to Christianity."[12] Familiar Christian concepts are used and applied inappropriately to very different bodies of belief. However, as David Lyon comments, "religious relationships and movements . . . are of increasing importance in today's modern world. Much secularization theory produced earlier in the twentieth century mistook the deregulation of religion for the decline of religion."[13] Moreover, as will be explained, secularists have neglected the rise of religion, that is *civil religion*, within the civil sphere of American and other cultures, for example, Islamic Indonesia.[14]

Although the definition of religion is still hotly contested, I believe the most suitable definition of religion is that it is a body of beliefs in which are embedded symbols, myths, and rituals that provide for an ordered whole and a program for the ideas, values, and lifestyle of a society that *ultimately* give meaning to life.[15] What is meant by

[11] Karel Dobbelaere, "The Meaning and Scope of Secularization," in *The Oxford Handbook of the Sociology of Religion*, ed. Peter B. Clarke, 600.

[12] Roger Trigg, *Religion in Public Life: Must Faith be Privatized?* (Oxford: Oxford University Press, 2007), 44.

[13] David Lyon, *Jesus in Disneyland: Religion in Postmodern Times* (Cambridge: Polity Press, 2000), 104. See the discussion by Charles Taylor, *A Secular Age* (Cambridge, MA: Belknap Press, 2007), 423–37; see also David Martin, *On Secularization: Towards a Revised General Theory* (Aldershot: Ashgate, 2005), 58–59, 123–28.

[14] See Robert Hefner, *Civil Islam: Muslims and Democratization in Indonesia* (Princeton, NJ: Princeton University Press, 2000).

[15] See Kevin J. Christiano, William H. Swatos, and Peter Kivisto, *Sociology of Religion: Contemporary Developments* (Walnut Creek, CA: Altamira Press, 2002), 9.

ultimately, however, can be interpreted in one of two ways: *substantively*, religion is oriented to supernatural beings, or *functionally*, every society has common values that answer questions about the ultimate meaning of life, for example, capitalistic values for some and Marxist values for others. Thus, we can say that religion is knowing who we are and why we act the way we act.

Thomas Luckmann defines religion functionally as "the capacity of the human organism to transcend its biological nature through the construction of objective, morally binding and all-embracing universes of meaning."[16] For Peter Berger functional religion is the human enterprise by which "the sacred cosmos is established."[17] For Catherine Wessinger, religion is "a comprehensive worldview that makes sense of the universe."[18] Anthropologist Clifford Geertz also identifies religion in a functionalist way, that is it provides a *meaningful order*, "[Religion is] a system of symbols which acts to establish powerful, pervasive, and long-lasting moods and motivations in men by formulating conceptions of a general order of existence and clothing these conceptions with such an aura of factuality that the moods and motivations seem uniquely realistic."[19]

With the decline on institutional religions, particularly in the Western world, more and more people are opting for the functional approach to religion. They search for individualized meanings that they cease to find in traditional religions. If the functional approach to religion is used, it is possible to agree, for example, with Robert Bellah, that the Western cultural revolution of the 1960s was really a religious crisis.[20] People struggled anew for *meaning* in their lives, resulting in all kinds of fundamentalist movements not just in the Western world but globally. Likewise, civil religions are examples of functional religions as will now be explained.

[16] Thomas Luckmann, cited by Arthur L. Greil and Lynn Davidman, "Religion and Identity," in *Sociology and Religion*, ed. James A. Beckford and N. J. Demerath (London: Sage, 2007), 554.

[17] Peter Berger, *The Sacred Canopy: Elements of a Sociological Theory of Religion* (New York: Doubleday, 1967), 25.

[18] Catherine Wessinger, *How the Millennium Comes Violently: From Jonestown to Heaven* (New York: Seven Bridges Press, 2000), 5.

[19] Clifford Geertz, "Religion as a Cultural System," in *Anthropological Approaches to the Study of Religion*, ed. Michael Banton (London: Tavistock, 1966), 4.

[20] See Robert Bellah, et al., *Habits of the Heart: Individualism and Commitment in America Life* (Berkeley: University of California Press, 1985).

Civil Religion and Fundamentalist Movements

Robert Bellah argues, correctly I believe, that every founding mythology, if it is to emotionally and cognitively bind people together in a culture, will contain "a common set of moral understandings" about what is collectively acknowledged as right and wrong. Bellah asserts that these moral understandings "must rest upon a common set of religious understandings." These religious perceptions encased in the founding mythology of a culture functionally provide an image of "the universe in terms of which the moral understandings make sense."[21] The mythology then gives both "a cultural legitimation" of the nation and a basic "standard of judgement" for evaluating the actions of the nation. Bellah calls this founding mythology a *civil religion*, that is, the "religious dimension, found in the life of every people, through which it interprets its historical experience in the light of transcendent reality." It is "perceived as a spontaneous common civic faith capable of sustaining a pluralistic culture by overriding its religious, ethnic, and social diversity."[22] Civil religions need not contain any reference to God or supernatural beings, or, if so, the meaning assigned to God is left very vague.

While the Soviet Union lasted, those in political authority attempted to create their own civic mythology with a set of symbols and rituals, and to impose them on the people. Rituals ranged, for example, from a mass political ritual such as that contained in the celebrations of the anniversary of the October Revolution, to rituals of initiation into various social and political collectives. Political leaders used the massed formations of people—marching, parading, flag swinging, and performing gymnastics—to integrate the individual into the collective.[23] Ultimately, this attempt at myth management from the top failed. The English civil religion has been shaped over centuries. The religious element, for example, as evident in the symbols and rituals surrounding coronations and state funerals, is assumed to be something from the distant past and is sufficiently

---

[21] Robert Bellah, *The Broken Covenant: American Civil Religion in Times of Trial* (New York: Seabury, 1975), ix.

[22] Marcela Christi and Lorne L. Dawson, "Civil Religion in America and in Global Context," in *Sociology*, ed. James A. Beckford and N. J. Demerath, 272.

[23] See Christel Lane, *The Rites of Rulers: Ritual in Industrial Society—The Soviet Case* (Cambridge: Cambridge University Press, 1981), 1–7, 276.

broad not to offend most citizens. Sociologists Edward Shils and Michael Young regarded the coronation of Elizabeth II in 1953 "as a ritual of communion, bringing the whole nation into a ritualistic dedication to the basic values of the society."[24]

Civil Religions: China and Brazil

Recently in China, Western-sounding names have come to be used for new apartment blocks, corporate towers, and gated housing estates to give them an aura of international and high-class quality, for example, "Cannes Water" and "Paris Spring." In March, 2016, the minister of civil affairs called for such foreign names to be removed because they offend "national sovereignty and dignity," that is, they insult the Chinese civil religion. This decree coincides with the recent moves by President Xi Jinping to insist on a return to "socialist core values."[25]

In 1950, Brazil hosted the Soccer World Cup. Its team famously lost to Uruguay. A journalist described the incident as a "national catastrophe . . . our Hiroshima." Again in 2014, Brazil lost the game. This humiliation left Brazilians shell-shocked because no other country has a more intimate identification with football. The sport provides Brazilians with a national narrative and cultural glue. In other words, football is an integral ritual in the civil religion of Brazil.[26]

There are three common forms of civic religion, state totalitarianism, sacred nationalism, and manipulated historical creeds. In practice, civil religions may be a mixture of all three, but one form will tend to dominate.[27]

---

[24] Robert Bocock, *Rituals in Industrial Society: A Sociological Analysis of Ritualism in Modern England* (London: George Allen and Unwin, 1974), 102; see also Edward Shils and Michael Young, "The Meaning of the Coronation," in *Sociological Review* 1, no.1 (1953): 63–81.

[25] *The Economist* (May 7, 2016): 26.

[26] See *The Economist* (July 12, 2014): 35.

[27] This section summarizes the expert analysis of civil religions by Marcela Christi and Lorne L. Dawson, "Civil Religion in America and in Global Context," in *Sociology*, ed. James A. Beckford and N. J. Demerath, 266–92.

State Totalitarianism

Bellah's analysis of civil religion is based on the writings of the sociologist Emile Durkheim (1858–1917) who believed that some kind of sacred symbolism is essential to moral and social stability.[28] For the symbolism and associated rituals to be effective, however, it ultimately requires the voluntary commitment of citizens. Civil religion, as understood by Durkheim and Bellah, is noncoercive. By contrast, Jacques Rousseau (1712–1778) believed civil religion involved a state-led ideology imposed with various degrees of coercion. When civil religion manifests as ideology, the state has the authority to compel belief and national unity. In this situation civil religion is used to support fundamentalist movements. In its most extreme form, there is little or no individual freedom as membership and participation are compulsory, as, for example, with Soviet Communism, Nazism, Italian Fascism, Franco's Spain, China during the time of the Cultural Revolution under Mao Zedong, State Shinto in Japan from 1868 to 1945, and Pinochet's Chile.[29] In Italy in 1939, almost half of the Italian population was connected in some way with a fascist organization. The apotheosis of Mussolini had become official policy. In 1936, a writer for the Italian newspaper, *Corriere della Sera*, reassured its readers, "When you are looking around and don't know who to turn to any more, you remember He is there. Who but He can help you?"[30] The "He" is not God but Benito Mussolini. Such also is the situation today with the leadership in North Korea.

Sacred Nationalism

Here the state in its development of its civil religion uses existing institutional religion to legitimize its authority. Such was the case in Spain with Franco's alliance with the Catholic Church and in Japan under State Shintoism. Likewise, in Saudi Arabia Wahhabism, a powerful fundamentalist sect, has been "harnessed with great political shrewdness, as an instrument of the state . . . to uphold the

[28] See Emile Durkheim, *Elementary Forms of Religious Life* (London, 1915).

[29] See Cristi and Dawson, "Civil Religion," 276–77.

[30] Cited by C. M. Clark, "Deep in the Volcano," *The New York Review of Books* (April 7, 2016): 60. Clark is the Regius Professor of History at Cambridge University.

king's absolute power."[31] The civil religion in Israel has gone through quite radical changes since the political state was first established in 1948. Prior to this date, Labor Zionists, while struggling to establish the state, vigorously rejected much of traditional Jewish life. However, particularly since the Six Day War in 1967 when Israel triumphed over Egypt, the mythology of traditional Judaism has been increasingly changed to become the civil religion of Israel.[32]

Historical Creeds: Manipulation

This occurs when a civil religious mythology is manipulated to serve biased political cult or sect purposes.[33] Sometimes individuals such as politicians seek to impose narratives of identities on people, selectively twisting history for their purposes. What we believe to be traditions passed from generation to generation have actually been deliberately invented by politically motivated people. It is thought, for example, that Scottish people have all worn kilts and played bagpipes from time immemorial. But my own lowland ancestors certainly did not because kilts and stylish bagpipes were all a political invention for fundamentalist nationalistic purposes in the early nineteenth century.

Nazism is an example of politicized identity, as earlier described, inasmuch as this sect demanded total allegiance from its followers. The Nazis, provoked by resentment of Germany's failure and humiliation following World War I, developed a narrative of the "pure German," untainted by the blood of "impure peoples," such as Jews, gypsies, homosexuals, the intellectually handicapped, and black people. However, even in democratic countries civil religion can be historically manipulated by governments and individuals to coerce people to be patriotic and to serve questionable political goals, "to legitimize special interests and inspire loyalty among political subordinates and allies."[34]

---

[31] Abdel Baru Atwan, *Islamic State: The Digital Caliphate* (London: Saqi Books, 2015), 198–99.

[32] See Charles S. Liebman and Eliezer Don-Yehia, *Civil Religion in Israel: Traditional Judaism and Political Culture in the Jewish State* (Los Angeles: University of California Press, 1983).

[33] See Christi and Dawson, "Civil Religion," 282.

[34] Ibid., 277.

Fundamentalism and Decontextualization

Indian sociologist T. K. Oommem defined fundamentalism as "text without context."[35] This means that religious works, which were always constituted "in a particular historical, cultural context, are decontextualized and held to be applicable without consideration to local circumstances; all other competing texts are rejected as having any corresponding claim to truth."[36] The following examples illustrate this point.

Religious Congregations

Sometimes religious congregations decontextualize their constitutions and consequently fall into the trap of fundamentalist thinking. For example, many religious congregations were founded to serve the poor, but prior to rapid urbanization the poor lived mainly in the countryside. Today, however, the poor are more often present in urban areas. Yet the same religious congregations insist they must move their ministries to rural areas to be faithful to their constitutions.

United States

During the McCarthy era the American Constitution was manipulated to bolster a civil religion as a political cultish instrument against an assumed Communist conspiracy. Presidents Johnson, Nixon, and George W. Bush deployed symbols of civil religion based on the Constitution to support their policies of war in Vietnam and Iraq. The National Rifle Association (NRA) in the United States is a fundamentalist cult founded in 1871. In 2013 its membership surpassed five million. Its primary purpose, built on the Second Amendment to the Constitution, is "To protect and defend the Constitution of the United States, especially with reference to the inalienable right of the individual American citizen guaranteed by such Constitution to acquire, possess, collect, exhibit, transport, carry, transfer

[35] Cited by Kevin J. Christiano, William H. Swatos, and Peter Kivisto, *Sociology of Religion*, 249.
[36] Ibid., 250.

ownership of, and enjoy the right to use arms."[37] In the mid-1970s the NRA changed its moderate support of gun control to an unconditional interpretation of the Second Amendment that protects the right of people to bear arms. The contemporary context is radically different from 1791 when the amendment was first passed. Guns have proliferated in number and quality. The results are tragic. In 2013 there were 33,169 deaths relating to firearms, yet the NRA continues to uphold the Second Amendment supported by a powerful political lobby.[38] In brief, the NRA is firmly committed to upholding the Second Amendment no matter what the cost to people's lives.

Britain

Efforts to re-define "Britishness" through narrative continue in United Kingdom due to rising immigration from Islamic countries, the fear that Northern Ireland, Wales, and Scotland will secede from Britain, and an antipathy towards the European Union.[39] Anti-European common market devotees, for example, today refer to the need to maintain British "sacred sovereignty" and "Britishness." They want to define the British civil religion in a fundamentalistly *exclusive* way. Likewise, in 1987, the minister of education proposed as a matter of urgency that a national curriculum in British schools be introduced to guarantee the continuation of an authentic British narrative and national identity. He stated, "There is so much distraction, variety, and uncertainty . . . that in our country today our children are in danger of losing any sense at all of a common culture and a common heritage." He ends with this statement: "The cohesive role of the national curriculum will provide our society with a greater sense of identity."[40] At first sight these comments look

[37] The National Rifle Association, cited in https://en.wikipedia.org/wiki/National_Rifle_Association (accessed February 3, 2016).

[38] In 2013 there were 84,258 nonfatal injuries in which firearms were used; 1.3 percent of all deaths were related to the use of firearms, https://en.wikipeda.org/wik/ Gun_violence_in_the_United_States (accessed March 3, 2016).

[39] See *The Economist* (January 14, 2007): 48–49. Britain voted by referendum in 2016 to withdraw from the European Union.

[40] Kenneth Baker, *The Times Literary Supplement* (September 25, 1987): 5.

logical and innocent, but the proposed national curriculum reflected an imperialist concept of a static white Anglo-Saxon culture that had ceased to exist. The reality is that through immigration the ethnic mixture is significantly diversifying. Any curriculum must mirror this. Moreover, the qualities of the former imperial Britain were very much the construct of an white upper-class system from which especially the working class was excluded. Contemporary "Britishness" is not something to defined by one class or ethnic group.[41]

Australia

In September 2001, contrary to international law, the Australian government prevented 433 Afghanistan asylum seekers from landing in Australia after they had been rescued from drowning by a Norwegian freighter. Their decision had widespread national support. The numbers trying to land were small but many Australians felt that the refugees, if they landed, would undermine the Anglo-Saxon identity of the nation.[42] A powerful residual myth in Australia behind this resistance to non-Anglo-Saxon migrants, even legitimate asylum seekers, is the White Australia Policy officially introduced in 1901. Though this policy was progressively dismantled after 1949, "Anglo-Saxonism" remains a residual myth that still lurks within the collective memory of the Australian nation as part of its civil religion.[43]

Cultural Trauma: Conducive to Fundamentalism

Trauma is defined as "an objective force that deprives a subject of some part of his normal sovereignty."[44] Sociologist Jurgen Habermas

[41] See Gerald A. Arbuckle, *Culture, Inculturation, and Theologians: A Postmodern Critique* (Collegeville, MN: Liturgical Press, 2010), 74–75.

[42] See *The Economist* (September 8, 2001): 30.

[43] See Catriona Elder, *Being Australian: Narratives of National Identity* (Sydney: Allen and Unwin, 2007), 118–27.

[44] Jurgen Habermas, *Legitimation Crisis* (Boston: Beacon Press, 1975), 3.

writes that social institutions can also experience trauma that dramatically threatens identity.[45] Cultural trauma (see figure 3.1), however, goes beyond individuals and institutions to embrace an entire culture.[46] Sociologist Neil Smelser defines cultural trauma as "an invasive and overwhelming event that is believed to undermine or overwhelm one or several ingredients of a culture or the culture as a whole."[47] When the founding mythology that emotionally and normatively binds the culture together, giving people a sense of collective identity, ceases to operate, cultural trauma is the result. People lose their sense of belonging: they feel stunned and rudderless, "subjected to a horrendous event that leaves indelible [paralyzing] marks upon their group consciousness."[48]

Sociologist Emile Durkheim long ago invented the term, "anomie," to describe the abrupt breakdown of meaning in life, but the term, "cultural trauma," is now anthropologically preferable since it focuses directly on the cultural quality of anomie. Cultural trauma is the crushing grief over the loss of the familiar, the radical disintegration of normative order and its accompanying emotional bonding.[49] This grief expresses itself in collective sadness, sorrow, anger, loneliness, anguish, confusion, shame, guilt, and fear.[50] There is a mythological

[45] Ibid., 1–3.

[46] See Ron Eyerman, "Cultural Trauma: Emotion and Narration," in *The Oxford Handbook of Cultural Sociology*, ed. Jeffrey Alexander, et al. (Oxford: Oxford University Press, 2012), 564–82.

[47] Neil Smelser, "Psychological and Cultural Trauma," in *Cultural Trauma and Collective Behavior*, ed. Jeffrey Alexander, et al. (Berkeley: University of California Press, 2004), 38.

[48] Jeffrey C. Alexander, "Toward a Theory of Cultural Trauma," in *Cultural Trauma and Collective Behavior*, ed. Jeffrey Alexander, et al. (Berkeley: University of California Press, 2004), 1.

[49] See Emile Durkheim, *Suicide*, trans. J. A. Spaulding and G. Simpson, ed. G. Simpson (London: Routledge and Kegan Paul, 1952), 258. Other sociologists, following Durkheim, also fail to focus on the *cultural* quality of cultural trauma. Robert K. Merton equates *anomie* with instability and refers in this connection to "demoralization." *Social Theory and Social Structure* (Glencoe: The Free Press, 1957), 136. Talcott Parsons sees *anomie* as "the polar antithesis of full institutionalization," as "the absence of structured complementarity of the interaction process or, what is the same thing, the complete breakdown of normative order." *The Social System* (Glencoe: The Free Press, 1951), 136.

[50] See Gerald A. Arbuckle, *The Francis Factor and the People of God: New Life for the Church* (Maryknoll, NY: Orbis Books, 2015), 61–84.

vacuum. People are no longer able to find an adequate mythological response to the stresses they are undergoing. Rollo May is right: "The loneliness of mythlessness is the deepest and least assuageable of all. Unrelated to the past, unconnected with the future, we hang as if in mid-air."[51] Little wonder, therefore, that newspaper reports following the murders of President John Kennedy and Swedish Prime Minister Olof Palme (1927–1980) described the nation as "stunned."[52]

When culturally traumatized, people find themselves at an impasse because there are no guidelines. Broadly, four reactions to gridlock are: (1) escape into an unreal golden age or a utopian past, (2) chronic paralysis, (3) attempting to move forward by seeking to refound or reform the culture in light of changing circumstances, and finally, (4) finding solace and meaning in fundamentalist movements. There is a causal link between cultural trauma/impasse and fundamentalist movements as the following six examples illustrate. As Karen Armstrong comments, "All fundamentalists feel that they are fighting for survival, and because their backs are to the wall, they can believe that they have to fight their way out of the impasse [and] on rare occasions, some resort to violence."[53] Notice in the examples how their charismatic leaders can draw on a mix of traditional and civil religions to enthuse their followers.

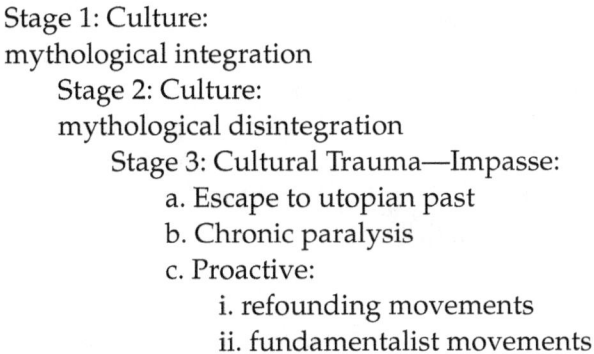

> Stage 1: Culture:
> mythological integration
> > Stage 2: Culture:
> > mythological disintegration
> > > Stage 3: Cultural Trauma—Impasse:
> > > a. Escape to utopian past
> > > b. Chronic paralysis
> > > c. Proactive:
> > > > i. refounding movements
> > > > ii. fundamentalist movements

Figure 3.1 Culture Change Model

[51] Rollo Mary, *The Cry for Myth* (New York: Delta, 1991), 99. Italics in original.
[52] See Eyerman, "Cultural Trauma," 565.
[53] Karen Armstrong, *Islam: A Short History* (London: Weidenfeld and Nicolson, 2001), 142.

Example 1: Ku Klux Klan

In the late 1820s and 1830s, the United States was in a period of cultural trauma. Older settlers resented the social and economic problems increasingly evident in the growing cities. Many feared for their jobs as the new immigrants, especially large numbers of Irish, were willing to work for minimal wages, intensifying anti-Irish and consequently anti-Catholic bigotry.[54] Protestant Americans were also suspicious about the institutional Catholic Church, believing it to be despotic, and holding values contrary to the American republican ideals.[55] Protestant leaders had become frightened by what they believed to be the dual dangers of Catholic growth and atheistic thinking. Not surprisingly, anti-Catholic, pro-white fundamentalist political movements emerged, for example, the Know-Nothings in the South before the Civil War, the American Protective Association in the Mid-West at the end of the nineteenth century, and the Klu Klux Klan in the early twentieth century.[56]

The Klan, a white supremacist sect, was founded as a terrorist movement, reaching its peak in the 1920s with over four million members. Their core belief is to restore America to being a white, Christian nation free from drugs, homosexuality, immigration, and race-mixing which the Klan believed caused (and continues to cause) the nation's decline. Their terrorist activities led to numerous killings and hate crimes against their perceived enemies. In brief, the major issue in the mind of the Klan in the 1920s became "a struggle between 'the great mass of Americans of the old pioneer stock' and the 'intellectually mongrelized Liberals.' "[57] According to Hiram Wesley Evans (1881–1966), the Imperial Wizard of the Klan from 1922 to 1939, the Klan spoke for those struggling with the moral decay and economic distress of the twentieth century.

---

[54] As John Cogley wrote: "Anti-Catholicism has been called America's oldest and most abiding prejudice." John Cogley and Rodger Van Allen, *Catholic America: Expanded and Updated* (Kansas City: Sheed and Ward, 1986), 8.

[55] See David Goldfield, *America Aflame: How the Civil War Created a Nation* (New York: Bloomsbury Press, 2011), 17–41.

[56] See Chester Gillis, *Roman Catholicism in America* (New York: Columbia University Press, 1999), 68.

[57] Richard Hofstadter, *Anti-Intellectualism in American Life* (New York: Knopf, 1966), 124.

Evans used three primary strategies to define his understanding of Americanism. The first firmly associated his organization with the nation's civil religious tradition—white Anglo-Saxon Protestantism. His second strategy was to use an intentional ambiguity describing Americanism as an intangible force that could not be concretely identified, but still existed and achieved a perceptible influence. The strategic use of ambiguity made it possible for the Klan to adopt all those qualities that he considered to be the symbolic signifiers of Americanism. The third strategy consisted of an extreme anti-alien sentiment that declared alienism to be *the* threat to the continuation of the civil religious experience. By defining the American civil religion as one shaped by Protestant considerations, with vaguely articulated ideas of Americanism, the Klan maintained a unified, all-encompassing vision for American political life that served them well throughout the 1920s.[58]

Example 2: Iran

In the Iranian Revolution (1977–1979), fundamentalist Ayatollah Khomeini in establishing a radical Islamic Shia state was able to build on the cultural trauma of the disaffected oppressed, who were primarily landless rural migrants and some of the urban working class. With Khomeini's leadership they reacted against the urban elite who had become the major agents and recipients of the Shah's dictatorial program of economic modernization.[59] Integral to the founding mythology of the Shia, historically oppressed by Sunnis, is the belief that they are called to be a righteous community to restore God's rule on earth. Khomeini rearticulated this mythology, giving hope of a better future for oppressed citizens of Iran.

Example 3: Political Populism and the Radical Right

The term "populism" is applied to a variety of political movements including fundamentalists, but the main quality they share is an

---

[58] See Nicolas Rangel, "Ambiguously Articulating 'Americanism': The Rhetoric of Hiram Wesley Evans and the Kland of the 1920s," *American Communication Journal* 11, no. 2 (2009).

[59] See Turner, *Religion and Modern Society*, 63.

appeal to the people as a whole, with an emphasis on the ordinary citizen as opposed to political power elites. The elites are described as trampling in an unlawful manner upon the rights, values, and voice of the legitimate people.[60] Populist leaders use extremist language and behaviour to assert that innocent citizens are "beset by remote, powerful and malign enemies,"[61] who must be named and marginalized or silenced. Populism is a reactionary movement that seeks to turn back the dominant developments of contemporary times and return to an unreal utopian past. Moises Naim writes that populists suffer from "ideological necrophilia," that is the blind fixation on dead ideas. Populists keep demanding social, economic, and political changes that have failed in the past and will collapse also in the future. Naim argues that there are many reasons why bad ideas endure, but perhaps the most important is people's need to believe in a leader amid rapid change and its resulting cultural trauma.[62]

Populism is increasingly evident in Asia, for example, Rodrigo Duterte in the Philippines, and on both sides of the Atlantic today.[63] It is feeding on the cultural trauma that people feel is overwhelming them. In the United States the Tea Party and Trumpism, both Republican insurgencies, claim that "the ruling elite has lost touch with the founding ideals of America, that the federal government is a bloated, self-serving Leviathan, and that illegal immigration is a threat to social order."[64] At the same time, right-wing populism is active in Europe: Marine Le Pen, leader of the Front National in France, once

[60] An early example in the United States was Populist Party in the 1880s and 90s, a grassroots, politically oriented alliance of agrarian reformers who were unhappy because of crop failures, falling prices, poor credit services, and assumed neglect by politicians in Washington, DC. See Chris Lehmann, *The Money Cult: Capitalism, Christianity, and the Unmaking of the American Dream* (Brooklyn, NY: First Melville House, 2016), 210–12.

[61] Michael Mann, ed., *Macmillan Student Encyclopedia of Sociology* (London: Macmillan Press, 1983), 298; see also Margaret Canovan, "Populism," in *The Social Science Encyclopedia*, ed. Adam Kuper and Jessica Kuper (London: Routledge and Kegan Paul, 1985), 629–31.

[62] See Moises Naim, "What Is Ideological Necrophilia?" *The Atlantic*, www.theatlantic.com/international/archives/2016/02/ideological-necrophilia.tru (accessed February 27, 2016).

[63] See Pippa Norris, *Radical Right: Voters and Parties in the Electoral Market* (New York: Cambridge University Press, 2005).

[64] *The Economist* (January 4, 2014): 7.

compared Muslims praying in the French street to the Nazi Occupation; Geert Wilders of the Party for Freedom believes that Muslim immigration should be halted; Siv Jensen, leader of the Progress Party in Norway, has achieved large popular gains through her attacks on Muslim immigration. In Germany in early 2016, the Alternative for Germany Party (AFD), achieved double-digit results in elections in three German states; party officials have said it may be necessary to shoot at migrants trying to enter the country illegally and they have bruited about the idea of banning mosques.[65] Unlike the Tea Party revolution within the existing Republican Party, the European right-wing parties are newly formed. The supporters of these movements are "angry people, harking back to simpler times."[66] They are angry because unemployment in Europe is high and rising and stagnant wages in America are hurting a large group of older working-class white men, whose jobs are threatened by globalization and technology. Moreover, beneath them "they complain, are immigrants and scroungers who grab benefits, commit crimes and flout local customs. Above them, overseeing the financial crisis and Europe's stagnation, are the impotent self-serving elites in Washington and Brussels."[67] In addition, particularly in Europe, the refugee crisis and international jihadist networks are eroding confidence that state governments can continue to protect their citizens.

Example 4: Trumpism and Extreme Populism[68]

As described above, cultural trauma was affecting both liberals and conservatives when Donald Trump sought the Republican presidential nomination. For liberals, the chief concern for past thirty-five

---

[65] See Jan-Werner Muller, www.nybooks.com/daily/2016/04/14/behind-new-german-right-afd?utm_medi (accessed April 17, 2016).

[66] *The Economist* (January 4, 2014): 7.

[67] *The Economist* (December 12, 2015): 1.

[68] See Harry Olsen and Dante J. Scala, *The Four Faces of the Republican Party: The Fight for the 2016 Presidential Nomination* (London: Palgrave Macmillan, 2016), 135–37. *The Economist* comments, "Trumpism looks set to earn its own dictionary entry: An unpleasant but often politically successful mix of populism, nativism and xenophobia, delivered with a dollop of cynicism." www.economist.com/blogs/economist-explains/2016/07/economist-explains-O (accessed July 5, 2016).

years has been the unfairness of the economy—virtual wage stagnation for most workers, huge gains for the top 1 percent, and the lax regulatory and enforcement regimes that have permitted these outcomes, along with slow recovery from the most recent recession.[69] For conservatives, for about the same period, the main worry is what is broadly called "culture," by which is really meant the anger and resentment felt by older white Americans about the fact that the country is no longer "theirs" and that their former status and authority no longer seem what they once were. The culture that they now loathe and fear embraces a number of issues— immigration, especially illegal immigration, same-sex marriage, and a black president in the White House. All these things conservatives parcel together under the detested label "political correctness." In their minds it is some sort of taint that has infected every institution in their once-great-nation and is destroying it daily before their eyes.[70]

When Donald Trump began to campaign with the slogan, "Make America Great Again," xenophobic right-wing populism reached a new level of vicious cultic fundamentalism in the United States. As a fundamentalist populist Trump became a "rage machine"[71] hitting out at whatever his followers felt angry and resentful about. He demanded a "total and complete shutdown" of America's borders to Muslim migrants and visitors, proposing to deport eleven million undocumented immigrants en masse and building a wall along the Mexican-American border to be paid for by the Mexican government. In addition to using derogatory words for women, he "referred to Mexicans crossing the border as rapists; called enthusiastically for the use of torture . . . advocated killing the families of terrorists."[72] The more vulgar and xenophobic he became the more his widespread

[69] In the United States while "American GDP per person grew by 14% in 2001–15, median wages grew by only 2%." *The Economist* (July 2, 2016): 9.

[70] See Michael Tomasky, "The Dangerous Election," *The New York Review of Books*, www.nybooks.com/aricles/2016/03/24/the-dangerous-election/?utm _medium=e (accessed March 4, 2016).

[71] See Michael Tomasky, "Trump," *The New York Review of Books*, www.nybooks. com/articles /2015/09/24/trump/?utm_medium=email&utm_cam (accessed December 14, 2015).

[72] *The Economist* (February 27, 2016): 9.

following. His popularity was built on fostering fear, hatred, and violence. Like his Tea Party followers he vowed to overturn Obamacare legislation that ensures the poor have medical insurance.[73] No one was spared his abuse, he even accused President Obama of having no legitimate American birth certificate.[74] He had little respect, and to some degree, outright antipathy, for his party's leaders.[75] And his followers could not get enough of his unrestrained conspiracy accusations and anger. All the time he returned to the founding experience of the nation, the civic religious belief that God destines America to be great and his task was to make it great again!

Example 5: Soka Gakkai, Japan

In Japan since the late 1930s, and especially since 1945 when the government removed its control over religious organizations, there developed a large number of religious fundamentalist sects. This was in response to the cultural trauma which had swept the country in the wake of a complete military defeat and unconditional surrender.[76] Sociologist Kiyomi Morioka describes the national cultural trauma, "[The new sects] largely attracted those people who were suffering from anxiety, disease, or shortages of material goods. From around 1955, when the Japanese economy began its high rate of growth, new religions offered the people guidelines for living, rather than resolving material problems."[77] One of the main reasons for the success of

---

[73] David M. Craig correctly comments, "The Affordable Care Act [Obamacare] and the Tea Party can be thought of as fratricidal twins. They grew up together. . . . The conflict is over America's values and their role in reforming US health care." *Health Care as a Social Good: Religious Values and American Democracy* (Washington, DC: Georgetown University Press, 2014), 183.

[74] See E. J. Dionne Jr., *Why the Right Went Wrong: Conservatism—From Goldwater to the Tea Party and Beyond* (New York: Simon and Schuster, 2015), passim.

[75] See Gerald Seib, "Trump Turning Republican Party Inside Out," *Wall Street Journal*, recorded by *The Australian* (February 24, 2016): 9.

[76] See Harumi Befu, *Japan: An Anthropological Introduction* (New York: Harper and Row, 1971), 117.

[77] Kiyomi Morioka, *Religion in Changing Japanese Society* (Toyko: University of Tokyo Press, 1975), 165.

Soka Gakkai, a new religion, has been its ability to organize "mostly the underdogs of society, those who previously had no organization to depend on," and to provide them with "an object with which they can identify and to which they can devote themselves."[78] Numerically and politically it is one of the more successful sects. As a sect it "holds to absoluteness not only in the commitment of the believer, but also in the absolute truth of its message,"[79] reconfirms traditional cultural values, and emphasizes lay evangelism rather than creating a sharp distinction between the sacred and profane. Soka Gakkai's beliefs are based on the teachings and practice established by Nickiren Daishonin, a Buddhist priest and philosopher who lived in thirteenth-century Japan, and his interpretation of the Lotus Sutra, which is believed to contain the ultimate and complete teaching of the Buddha. In 1964, the sect, under charismatic leadership, developed the Komeito (Clean Government Party) as a successful political party.

Example 6: Australia

In the 1990s, rural Australia was facing an increasing economic and social decline that led to cultural trauma, particularly among white Anglo-Saxon rural Australians. A nationalistic political party called One Nation emerged under the leadership of Pauline Hanson and initially had a significant impact on voters. Marilyn Lake comments that Hanson's rhetoric spoke "to the subjectivities of [Anglo-Saxon] men—marginalized, rural, white men—tapping into their pervasive sense of loss . . . mourning for jobs, past glories, lost power and . . . the loss of national sovereignty" due to immigration and globalization."[80] Among the reasons Hanson gave for the notable decline in incomes of rural white Australians, and for the resulting cultural trauma, were globalization, Asian immigration, and welfare payments to Aboriginal peoples.

[78] Takeshi Ishida, *Japanese Society* (New York: Random House, 1971), 42.

[79] H. Byron Earhart, *Japanese Religion: Unity and Diversity*, 2nd ed. (Belmont, CA: Wadsworth, 1974), 115.

[80] Marilyn Lake, "Pauline Hanson: Virago in Parliament, Virago in the Bush," in *Two Nations*, ed. Robert Manne (Melbourne: Bookman Press, 1998), 118.

Fundamentalism in the United States: Analysis of a Case Study

The biggest difference between the United States and most parts of western Europe . . . lies in the degree to which religion continues to be embedded in America popular culture.[81]

—Hugh McLeod

The civil religion of the United States and its connection to the founding mythology of the nation has already been briefly referred to. This section will examine this connection more in depth and then show why fundamentalist movements inevitably emerge whenever the nation experiences cultural trauma. Of America, Karen Armstrong states that "Fundamentalism is not going to disappear. In America religion has long shaped opposition to government."[82] Fundamentalist movements will not disappear simply because the founding mythology of God-decreed success cannot allow the American nation to tolerate failure for any lengthy period. These movements under charismatic leaders offer quick-fix, simplistic solutions to periodic national cultural trauma. Steve Bruce points out that "Although ethnic and racial considerations are not entirely absent, American fundamentalism is essentially a voluntary association of self-selecting individuals, competing to define the culture of a stable nation state."[83]

Founding Mythology: God-Decreed Success

The function of a founding mythology, as explained in the previous chapter, is to explain where we fit in a comprehensible and safe world. The founding mythology of the United States, that is, the country's civil religion, as incorporated in the Great Seal of the nation (and which is copied on one side of the one-dollar bill), reminds Americans that God, or some extraordinary destiny, calls them to participate in a new biblical Exodus, a new journey from the poverty and oppression of other nations, in order to build *successfully* a new promised

---

[81] Hugh McLeod, *The Religious Crisis of the 1960s* (New York: Cambridge University Press, 2007), 255.

[82] Armstrong, *The Battle for God*, 362.

[83] Steve Bruce, *Fundamentalism* (Cambridge: Polity, 2000), 10.

land. America is to be "a new order of ages" (*Novus ordo seclorum*), under the ever-watchful Eye of Providence (*annuit coeptis*). Success is the sign that God is with Americans, keeping his side of the covenant. The Constitution, and its supportive sentiments of equality, freedom, and respect for individual rights, provides a system of social organization that guarantees a person's rights to be a part of this journey into the promised land. The fact that Americans have been called by God to participate in this work of building this earthly dreamland, while others struggle in abject poverty and oppression elsewhere, is a vision that instills within them a sense of pride. It gives them a reason for continuing to struggle, to succeed in life, no matter how enormous the obstacles, and to express that achievement through visible material symbols. That is, this mythology gives meaning to the lives of Americans by fitting them into a coherent cosmology. Every American politician who wishes to win power must legitimize their policies by reference to this creation mythology in some way or other. Charismatic politicians like Ronald Reagan and Bill Clinton had the gift of communicating this national truth.

There is a second feature in the founding mythology of the United States—the lone cowboy and the West so well portrayed in the *Lone Ranger* films in earlier days. The Lone Ranger in the frontier West would gallop ahead to solve an injustice, thus rescuing the oppressed from the impasse of cultural trauma; having succeeded he would again gallop west into the lonely evening ready to respond successfully to yet another injustice most likely caused by a corrupt government official.[84] In later American Westerns, as in *Shane* (1953) or *Cat Ballou* (1965), the hero is also a strong, self-contained individual unknown to or not fully accepted by society, who possesses exceptional abilities that he uses successfully to defend a powerless society against the evil actions of the villain. The society finally accepts the savior it had earlier rejected. The cowboy hero of Western films has now been modernized through the *Rocky* and *Rambo* films of Sylvester

---

[84] Daniel Boone, the great champion of the American frontier, became "a psychological repository of American virtues of courage, martial spirit, fierce individual autonomy, defiance of authority, and near-mystical combinations of continuous movement, pervasive entitlement, and dynamic achievement." Robert Jay Lifton, *The Protean Self: Human Resilience in an Age of Fragmentation* (New York: Basic Books, 1993), 35.

Stallone and in, more recent times, the *Terminator* films of Arnold Schwarzenegger and Bruce Willis defeating successive sets of terrorists in *Die Hard* (1988), *Die Harder* (1990), and *Die Hard: With a Vengeance* (1995). The vigorously individualistic, macho, physically strong, thoroughly self-contained and silent person, the "truly American" hero, is center stage once more, destroying villains with modern firepower, using helicopters in place of horses, restoring the morale of the American people, and prepared to return when needed to uphold the American way of life. The individual hero will always return the people to a journey of success.

Updated Superman

Television sitcoms and Hollywood commonly mirror the current collective depression of the American people and what must be done to restore hope and success intrinsic to the American founding mythology.[85] In 2013, a time when the Republican Tea Party was decrying the federal government's involvement in healthcare reform for the uninsured, several Hollywood films vigorously expressed distrust of the ruling classes. One film (*World War Z*) was about a plague that caused the overthrow of the government and leaves Americans under military law. A second film (*Elysium*) described a narcissistic elite which has fled to a garrisoned Nirvana, leaving 99 percent to struggle to live on a shantytown-like Earth. In the third film (*The Hunger Games: Catching Fire*) debauched big shots lolling "about in a thinly disguised Washington, D.C., oppressing the masses and making youngsters kill one another on reality TV."[86]

But the population could not remain in collective cultural trauma for long. An updated Superman film, *Man of Steel*, reminded patrons that the nation would again be restored to a journey of success. It begins with most Americans feeling desperately depressed, impotent, and with alien forces destroying a Manhattan-like city and its citizens. But Superman returns

---

[85] See Gerald A. Arbuckle, *Laughing with God: Humor, Culture, and Transformation* (Collegeville, MN: Liturgical Press, 2008), 95.

[86] See *The Economist* (June 22, 2013): 38.

alone to bring hope that all can be restored once more to the American dream of success. During the Great Depression he had fought capitalist tyrants, while throughout the Cold War he had confronted crooks with atomic bombs. And in 1978 "he tackled an urban crime-wave as a sort of super-cop, his heroism wrapped in just enough camp irony to win over jaundiced, post-Watergate, post-Vietnam audiences."[87] It happens again, in a nation where only about one-in-ten Americans trusts Congress and the dependable military has no solutions, Superman as man of steel saves the nation. Superman, a super lone ranger, relives the founding story of the nation. All are now back on the journey to success.

Civil Religion: Pervasive Power

Bellah further refines our understanding of the civil religion of the United States: it is a "genuine apprehension of universal and transcendent religious reality as seen in or . . . as revealed through the experience of the American people."[88] He wrote that the "words and acts of the founding fathers, especially the first few presidents, shaped the form and tone of the civil religion as it has been maintained ever since. Though much is selectively derived from Christianity, this religion is clearly not itself Christianity."[89] No reference is made to Jesus Christ. By reviewing various Presidential statements, Bellah noted how often references to God are a central quality of public communication.[90] For example, Harry S. Truman invoked Thomas Jefferson, "We believe as Jefferson did, that [the] 'God who gave us life gave

---

[87] Ibid.

[88] Robert Bellah, "Civil Religion in America," *Daedalus: Journal of the American Academy of Arts and Sciences* 96, no. 1 (1967), www.robertbellah.com/articles_5 .htm (accessed February 24, 2016).

[89] Ibid.

[90] David Goldfield writes, "Historians debate whether Abraham Lincoln was a religious man. He was. His religion was America, and that faith ran very deep." *America Aflame: How the Civil War Created a Nation* (New York: Bloomsbury Press, 2011), 103. In other words, Lincoln was strongly committed to American civil religion.

us liberty.'"[91] Aspects of this civil religion contain the idea that God actively participates in, and critiques, American public life; a belief that the American nation has been especially chosen by God; therefore, Americans must respect this choice and act accordingly. This civil religion is steeped in biblical imagery: "Exodus, Chosen People, Promised Land, New Jerusalem, Sacrificial Death and Rebirth."[92] But it is neither "sectarian nor in any specific sense Christian."[93] Although its symbols are Christian in origin, paradoxically they do not stand for any God, church, or denomination in particular.

As in other religions, America's civil religion has its own collection of symbols, rituals, sacred texts and sites, martyrs, and prophets, such as George Washington, Abraham Lincoln, John F. Kennedy, and Martin Luther King Jr., events such as Gettysburg, and rituals such as Thanksgiving Day, Memorial Day, and saluting of the flag.[94] All help to integrate families into the civil religion, or to unify the community around its values. "Beneath diversity and apparent secularity lies a hidden religion firmly tied to the nation's history and institutions, and providing the essential integration around sacred things."[95] In brief, the American civil religion as encased in the founding mythology, "provides religious legitimation to political authority, gives the political process a transcendent goal, serves as carrier of national identity and self-understanding, and serves as a resource for morally judging the nation."[96]

[91] Cited in Jon Meacham, *Thomas Jefferson: The Art of Power* (New York: Random House, 2012), 502.

[92] Bellah, "Civil Religion," 18.

[93] Ibid., 8. Bellah's first description of American civil religion in 1967 was widely understood to mean that it had a belief system which both moulded and legitimized the historical experience of the American people, but in his later work in 1975 he corrected this interpretation by describing it as an absolute and independent truth, by the standards of which contemporary American society is to be judged. American civil religion for Bellah did not legitimize the social and political status quo but rather it could become an instrument for social transformation.

[94] See Christi and Dawson, "Civil Religion in America," 271.

[95] *Macmillan Student Encyclopedia*, 44.

[96] Ibid., 272.

Table 3.1

US Presidents	Mythology of Success Fails: National Cultural Trauma	Fundamentalist Reactions
Franklin D. Roosevelt (1933–1945)	Great Depression. New Deal Policies. Fear of World War.	Fr. Charles Coughlin: National Union For Social Justice: anti-New Deal/anti-Semitism. America First Committee (1940–1941).
Harry Truman (1945–1953)	Fear of Communism: Soviet Union's acquisition of atomic bomb. Korean War Setback (1950–1953).	McCarthyism. John Birch Society.
Dwight Eisenhower (1953–1961)		Christian Libertarianism: No need for government-provided social services.
John F. Kennedy (1961–1963)	Russian space success. Nuclear threat: Cuban Missile Crisis/Bay of Pigs disaster. JFK assassination (1963).	
Lyndon Johnson (1963–1969)	National identity crisis: Civil Rights Act (1964). Malcolm X, Black Muslim Leader, assassinated (1965). Civil Rights and Urban Riots, e.g., Watts Los Angeles (1965). Anti-Vietnam War protests. Democratic Convention, Chicago, under siege (1968). Martin Luther King Jr. assassinated (1968). Robert Kennedy assassinated (1968). Institutions under attack, e.g., governments, traditional religions/churches.	Expressive (counter-culture) revolution emerges. New religious sects/cults: – Self-religions, that is, new personal identity self-help, e.g., therapy cults, Scientology. – Total sects: new identity from submission to group, e.g., Unification Church, Hare Krishna. Political reactionary groups, e.g., Ku Klux Klan revitalised.
Richard Nixon (1969–1974)	Continued protests against Vietnam War. Excerpts of "Pentagon Papers" published detailing government lies (1971). Watergate scandal (1972–74).	

	Vice-President Agnew scandal/resignation (1973).	
Gerald Ford (1974–1977)	Controversial pardon for Richard Nixon (1974).	
Jimmy Carter (1977–1981)	Iran hostage crisis (1979–1981): failure to free hostages (1980). Energy crisis speech (1979). Economic stagflation, i.e., a portmanteau of stagnation and inflation— inflation is high, economic growth rate slows, unemployment high.	
Ronald Reagan (1981–1989)	Malaise: result of previous presidencies. Cut budget on: Medicaid, food stamps, federal education programs; attempted to purge many with disabilities from Social Security disability rolls. Iran-Contra scandal.	"Reaganomics": laissez-faire philosophy and free-market fiscal policy; environment subject to market forces. New Right groups, e.g., Richard Viguerie, Jerry Falwell (Moral Majority).
George H. W. Bush (1989–1993)	Lack of vision. Failed to keep promise not to raise taxes. Economic recession.	
Bill Clinton (1993–2001)	Healthcare Reform failure. Monica Lewinsky scandal. Impeachment proceedings (1999).	Jerry Falwell: "with the election of Bill Clinton to the presidency, Satan had been let loose in the United States."[97] "Small government utopia" Republican campaign (Newt Gingrich).[98]
George W. Bush (2001–2009)	Terrorist attack (9/11/2001). Afghanistan war begins (2001). Iraq war begins (2003).	

[97] Karen Armstrong, *The Battle for God: Fundamentalism in Judaism, Christianity and Islam* (London: HarperCollins, 2000), 362.

[98] See E.J. Dionne, *Why the Right Went Wrong: Conservatism—From Goldwater to the Tea Party and Beyond* (New York: Simon and Schuster, 2016), 124–59.

	Torture policy uncovered. Hurricane Katrina (2005). Severe economic recession begins (2007). National debts rises. Unemployment rises. Median household income drops; poverty increase.	Neoconservatism revitalized, i.e., promotion of U.S. national interests in international affairs, including by means of preemptive military force and the use of torture.
Barack Obama (2009–2017)	Recession impact continues. Income inequality. Stagnant middle-class income. Patient Protection and Affordable Health Care Act (Obamacare) (2010): vigorous Republican opposition.	Tea Party (began in Republican Party in 2009): opposes Obamacare; laissez-faire economics. "Trumpism": extreme right-wing political policies, including anti-Muslim and anti-Mexican immigration.

Table 3.1 sets out various national experiences of cultural trauma since the time of President Franklin Roosevelt that have become catalysts for fundamentalist reactions. The Great Depression of the 1930s was, of course, a major assault on the mythology of success and the National Union for Social Justice was a fundamentalist reaction to the economic remedies of the New Deal. This extreme right-wing union was led by a Catholic priest Father Charles Coughlin in a Michigan parish, a young pastor and skilled communicator. At first in his Sunday afternoon radio broadcasts, he was a strong advocator of the New Deal: "Roosevelt or Ruin!" Supported by millions of supporters he quickly and bitterly turned against Roosevelt, the slogan changing to: "Roosevelt *and* Ruin!" While asserting that the New Deal was communist-inspired, he also adopted overt anti-Semitism.[99]

Fundamentalist McCarthyism and the John Birch Society later flourished during the national trauma years under President Truman; many Americans had become obsessed with the fear of communism. Under Lyndon Johnson the mythology of success once more miser-

---

[99] See Cogley and Allen, *Catholic America*, 78–79; Chester Gillis, *Roman Catholicism in America* (New York: Columbia University Press, 1999), 231–32.

ably failed with the nation haunted by the ongoing Vietnam disaster and its accompanying political turmoil. Gerald Howard considers the period as "a spirited, wildly inventive era—a decade of great social and political upheaval when ideas and customs collided in every corner."[100] A wide variety of postmodern fundamentalist reactions developed in the midst of the bewildering 1960s' Expressive Revolution. There emerged the New Religion Movements, often with fundamentalist qualities, for example, the Children of God (1968), Hare Krishna (1964), Scientology (1960s), First Unification Church (1970s) commonly known as the "Moonies," Maharaj Ji's Divine Light Mission (1971), and Healthy, Happy, Holy, an offshoot of Indian Sikhism (1968).[101] These religions responded to the bewilderment and frustration of people caught up in the turmoil of the Expressive Revolution: people impoverished by inflation and unemployment, confused by changes in sexual mores, and terrified by crime in the streets.[102]

Cultural trauma once more engrossed the nation's attention as a consequence of political and economic malaise during and following the presidencies of Richard Nixon, Gerald Ford, and Jimmy Carter. Many millions of Americans had become dismayed and frustrated by the corruption in the government and the feeling of powerlessness to do anything about it. Ronald Reagan conveyed hope, a return to a national journey of success. Under Reagan, in reaction to the trauma evoked under the previous three presidents, New Right fundamentalism emerged in politics, economic policies, and among Evangelical Christians. The Moral Majority, founded in 1979 under the influence of Jerry Falwell, became a significant force that inspired Evangelicals to become committed to the right-wing economic strategies of Reagan.

[100] Gerald Howard, *The Sixties: The Art, Attitudes, Politics and Media of Our Most Explosive Decade* (New York: Washington Square Press, 1982), 4; see also Gerald A. Arbuckle, *Violence, Society, and the Church: A Cultural Approach* (Collegeville, MN: Liturgical Press, 2004), 153–79; Bernice Martin, *A Sociology of Contemporary Cultural Change* (Oxford: Basil Blackwell, 181) 27–52; and Sharon Monteith, *American Culture in the 1960s* (Edinburgh: Edinburgh University Press, 2008).

[101] See John A. Saliba, *Perspectives on New Religious Movements* (London: Geoffrey Chapman, 1995).

[102] See Marvin Harris, *America Now: The Anthropology of a Changing Culture* (New York: Simon and Schuster, 1981), 141–65.

Falwell and other evangelical adherents became vociferous enthusi-
asts of supply side Reaganism.[103]

The Moral Majority capitalized on the ill-defined but conservative
feelings of many Evangelicals and others; Falwell proudly called the
movement "fundamentalist."[104] It has been estimated that "during
the 1960s and 1970s four out of every ten households in the United
States tuned in to his station in Lynchburg, Virginia."[105] It became the
age of the television evangelists and "video cults." Most of these cults
projected the American civil religious gospel of wealth and success.[106]
Believers did not have to physically go to a church; all they had to
do was to turn on their television "to participate in the healing and
soothing powers of a caring and supportive fellowship."[107] Financially these video cults became overwhelmingly prosperous. The best
way for televangelists to prove their credibility was obviously to
succeed materially themselves. And many did![108] Certainly the success of these fundamentalist cults did not depend only on the adroit
marketing of Jerry Falwell and other televangelists. Elements of
American civil religion were favourable to this literalistic form of
faith, and they provided them with a fertile soil.[109] Right-wing fundamentalism continues today, especially within the Republican Party,
for example in the emergence of the Tea Party[110] and Trumpism.[111]

[103] See Lehmann, *The Money Cult*, 312–25. Jerry Falwell wrote: "Ownership of
property is biblical. Competition in business is biblical. Ambitious and successful business management is clearly outlined as part of God's plan for His people."
Listen America! A Conservative Blueprint for Moral Rebirth (New York: Bantam,
1981), 7.

[104] See George Marsden, "Preachers of Paradox: The Religious Right in Historical Perspective," in *Religion and America*, Douglas and Tipton, 150–68.

[105] Armstrong, *The Battle for God*, 275.

[106] See Lehmann, *The Money Cult*, 307–8.

[107] Harris, *America Now*, 158.

[108] Jim Bakker and his wife Tammy grossed over fifty million dollars in 1980
for their Praise The Lord Club. See Harris, *America Now*, 159.

[109] See Armstrong, *The Battle for God*, 355.

[110] Opposition to immigration reform is a key feature of Tea Party politics. See
E. J. Dionne, *Why the Right Went Wrong*, 447.

[111] Ibid., 236–60.

Expressive Revolution: Impact on Mainline Churches

During the Expressive Revolution there was widespread erosion of the legitimacy of traditional institutions: business, government, education, traditional churches, and the family. Mainline churches experienced widespread malaise, a loss of institutional vitality and direction; they were ill-equipped to respond to the spiritual and ideological trauma of the time. Significant numbers of young people felt these churches had not only compromised with secular values, but had become so bureaucratic and unfeeling that they could no longer provide the desired havens of understanding and meaning. While the demands for social justice that characterized many movements in the revolution conformed closely to the traditions of Judaism and Christianity, the churches themselves were perceived to have colluded with oppression. Hence they were excluded from influencing the revolution and from developing a following despite the leadership of religious people like Martin Luther King Jr.[112]

Refounding Narratives: Not Fundamentalist

Refounding is a process of storytelling whereby imaginative leaders are able to inspire people collaboratively to rearticulate the founding mythology of an institution and apply it to contemporary needs through creative dialogue with the world. The purpose of refounding narratives is to find a positive way out of trauma by allowing people to reenter the sacred time of their founding with imaginative leaders who are able to rearticulate the founding mythology in narratives adapted to the changing world. The founding mythology again becomes *regenerative*, a process described by anthropologist Bronislaw

---

[112] See Arbuckle, *Violence, Society*, 161; Hugh McLeod, *The Religious Crisis of the 1960s*, 125–60; Wade Clark Roof, "America's Voluntary Establishment: Mainline Religion in Transition," in *Religion and America: Spirituality in a Secular Age*, ed. Mary Douglas and Steven M. Tipton (Boston: Beacon Press, 1982), 130–49.

Malinowski as "a narrative resurrection of a primeval reality."[113] That is, inspired by the re-owning of the founding mythology, people are motivated to develop "quantum leap" imaginative methods that apply the original founding experience to the very different modern-day conditions. The creative jump means breaking with the past, an act of dissenting.

A refounding narrative radically differs from a fundamentalist narrative because the latter is closed to dialogue and responsible dissent. Refounding is a process of an ongoing dialogue and creative response to changing times. People involved in a refounding narrative never feel they have all the answers to the challenge to adapt the founding mythology to the complex contemporary world. There is always a constant search for innovative responses as the context changes. Fundamentalists, however, believe they have absolutely certain solutions to the problems around them. For them the world may be complex, but they have neatly pre-packaged solutions, if only the world would listen!

In 1984 the United States was still recovering from the cultural trauma of the Richard Nixon and Jimmy Carter years. With the Soviet Union boycotting the Olympic Games in Los Angeles, President Reagan, the new political superman, led a dramatically innovative revitalizing ritual at the opening of the games. The ritual's narrative ingeniously involved symbols of American success, for example, eighty-four grand pianos played simultaneously. Americans felt good again. Creativity was adapted to present realities reinspire them. To use Eliade's language, in regeneration rituals, sacred time breaks into profane time. Sacred time is ritual time. It consists of those ritual narratives in which people re-enact the holy, aboriginal events of their culture but which are now adapted to contemporary conditions never foreseen in the original founding times.[114]

The refounding narrative is also not synonymous with renewal. The renewal narrative tackles only the symptoms of problems, but refounding seeks to make "quantum-leap" responses to their causes. For twelve years (1984–1996) Steve Jobs worked to renew or improve existing computer models. However, dramatic success came only

---

[113] Bronislaw Malinowski. *Magic, Science and Religion, and Other Essays* (Glencoe, IL: Free Press, 1948), 101.

[114] See Mircea Eliade, *The Sacred and Profane* (New York: Harcourt, 1959), 95.

when he realized that computing in the future would simply not resemble computing in the past. Then he truly began refounding Apple with the inventions of the immensely successful iPod, the iPhone, and the iPad. Future computing would not take place by simply renewing conventionally shaped computers. By simply repeating past narratives, fundamentalists are more like renewalists than refounders.[115]

Summary Points

1. External factors, particularly cultural trauma experiences, deeply influence the development of fundamentalist movements.

2. In a cultural trauma the mythological certitudes of a people disintegrate and this shatters their sense of order and identity. People are then more likely to listen to fundamentalist leaders who offer them simplistic solutions to their loss of belonging, order, and vision.

3. Since religion is an important basis of moral certainty, people frequently turn to it as a motivating force in shaping fundamentalist values and movements. Functionally religion offers people a mythological way of understanding the world in which they live; understood in this way, religion is today rapidly on the increase although traditional institutional religions are on the decline in the Western world.

4. Civil religion refers to the symbols, myths, and rituals that legitimate the social system, create solidarity, and mobilize a community to attain common political aims. In a number of countries, where formal religion is weakly present, civil religions powerfully influence the development and maintenance of fundamentalist groupings, for example, in the United States.

5. A refounding narrative radically differs from a fundamentalist narrative because the latter is closed to dialogue and responsible dissent.

[115] See Gerald A. Arbuckle, *Catholic Identity or Identities? Refounding Ministries in Chaotic Times* (Collegeville, MN: Liturgical Press, 2013), 100–102.

Discussion Questions

1. Pope Francis writes, "The message [of the Gospel] that we pro-claim always has a certain cultural dress, but we in the Church can sometimes fall into needless hallowing of our own culture, and thus show more fanaticism than true evangelizing zeal."[116] As you reflect on the history of your community or nation can you identify symptoms of fanaticism?

2. Does your culture encourage you to look down on other peoples, even to blame them for the problems of your nation? Think of the times when Jesus condemned this behavior.

3. Pope Francis writes, "Saint Therese of Lisieux invites us to prac-tise the little way of love, not to miss out on a kind word, a smile or any small gesture which sows peace and friendship."[117] What can you do to implement the "little way of love" today? At home? At work?

[116] Pope Francis, *The Joy of the Gospel (Evangelii Gaudium)* (Strathfield, Australia: St. Pauls, 2013), par. 117.

[117] Pope Francis, *Care for Our Common Home (Laudato Si')* (London: St. Pauls Publishing, 2015), par. 230.

Chapter 4

Catholic Fundamentalism: An Analysis

Fundamentalism is a sickness that is in all religions. . . . Religious fundamentalism is not religious, because it lacks God. It is idolatry, like idolatry of money. . . . We Catholics have some—and not some, many—who believe in the absolute truth and go ahead dirtying the other with calumny, with disinformation, and doing evil.[1]

—Pope Francis

We know well that even in this Holy See . . . abominable things have happened. . . . We intend to use all diligence to reform the Roman Curia.[2]

—Pope Adrian IV, 1523

Key Points

- "Integralism" as a theological fundamentalist movement

- The emergence of traditionalist/schismatic and conservative/nonschismatic fundamentalist movements due to Vatican II

---

[1] Pope Francis, comments to journalists on the plane returning from Africa (November 30, 2015), www.lifesitenews.com/news/pope-francis-attacks-fundamentalist-catholics-dismisses-condom-ban-as-unimp (accessed March 26, 2016).

[2] Pope Adrian VI, cited in Luigi Accattoli, *When a Pope Asks for Forgiveness* (New York: Alba House, 1998), 7.

- Delegated to lead reform of the church, the Roman Curia errs on the side of fundamentalism

- Pope Francis' definitive "no" to restorationism

At the close of the eighteenth century the French Revolution helped to destroy the stable socio-political order with which the church had been allied for centuries. Napoleon aimed to place the church directly under the control of the state, thus modelling for the rest of Europe a new form of state-church relationships. As the nineteenth century developed the church had to confront an entirely different and anxiety-evoking situation at all levels of human endeavour: the vigorous power of an anti-clerical state system, the growing impact of the Industrial Revolution on society, the Enlightenment values of naturalism, rationalism, liberalism, and democracy, and the growing fascination of the world for the new empirical sciences and methods of historical research. The efforts to turn back these radical ideas and movements and to restore the pre-Revolutionary alliance of throne and altar failed in the revolutions of 1830 and 1848, while the popes Gregory XVI and Pius IX struggled vainly to withstand the forces of modernity even within the papal states.[3]

Fundamentalist Reactions to Modernism

The more the church's leadership struggled to resist the revolutionary insights and values emerging within the Western world, the more the church withdrew from what was taking place in history and in people's lives. It increasingly became sect-like and fundamentalist in the face of the dramatic changes in society. For example, Rome fostered a form of scholastic philosophy, neoscholasticism, which provided the church with a coherent intellectual framework. Yet this philosophy had one serious disadvantage, namely, it was so self-contained that its supporters saw no need to listen to, and even learn

[3] See Gerald A. McCool, *Catholic Theology in the Nineteenth Century* (New York: Seabury Press, 1977), 23–27.

from, other philosophies.[4] The church as a culture became progressively closed or inward-looking, defensive and protective of its members, compelled to live in a world considered to be under the direction of evil and subversive forces. Detailed rules and laws were invented just to keep Catholics safe from contact with these agencies. The assumption that had existed for centuries, namely, that people had to be changed by religion, not religion changed by the culture, was reinforced throughout the nineteenth century and right up to Vatican II.[5] In 1907, Pope Pius X condemned so-called Modernists within the church, that is, Catholics who sought to understand and use the new scientific ideas in the service of religion.

For Pius, Modernism was "the synthesis of all heresies." Yet it was a much-needed "self-conscious, if inchoate and loosely organized, attempt by certain European Catholic exegetes, historians, philosophers, and theologians to construct a viable synthesis between the ancient faith and modern (post-Kantian) thought."[6] His condemnation sparked off a tragic witch-hunt craze that stifled creative theological reflection for decades. The church had the total truth, it was assumed, so it felt it had nothing to learn from the changing world of ideas and technologies—a tragic symptom of fundamentalist thinking. Moreover, the church was thought to possess and live the "pure Gospel." It did not see itself as a culture in its own right with layer upon layer of uncritically accepted Eurocentric customs, aristocratic values, and habits. The church was not a pilgrim people in search of redemption. Rather it was described as a static, *perfect* society. It contained all the means for our own salvation; it did not need to learn from the world. The refusal of the world to listen to the church only confirmed the point that evil resided in the hearts of secular governments and people!

---

[4] Blessed John Henry Newman (1801–1890) found the neoscholastic method of teaching of his day arid, "rigorously abstract, ahistorical and deductive." Nicholas Lash, "Waiting for Dr. Newman," *America* (February 1–8, 2010), 13.

[5] See John W. O'Malley, "Reform, Historical Consciousness, and Vatican II's Aggornamento," *Theological Studies* 32, no. 4 (1971): 591 and passim.

[6] William D. Dinges, "Roman Catholic Traditionalism," in *Fundametalisms Observed*, ed. Martin E. Marty and R. Scott Appleby (Chicago: University of Chicago Press, 1991), 82.

These theological beliefs, rigidly protected from Rome, became known as *integrisme* in French, "integralism," in English, the Catholic fundamentalist counterpart of American Protestant fundamentalism, and it flourished from the First to the Second Vatican Councils.[7] That is, the foundation of Protestant fundamentalism was the literal interpretation and inerrancy of the Scriptures while Catholic integralists asserted that their fundamentalism rested on "a literal, a historical, and nonhermeneutical reading of papal pronouncements, even *obiter dicta*, as a bulwark against the tides of relativism, the claims of science, and the inroads of modernity."[8]

Impact of Vatican II: Cultural Trauma and Fundamentalism

Vatican II radically affected the church's contemporary expression of its foundational mythology of integralism in three ways, and the result had to be the confusion and malaise of cultural trauma.[9] First, it sought to reintroduce a much-needed *balance* within the mythology; for example, the principle of collegiality was highlighted in order to counter centuries-long overemphasis on papal authority. The theology of Vatican II is filled with tension caused by ambiguity, resulting from the reintroduction of the polar opposites of key myths within the creation mythology. Gone are the unequivocal certainties of the pre–Vatican II apologetics premised on the assumption that theological opposites do not exist. Here are three ambiguities to ponder:

- The church is an institution under the leadership of the bishops *but* it is also the people of God who as pilgrims are not concerned about rank.

---

[7] See Massimo Faggioli, *Vatican II: The Battle for Meaning* (Mahwah, NJ: Paulist Press, 2010), 24–37; Joseph A. Komonchak, "Modernity and the Construction of Roman Catholicism," in *Modernism as a Social Construct*, ed. George Gilmore, et al. (Spring Hill, AL: Spring Hill College, 1991), 11–41; and Gabriel Daly, *Transcendence and Immanence: A Study in Catholic Modernism and Integralism* (Oxford: Clarendon, 1980).

[8] Malise Ruthven, *Fundamentalism* (Oxford: Oxford University Press, 2004), 46.

[9] See Gerald A. Arbuckle, *Refounding the Church: Dissent for Leadership* (New York: Orbis Books, 1993), 41–43.

- The church is universal, *but* it is to be incarnated within local churches to reflect their diversities of culture.

- Priesthood is a sacrament and ministry established by Christ, *but* all who are baptized are priests.

Nowhere in the documents does the council spell out precisely *how* these polar opposites are to be balanced in real life, and, in fact, it simply could not do so. If it had done so, the council would have fallen into a fundamentalist trap. Rather, the council challenged Catholics to struggle in faith to develop *a living balance* between the opposites. Ultimately this balance can be achieved over time only if all sides interiorize the vision of the church as Christ's Mystical Body as given to us by St Paul: "Now there are varieties of gifts, but the same Spirit . . . and there are varieties of activities, but it is the same God who activates all of them in everyone. To each is given the manifestation of the Spirit for the common good. . . . As it is, there are many members, yet one body. . . . Now you are the body of Christ and individually members of it" (1 Cor 12:4-7, 20, 27).

For example, the people and the structures of the local and the universal church will work together *only* if they recognize that they must pursue a common task—Christ's mission to the world. This does not mean abdicating the gifts and authority given them by the Lord; in fact, as Paul so eloquently describes, the church cannot truly be itself if any structure claims it can function without structures representing the polar opposites in the church's mythology. Nor can they work together constructively through dialogue unless each is accountable to the other and to the whole. Thus, the council established the synod of bishops and episcopal conferences to model to the rest of the church how Rome and the bishops must be accountable to one another for the sake of mission.

Of course, historically, the council's call to foster, through dialogue, a living balance between the mythological opposites has all too rarely been heard and owned. Following the council, people opted with growing emotional intensity for one pole or the other. For example, one group would say, "The council says that the church is universal and this must be respected above everything else!" Another would say, "The particular churches must take precedence because that is what the council decrees!" Theological, pastoral, and liturgical controversies rapidly emerged, and especially in the early years after the council protagonists were able to grab media headlines, which added fuel to the fire of resistance between opposing groups. Such reactions generated an atmosphere in which opposing sides did not trust one another. When this happened each pole of the tension became closed to the other, which is a fundamentalist response.

The second quality in these documents—a quality that radically undermined static fundamentalist thinking at the time—is their emphasis, following Cardinal Newman in his 1845 book, *An Essay on the Development of Christian Doctrine,* on the fact that doctrines develop over time.

> The Tradition that comes from the apostles makes progress in the Church, with the help of the Holy Spirit. There is a growth in insight into the realities and words that are being passed on. This comes about in various ways. It comes through the contemplation and study of believers who ponder these things in their hearts.[10]

Catechesis Failure

The third quality of the documents that intensified cultural trauma was the council's decision, in contrast to previous councils, not to give a sharp focus to its deliberations. "Nothing," writes Father John O'Malley, SJ, "is more characteristic of Vatican II than the breadth of its concerns, never neatly packaged into a central issue."[11] The council said, "take the Good News out to the world, but listen to its needs and be prepared to learn and be changed by it!" It could not tell us how to respond to this imperative pastorally, just as it could not spell out how to reconcile the polar opposites in the myths listed above.

As a theologian I am grateful for the council's documents and regret that the council was not called earlier, but as an anthropologist I believe the council was naïve about the effect its statements would have on Catholics culture. It failed to remind Catholics that the radical

---

[10] *Documents of Vatican II*, ed. Austin P. Flannery (Grand Rapids: Eerdmans, 1975), "Dogmatic Constitution on Divine Revelation," (*Dei Verbum*), par. 8.

[11] John W. O'Malley, "Developments, Reforms, and Two Reformations: Toward a Historical Assessment of Vatican II," *Theological Studies* 44, no. 3 (1983): 395.

mythological changes called for by the council would inevitably lead to a period of lengthy painful and confusing cultural trauma.[12] For centuries Catholics had been treated like dependent children in that they were told by a clerical leadership exactly how to win salvation, usually by obeying a list of detailed rules. Suddenly the council says Catholics are to stand on their own feet and make decisions for themselves in light of the needs of the world, the Gospel, and church teaching.

> Many Catholics were left with the impression that what they had viewed as . . . absolute in form and structure was . . . subject to redefinition and cultural and territorial variation. Changes in Catholicism's core corporate ritual also suggested the troubling possibility that other constituent elements of the Church were not objective, superimposed "givens," but that they too had been (and could be) sociologically and historically constructed and reconstructed.[13]

The fact is that Vatican II radically altered the existing mythos of the church and no such change is possible without being catastrophic. The resulting fundamentalist turmoil on the left and right in the church should have been expected and a better catechesis prepared to explain the inevitable chaotic, yet potentially creative, consequences of the council's decisions. We must recall the anthropological axiom that any rapid change in people's mythology, even a rumor of possible change, will intensify anxiety. Further, when identity is destabilized chaos is a real, even inevitable, possibility.[14]

In fairness to the council fathers, they were but men of their times and we moderns are rarely attuned to appreciate the devastating nature of radical mythological changes. Few bishops left the council aware that cultural changes of the profound nature required by the council would have to be slow and hesitant. They could not be

[12] See Arbuckle, *Culture, Inculturation, and Theologians: A Postmodern Critique* (Collegeville, MN: Liturgical Press, 2016), 35–36.
[13] Dinges, "Roman Catholic Traditionalism," 97.
[14] See Arbuckle, *Culture, Inculturation*, 19–34.

achieved overnight simply by episcopal decrees.[15] As canonist Father Ladislas Orsy, SJ, writes, "The insights of the Council [were] so penetrating and far reaching that they [could] be grasped only slowly—even for those who took part in it . . . To work on the unfolding of the mystery remains the task of the coming generations."[16] We are accustomed to seeing entire landscapes being destroyed and redeveloped over a short time. In our naïve appreciation of the power of technology, we assume that the same destruction and redevelopment can occur within cultures. We assume that symbolic landscapes of peoples can be destroyed and that the familiar sights, sounds, and routines in which peoples are nurtured can be obliterated overnight without particularly negative results.

This is simply not so. Symbols, myths, and rituals are not replaced as quickly or easily as buildings or landscapes or mass produced as neatly as automobiles or toothbrushes. The uprooting of the inner framework of cultures, even when there is conscious and intellectual assent to what is happening, destroys the stable sense of belonging and people's identities. They are bound to experience periods of intense loss. Consider the example of the civil rights movement in the United States in the 1960s. Many white Americans agreed wholeheartedly in principle to extend civil rights to African Americans and other minority groups. However, when the legal changes required that they *themselves* attitudinally and behaviourally alter their long established, white-centred interpretation of the founding story, they experienced all kinds of personal and collective turmoil. Remember that a key fact in this analysis of fundamentalism is that myths relate primarily to the heart. We can change our ideas and make all kinds of rational plans with ease, but dramatic change in mythic structures are bound to be traumatic, since the mythic structure is the way we impose felt order or meaning on the world and hold back chaos and its accompanying cultural trauma.

[15] See Gerald A. Arbuckle, *Humanizing Healthcare Reforms* (Philadelphia: Jessica Kingsley, 2013), 14–15.

[16] Ladislas Orsy, *Receiving the Council: Theological and Canonical Insights and Debates* (Collegeville, MN: Liturgical Press, 2009), 84.

Catholic Fundamentalist Movements

The mythology of Vatican II is radically different from that of integralism, so it is not at all surprising that Catholic fundamentalist movements resulted, namely, traditionalist/ schismatic and conservative/nonseparatist. In an effort to control what was happening, Rome increasingly sided with conservative fundamentalists.[17]

Traditionalist/Schismatic

The Catholic traditionalist movement began as a religious protest, a remonstration against what its followers perceived to be to the heretical disastrous event of Vatican II. The most notable leader of the traditionalists was Archbishop Marcel Lefebvre (1905–1991), founder of the Society of Pius X. Under his leadership traditionalists denounced the council as schismatic and they publicly attacked "modernist" and "Masonic" influences among the hierarchy and denounced the new liturgy as a "bastard rite."[18] They felt that the internal move to destroy the church from within had to be halted and demanded a return to the static, ahistorical theology, structures, and rituals of the pre-council church. Some of the key features of Catholic traditionalist fundamentalism as summarized by William Dinges are:

— Theological Foundation: "Catholicism is an exclusive deposit of doctrinal and moral truths"[19] handed down with no change from century to century.

— Faith is Cognitive: "Faith for Catholics is certain, objective, and devoid of any human subjectivity; faith is something to which one merely 'submits.' "[20]

— Liturgy: The Tridentine Mass alone is authentic.

— Ecumenism: There is no room for ecumenical dialogue because the Catholic Church alone is the one true church.[21]

---

[17] See Gerald A. Arbuckle, *The Francis Factor: New Life for the People of God* (Maryknoll, NY: Orbis Books, 2015), 161–92.

[18] See Dinges, "Roman Catholic Traditionalism," 76.

[19] Ibid., 82.

[20] Ibid., 85.

[21] Ibid., 87.

— Elitist and Exclusivist: "Traditionalism is . . . an action-oriented ideology. It is a position that seeks not merely to state an ecclesiology within the Catholic tradition but to discredit and eliminate all others."[22]

— Conspiracy Theories: "In addition to Satanic, communist, and Masonic allegations, traditionalist conspiracy theories have also been interwoven with anti-Semitic motifs, although the latter are a less prominent feature of traditionalist ideology."[23]

— Worldview: The world is basically evil.[24]

— Right-Wing Politics: Traditionalists have tended to support right-wing political movements like the John Birch Society in the United States and the reactionary movement of Jean-Marie Le Pen in France.[25]

Conservative/Nonschismatic

As cultural chaos developed in the church, further restorationist or fundamentalist movements, hoping for a return to a utopian past purified of "dangerous ideas and practices," continued to develop, for example, the Catholics United for the Faith (CUF), the Neo-Catechumenate, Opus Dei, and Communion and Liberation.[26] These movements sought to engage the support of Rome in their cause by the "co-option of [its] central executive and legislative power."[27] While not schismatic, nonetheless they have characteristics of fundamentalist integralism.

— Nostalgia for a pre–Vatican II golden age, when it is assumed that church never changed and existed as a powerful presence

---

[22] Ibid.

[23] Ibid., 90.

[24] Ibid., 99.

[25] Ibid., 91–92.

[26] See Arbuckle, *Violence, Society, and the Church: A Cultural Approach* (Collegeville, MN: Liturgical Press, 2004), 208–13. Communion and Liberation developed in the 1960s and 1970s mainly among university students in reaction against the revolutionary radicalization and moral decay of Italian society.

[27] Patrick Arnold, "The Rise of Catholic Fundamentalism," *America* (April 11, 1987): 298.

and political force in the world, undivided by misguided devotees of the council's values. The fact is that the church and its teachings have often changed. Today the pope alone can appoint a bishop, but this has not always been the case, for example, Pope Celestine I (c. 425) decreed that "No bishop should be installed against the will of the people," and Pope Leo IX in 1049 proclaimed that "Bishops are to be elected by clergy and people."[28] Some statements have been shown to be wrong and were either repealed or allowed to lapse; for example, for centuries the church assumed that slavery was morally acceptable.[29]

— A highly selective approach to what fundamentalists think pertains to the church's teaching: statements on *incidental* issues are obsessively affirmed, but papal or episcopal pronouncements on social justice are ignored or considered matters for debate only.

— The vehemence and intolerance with which they attack co-religionists who are striving to relate the Gospel to the world around them according to Vatican II. An elitist assumption that fundamentalists have a kind of supernatural authority and right to pursue and condemn those who disagree with them, including bishops and theologians. Jesus Christ is portrayed as an unforgiving and punishing God; the overwhelming compassion and mercy of Christ are overlooked.

Rome Supports Fundamentalist Reactions

Once the euphoria of the council began to fade, its inherent unaddressed weaknesses became more obvious. As long as these weaknesses remained unresolved, the cultural trauma among the people of God intensified. The council did not establish an appropriate process to implement its mythological changes. To fill the administrative

---

[28] See Maureen Fiedler and Linda Rabben, eds., *Rome Has Spoken: A Guide to Forgotten Papal Statements, and How They Have Changed through the Centuries* (New York: Crossroad, 1998), 92.

[29] Ibid., 81–90; see also William D. Dinges, "Roman Catholic Traditionalism," 66–101.

vacuum, in 1967, the unreformed bureaucratic curia would be responsible for the implementation of the council's major decrees.[30] This was an unfortunate move. An unreformed curia could scarcely be expected to lead a reform when its influential leaders did not believe in Vatican II. The curia, therefore, quickly and inevitably began to restore the preconciliar fundamentalist mythology. Responsible dissent[31] was increasingly forbidden by the curia and its supporting hierarchies around the world.[32] This section summarizes the ways in which Rome, in the midst of the cultural trauma following the council, aimed to draw the church back to embrace preconciliar theology and structures.

The Curia: A Fundamentalist Bureaucracy

Max Weber, having described the ideal type of bureaucracy, warns against its potential to dominate people's lives by becoming fundamentalist.[33] The following are interconnected negative qualities of bureaucracies that Weber and others have identified, each generating its own particular brand of organizational fundamentalist subjugation (see chapter 2):[34]

Abuse of Information. Bureaucrats are expected to implement policies by people in authority, but their control of the implementation gives them the chance to reinterpret the material of the policies, as well as to delay or even obstruct its introduction.[35]

---

[30] See John W. O'Malley, *What Happened at Vatican II* (Cambridge, MA: Belknap, 2008), 283; Hans Kung, *Can We Save the Church* (London: William Collins, 2013), 201–5.

[31] "To start with, theological dissent is the public expression by a theologian or group of theologians of a possibility for authentic Christian experience that differs from the official formulations of the range of possibilities of that experience received from the past and defined by the magisterium of the church." See Daniel Speed Thompson, *The Language of Dissent: Edward Schillebeeckx on the Crisis of Authority in the Catholic Church* (Notre Dame, IN: University of Notre Dame Press, 2003), 151.

[32] See Faggioli, *Vatican II*, 37.

[33] See Gareth Morgan, *Images of Organization* (London: Sage, 1986), 277–87.

[34] See Arbuckle, *Violence, Society*, 109–11.

[35] See Andrew Heywood, *Politics* (London: Macmillan, 1997), 351.

Detachment. In bureaucratic rationality the most important quality is *instrumental* reason, that is, *how* to do something rather than *why* to do it. The bureaucrat becomes detached from values and people and concerned for practical implementation. The culture allows separation of ethics from instrumental rationality, with the possibility that rational means will displace moral ends.[36]

No Personal Accountability or Dissent. Organizationally, the overall aim of a bureaucracy is divided among different offices, each of which has responsibility for a small section. It is not for people at each level to question their seniors; their task is to do what is asked of them. No responsible dissent encouraged.

Siloism. Bureaucracies are prone to siloism, that is, departments tribally operate independent of one another; they are secretive and resist sharing information across their boundaries.[37] This jealously guarded departmental individualism is inimical to the development of teamwork across the silo barriers.[38]

Facts over Feelings. To the bureaucrat, the world is a world of facts to be assessed according to pre-established rule, impersonally and unemotionally.

Self-Perpetuating Succession. A bureaucracy takes on a life of its own. The danger is that it will do anything to keep perpetuating itself, so people are recruited who will maintain the status quo.[39]

At the beginning of the council, the curia had the above bureaucratic failings and they remained intact up to the time of Pope Francis. In his address to the Roman Curia on December 22, 2014, the pope strongly censured the curia. It was, he said, suffering from fundamentalist bureaucratic diseases, which he unambiguously named as: "neglecting the need for regular

[36] See Zygmunt Bauman, *Modernity and the Holocaust* (Cambridge: Polity Press, 1989), 206.

[37] See Gillian Tett, *The Silo Effect* (London: Little Brown, 2015), 13.

[38] See Henry Mintzberg, *Managing* (Harlow: Pearson, 2009), 169–70.

[39] See Robert Michels, *Political Parties* (New York: Free Press, 1949); Jim McGuigan, *Modernity and Postmodern Culture* (Buckingham: Open University, 1999), 45–46.

check-ups"; having a "pathology of power"; having "poor co-ordination"; paralysed by "mental and spiritual 'petrification'"; crippled by "rivalry and vainglory"; restricting "themselves to bureaucratic matters, thus losing contact with reality, with concrete people"; "indifference to others"; and operating as "closed circles."[40]

Responsible Dissent Is Discouraged

By the early 1970s, theologians had begun to voice their growing anxiety at the curia's obstructive behaviour and bemoaned lost opportunities to implement the council's vision for the church. In 1974, Father Karl Rahner, SJ, forthrightly wrote that "[There] is no Christian principle to the effect that the conservatives must always be right when a choice has to be made between [the Roman Curia and its supporters and future-oriented people]."[41] Of theologians, James Provost, then professor of canon law at The Catholic University of America, wrote in 1989, "The rejection of any type of 'dissent' from non-infallible positions has been severe, despite the exception made for many years in the case of Archbishop Lefebvre. There has been an on-going harassment of theologians . . . which often appears as an attempt to appease influential minorities." Provost commented that the way this authority is being used on occasions "has the appearance of a defensive effort to exercise centralized control—defensive against the 'evil' world in contrast to the Second Vatican Council's views . . . defensive of a very limited school of theology."[42] This harassment of theologians significantly continued through Pope Benedict's pontificate.

As in all witch hunts, disrespect for truth and human rights can take place, as the following description of the judicial process formed

---

[40] Pope Francis, www.w2.vatican.va/content/francesco/en/speeches/2014/december/documents/papa-francesco_20141222_curia-romana.html (accessed April 21, 2016).

[41] Karl Rahner, *The Shape of the Church to Come* (New York: Seabury Press, 1974), 49.

[42] James Provost, "The Papacy: Power, Authority, Leadership," in *The Papacy and the Church in the United States*, ed. Bernard Cooke (New York: Paulist Press, 1989), 205.

by the Congregation for the Doctrine of the Faith (CDF) shows.[43] It remains substantially unaltered since it was inaugurated in 1971:[44] CDF is prosecutor, judge, and jury; the person being investigated is not told of the inquiry until stage thirteen (of eighteen stages) and may never know the identity of their accusers; the defendant is unable to choose their defender or even know the latter's identity, nor is there access to material relating to the allegations against the accused; no publicity is permitted concerning the proceedings and there is no right of appeal.[45] Serious injustices can happen. For the CDF secrecy is important in the judicial process. Secrecy is a powerful weapon of control in witch hunting and it is a particular quality of hierarchical cultures. It is a way for elites to maintain power through the possession of special knowledge, and by nonelites in order to protect themselves against the obtrusive interference of the elite.[46] In 2009, Ladislas Orsy repeated his concern that creative theologians in

[43] For further explanation, see Gerald A. Arbuckle, *Catholic Identity or Identities? Refounding Ministries in Chaotic Times* (Collegeville, MN: Liturgical Press, 2013), 15–20.

[44] The Holy See published new rules in 1997 called "Regulations for the Examination of Doctrines," which modified existing norms governing the scrutiny of theologians. However, they do not substantially change the previous rules. As canonist Ladislas Orsy writes, "for anyone educated in the sensitivities of jurisprudence, [they] do not respond, as they were intended, to the demands of the present day. . . . They have their roots in past ages; they were not born from the vision of human dignity and the respect for honest conscience that is demanded the world over today. . . . They are not rooted in any divine precept." *Receiving the Council: Theological and Canonical Insights and Debates* (Collegeville, MN: Liturgical Press, 2009), 102–3.Theologian Elizabeth Johnson had not heard that the Committee on Doctrine of the United States Bishops Conference had examined and rigorously criticized her book, *Quest for the Living God*, until the day prior to the publication of their document. She had never been invited to meet and dialogue with the committee. See Richard R. Gaillardetz, "The Elizabeth Johnson Dossier," in *When the Magisterium Intervenes: The Magisterium and Theologians in Today's Church*, ed. Richard R. Gaillardetz (Collegeville: Liturgical Press, 2012), 178.

[45] This description comes from B. Quelquejeu and is quoted by Richard A. McCormick and Richard P. O'Brien, "L'Affaire Curran II," *America* 163, no. 6 (1990): 128.

[46] See Donald N. Levine, *The Flight from Ambiguity: Essays in Social and Cultural Theory* (Chicago: University of Chicago Press, 1985), 33; Gerald A. Arbuckle, *Confronting the Demon: A Gospel Response to Adult Bullying* (Collegeville, MN: Liturgical Press, 2003), 65–94.

constant fear of being silenced endangered the church's future: "creative thinkers are one of the greatest assets of our church: they let the
internal riches of the evangelical message unfold."[47] In brief, the task
now assigned to theologians became increasingly reduced to explaining the authoritative pronouncements of the official church. This is
a return to pre–Vatican II practice.

The theologian Father Charles Curran, when assessing in 2012 the
growing censuring of theologians and anyone who questions Rome's
authoritarian decision-making processes, concludes that it is now
only concerned to maintain "a remnant church—a small and pure
church that sees itself often in opposition to the world around it."
This model of the church, he argues, "is opposed to the best understanding of the Catholic Church." He continues, "The church embraces both saints and sinners, rich and poor, female and male, and
political conservatives and liberals. Yes, there are limits to what it
means to be a Catholic, but the 'small "c" catholic' understanding
insists on the need to be as inclusive is possible."[48]

Collegiality Downplayed

The revised Code of Canon Law promulgated in 1983 also very
clearly gave the message to the universal church that Rome was
turning its back on the council. Orsy noted in 1991 that the revised
code "offers little or no help for [the] evolution of [particular churches]
and we are all the poorer for it."[49] Rome weakened the authority of

---

[47] Ladislas Orsy, *Receiving the Council*, 103.

[48] Charles Curran, www.ncronline.org/news/condemnation-just-love-not
-surprise-day-and-age (accessed June 7, 2012). John L. Allen thinks that Benedict
XVI no longer believes in the notion of a "remnant church," that is, a church that
is smaller in order to be more pure. To support his view Allen cites the pope's
commitment to a New Evangelization, which aims to draw lapsed Catholics
back to the church in the Western world and to reach out to others who feel
alienated by postmodernity, www.ncronline.org/blogs/all-things-catholic
/benedict-xvi-pope-ironies (accessed May 1, 2012).

[49] Ladislas Orsy, "The Revision of Canon Law," in *Modern Catholicism: Vatican
II and After*, ed. Adrian Hastings (London: SPCK, 1991), 22; see also Knut Walf,
"The New Canon Law-The Same Old System: Preconciliar Spirit in Postconciliar
Formulatio," in *The Church in Anguish: Has the Vatican Betrayed Vatican II?*, ed.
Hans Kung and Leonard Swidler (San Francisco: Harper and Row, 1986), 90.

the episcopal conferences and the bishops' synod; the new code speaks about the collaborative rights of episcopal conferences in about ninety places, but on careful evaluation it is clear that allowances for decentralization are outweighed by the emphasis given to Rome. For example, the USA Episcopal Conference in 1983 was told by Rome that it did not have the skills to write a pastoral letter on peace.[50]

The Church as "the People of God" Edited Out

The 1985 Extraordinary Synod met to evaluate the role of the council in the postconciliar church, but "its abandonment of 'the People of God' as the key concept in understanding the Church and its 'pessimistic' re-editing of 'the signs of the times,' [were] further evidence of the dismantling of the heritage of Paul VI"[51] and the council, thus evoking more disappointment and sadness in the church. In 1985, Cardinal Joseph Ratzinger's (later Pope Benedict XVI) published an evaluation of the post–Vatican II church, which initiated further alarm and grief among evangelizers committed to a culture of openness and apostolic boldness within the church.[52] Even allowing for obvious excesses following the council, the emotional and condemnatory expressions he used of the postconciliar years are disturbing, calling it, for example, a period of "self-destruction," "discouragement," and "decadence."[53] The model of the church as "the people of God" caused him anxiety,[54] as also the prominence given to the teaching role of episcopal conferences. He highlighted the relevance using the threat of excommunication as a way ultimately to control theologians or others judged to be endangering the "purity" of the church's teaching and boundaries.[55] Overall, there was a negativity and an undisguised fear of the new throughout his book. He said nothing about

[50] See Peter Hebblethwaite, "The Pope and the Bishops," *The Tablet* (April 30, 1983): 400–402.

[51] Peter Hebblethwaite, *Paul VI: The First Modern Pope* (New York: Paulist Press, 1993), 7.

[52] See Joseph Ratzinger with Vittorio Messori, *The Ratzinger Report: An Exclusive Interview on the State of the Church* (San Francisco: Ignatius Press, 1985).

[53] Ibid., 28.

[54] Ibid., 48–49.

[55] Ibid., 24–26.

the need to interact with the postmodern world or the role of prophetic persons and institutions that risk the new for the building of the Kingdom.

Liturgical Reform Centralized

In 2001, Rome issued *Liturgiam Authenticam*, a document firmly asserting that Rome has the right to intervene in liturgical matters.[56] It undermines what is at the center of Vatican II ecclesiology by further centralizing power in the curia and by demanding that local cultures implement an essentially Roman form of worship.[57] The curia-centered control is not to be confined to liturgical matters only but to embrace all aspects that relate to faith and culture including such matters as interreligious dialogue and social justice. Finally, in 2010, for many Catholics frustration with monarchical Rome reached a breaking point when it imposed a new English translation of the Roman Missal on the English-speaking world.[58] Rome refused to listen not just to angry experts in the English language but also to believers in the pews who found the translation to be archaic and not infrequently unintelligible. Not only is the language exclusive, but the translation slavishly follows the Latin style of long sentences broken up into numerous clauses. Justly, Eamon Duffy writes of "craven acquiescence of the English-speaking conferences [of bishops] in the ghastly translation of the Missal which now afflicts us."[59]

Lack of Transparency

In the early 1990s, the sex abuse scandals, including cover-ups by Rome and some bishops, began to hit the media and have continued

---

[56] For a liturgical critique of this document, see Gerard Moore, "Let Justice Find a Voice," *Worship* 90 (2016): 206–24.

[57] See John L. Allen, "New Document Replaces 35 Years of Liturgy Work," *National Catholic Reporter* (May 25, 2001): 13.

[58] See Philip Endean, "Worship and Power," *The Tablet* (August 28, 2010): 8–9; Peter J. Cullinane, "Liturgy and the Role of Bishops," *The Tablet* (July 30, 2011): 17–18; Seasoltz, *A Virtuous Church: Catholic Theology, Ethics, and Liturgy for the 21st Century* (New York: Orbis, 2012), 200.

[59] Eamon Duffy, "Style is Not Enough," *The Tablet* (March 8, 2014): 7. Duffy is professor of the history of Christianity at Cambridge University.

ever since.[60] Not just anger and compassion for the victims, but also an ever-increasing sense of shame has become the daily burden of a grieving church. Trust was broken and morale shattered, resulting in thousands leaving the church. Rome's moral integrity and credibility was undermined.[61] The church is now seen to lack the transparency and accountability demanded by the council, a church "more concerned with protecting the reputation of the institution and the clerical profession than in safeguarding real or potential child victims."[62] Even George Weigel, a very conservative observer, complained that "the People of God are treated as if they were cattle, not sheep to be nourished and shepherded."[63] When the cardinals met in 2005, they urged as a priority the reform of the curia, but this reform did not take place under Benedict XVI; the situation further deteriorated during his pontificate.[64] John Thavis commented that Benedict XVI "faced with actual evidence of impropriety and infighting in his own city-state . . . appeared uninterested."[65] In 2013, Thavis described the bureaucratic dysfunctionality in the curia with its silo mentality:

> [A] patchwork of departments, communities and individuals, all loosely bound by a sense of mission but without comprehensive management or rigorous oversight . . . where each agency of the Roman Curia jealously guards its turf, where the little guys and big shots may work at cross-purposes and where slipups and misunderstandings are common.[66]

---

[60] See Philip Jenkins, *Pedophiles and Priests: Anatomy of a Contemporary Crisis* (Oxford: Oxford University Press, 1996), 46–47.

[61] The bishops of New Zealand, in their address to the Pope in 1998, reflected the ongoing frustration of many episcopal conferences: "[W]ithin the household of the Catholic Church itself, Discasteries [i.e., curia] of the Holy See occasionally make norms which impinge on the ministry of bishops with little or no consultation of the episcopate as such. This seems inconsistent." Bishop Peter J. Cullinane, "A Time to Speak Out," *The Tablet* (November 22, 1998), 1589.

[62] Jenkins, *Pedophiles*, 3–4.

[63] George Weigel, *Evangelical Catholicism: Deep Reform in the 21st Century Church* (New York: Basic Books, 2013), 251.

[64] See Weigel, *Evangelical Catholicism*, 250.

[65] John Thavis, *The Vatican Diaries* (London: Penguin, 2013), 302.

[66] Ibid., 5.

Examples of this organizational sickness became sadly evident in such things as the lengthy delay—despite the extent of the evidence available—in admitting the scandalous behavior of Marcial Degollado Maciel, [67] founder of the Legionaries of Christ,[68] and the failure to research Bishop Richard Williamson's background as a member of the schismatic Society of St Pius X.[69]

Scapegoating Women Religious

Three groups within the church are relatively powerless: women, theologians, and the poor.[70] For this reason they are in constant danger of becoming the objects of ecclesiastical witch hunting. Certainly the scapegoating of theologians and women intensified in this period from the later 1980s onwards. In 2009, Benedict XVI deputized Cardinal Franc Rode, Prefect of the Congregation for Religious, to lead a review of American women's religious communities. Thousands of women religious who had loyally given their lives to frontline evangelization, often with minimal financial support, came under suspicion by Rome. Many are now elderly and not infrequently living close to the poverty line. However, the months-long investigation quickly lost credibility and momentum when pictures were published of the cardinal robed in a medieval, expensive scarlet *capa magna* ordaining deacons. The contrast between the cardinal's symbols of monarchical power and prestige stood in vivid contrast to the simple lifestyles of the religious women. In 2012, the Congregation for the Doctrine of the Faith (CDF) announced that it would begin an assessment of the theological orthodoxy of the Leadership Conference of Women Religious (LCWR). This decision was made without consultation or knowledge of the Cardinal Braz de Aviz, Prefect of the Congregation for Institutes of Consecrated Life and Societies of Apostolic

---

[67] See Weigel, *Evangelical Catholicism*, 186–87.

[68] See Thavis, *The Vatican Diaries*, 69–116.

[69] Ibid., 144–82. Williamson denied that the Jewish holocaust had occurred.

[70] See Daniel S. Thompson, *The Language of Dissent: Edward Schillebeeckx on the Crisis of Authority in the Catholic Church* (Notre Dame: University of Notre Dame Press, 2003), 1–9; Bradford E. Hinze, "A Decade of Disciplining Theologians," Gaillardetz, *When the Magisterium Intervenes*, 3–39; Arbuckle, *Violence, Society*, 144–46.

Life—a sad example of the bureaucratic compartmentalization or siloism.

Anthropological Reflection

Anthropologist Mary Douglas describes one particular model of culture, which she terms *strong group/strong grid*,[71] that helps to explain the nature of the culture Rome was trying to reimpose on the people of God. In this model the boundaries of the culture and the way individuals are to relate to one another within these boundaries are rigidly defined and maintained.[72] The wider threatening world of change must be kept at bay for fear that it will destroy the purity of the culture. They are orthodox in that people are expected to fit into a tradition-based, bureaucratic, hierarchical, and patriarchal system. Dress codes are formal. The cosmology of the culture mirrors and reinforces this static system. Identities are normative,[73] that is, they are imposed by tradition and are commonly reduced to one dominant identity, namely, unquestioning submission to the status quo. Since responsible dissent is forbidden, those who dare to dissent are marginalized. They become "non-people." Since the role of official leaders is to maintain the status quo, they emphasize ceremonies or formal displays of power, rather than ritual, which is transformative, whereas ceremony reinforces the cultural status quo.[74] Inaugurals are ceremonies and funerals are rituals.

---

[71] See particularly the following studies by Mary Douglas, *Natural Symbols: Explorations in Cosmology* (New York: Pantheon Books, 1970), and *Purity and Danger: An Analysis of the Concepts of Pollution and Taboo* (London: Routledge and Kegan Paul, 1966).

[72] For a fuller explanation of this model as applied to the church, see Arbuckle, *Refounding the Church*, 80–85.

[73] See Arbuckle, *Catholic Identity*, 3–4.

[74] Victor Turner distinguishes ritual from ceremony: "Ritual is transformative, ceremony confirmatory." *The Forest of Symbols: Aspects of Ndembu* (Ithaca: Cornell University Press, 1976), 164. Ceremonies confirm and reinforce the pre-existing order of status and roles; rituals are concerned with the change in status or role. Turner sees that ritual is the temporary suspension of social hierarchies, the remaking of personal identities, and the stimulation of cultural creativity; Arbuckle, *Culture, Inculturation*, 81–98.

Many of the people of God felt betrayed by the fundamentalist Roman cultural imperialism. And the shame resulting from the publication of more and more scandals—both sexual and institutional—evoked a collective depression that is characteristic of cultural trauma. Hans Kung concluded that the church was in such suppressed grief that it was now suffering from a "debilitating and potentially terminal illness."[75] Anthropologically, he is correct. Vatican II had theoretically returned the church to the mythology of the Gospel raising the expectations of the people of God. Yet, the more the institutional church encouraged the mythology of the precouncil era to resurface the more those who remained in the church were tempted to despair. Those who had believed in the council's vision felt betrayed by the institutional church's failure to live up to the promise of its vision.

Pope Francis: "No" to Fundamentalism

More than by fear of going astray, my hope is that we will be moved by the fear of remaining shut up within structures which gives us a false sense of security, within rules which make us harsh judges, within habits which make us feel safe, while at our door people are starving and Jesus does not tire of saying to us: "Give them something to eat" (Mark 6:37).[76]

—Pope Francis

The residual founding mythology of the church itself, not the preconciliar mythology, has slowly begun to resurface under the leadership of Pope Francis, a wisdom figure. Through his actions and words he is leading the church in a ritual of letting go of attachments to a monarchical papacy and its theological foundations. At last, the people of God have permission to mourn publicly. Despite the cul-

[75] Hans Kung, *Can We Save the Catholic Church?* (London: William Collins, 2013), 1.
[76] Pope Francis, Apostolic Exhortation, *The Joy of the Gospel* (*Evangelii Gaudium*) (Sydney: St. Pauls Publications, 2013), par. 49.

tural resistance from the curia and others, Pope Francis struggles to build governance structures to ensure that the Vatican II mythology is finally and firmly embedded in the church's culture. From the moment of his election he adopted a new style of leadership based on the founding mythology of the Church. By his words and behavior he has said a definite "no" to deadening fundamentalist restorationism with its insistence on coercive rules, and an unambiguous "yes" to be involved in the hopes and frustrations of people and their cultures.

> If the Christian is a restorationist, a legalist, if they want everything clear and safe, they will find nothing. . . . Those who today always look for disciplinarian solutions, those who long for an exaggerated doctrinal "security," those who stubbornly try to recover a past that no longer exists—they have a static and inward-directed view of things. . . . God is in every person's life. Even if the life of a person has been a disaster. . . . You must try to seek God in every human life. Although the life of a person is a land full of thorns and weeds, there is always a space in which the good seed can grow. You have to trust God.[77]

A church that is fearful of the world becomes a church of protective rules, a fortress church of the preconciliar type. Francis will have none of this. As Cardinal he had said that the church had become "too wrapped up in itself . . . too navel-gazing . . . 'self-referential'" and this had "made it sick . . . suffering a 'kind of theological

---

[77] Pope Francis, www.americamagazine.org/pope-interview (accessed October 1, 2013). A group of forty-five priests and theologians criticised the 2016 apostolic exhortation, *The Joy of Love* (*Amoris Laetitia*) of Pope Francis. They claim there are several statements "whose vagueness or ambiguity permit interpretations that are contrary to faith and morals, or that suggest a claim that is contrary to faith and morals without actually stating it." They are asking for "definitive and final" clarifications of the texts. Theologian Gerald O'Collins, SJ, correctly points out that this is impossible, as the exhortation notes by referring to the teachings of St. Thomas Aquinas (par. 304). "General rules," writes O'Collins, "have a clarity that is often not available in the actions that constitute the concrete life of human beings." "An Illusion of Certainty," *The Tablet* (July 30, 2016): 8. The complainants are asking for "exaggerated doctrinal 'security'" where this is impossible in the exhortation; their request suggests theological fundamentalism.

narcissism.' "[78] As pope he has written, "I prefer a Church which is bruised, hurting and dirty because it has been out in the streets, rather than a Church that is unhealthy from being confined and from clinging to its own security."[79] Neither the church nor the evangelizer is to be the focus of our concern, but rather the "center is Jesus Christ, who calls us and sends us forth."[80] The church's primary task is to evangelize, not to protect itself from the sufferings of others especially people who are poor and vulnerable.

> Mere administration can no longer be enough . . . I dream of a "missionary option," that is, a missionary impulse capable of transforming everything, so that the Church's customs, ways of doing things, times and schedules, language and structures can be suitably channeled for the evangelization of today's world rather than for her self-preservation.[81]

His primary model of the church, therefore, is not hierarchical but the people of God: "The image of the church I like is that of the holy, faithful people of God. . . . There is no full identity without belonging to a people."[82] And Francis expresses this identity personally by openly proclaiming, "I am a sinner." Little wonder that Francis is such a powerful communicator. People feel he understands them.

Culture and Inculturation

Francis has a particularly sensitive feeling for the power and importance of cultures. A culture is not something static or mechanistic.

[78] Cardinal Jorge Bergoglio to cardinals meeting in conclave, cited by Paul Valllely, *Pope Francis: Untying the Knots* (London: Bloomsbury, 2013), 155. During the Easter rituals in 2013 Francis warned the clergy against becoming mere "managers" or "antique collectors" obsessed with liturgical niceties, urging them to leave their sacristies to change the secular world. See William Pfaff, "Challenge to the Church," *The New York Review of Books* (May 9, 2013): 11.

[79] Pope Francis, *The Joy of the Gospel*, par. 49.

[80] Pope Francis, www.ncronline.org/news/spirituality/pope-francis-ecclesi ology-rooted-emmaus-story (accessed August 7, 2013).

[81] Pope Francis, *The Joy of the Gospel*, pars. 25, 27.

[82] Pope Francis, www.americamagazine.org/pope-interview (accessed April 1, 2014).

Rather it "is a dynamic reality which a people constantly recreates."[83] For this reason he forthrightly believes in inculturation, namely, the need to begin theology with the realities of people's lives, hearts, and cultures, not placing metaphysics as its center. Inculturation has too long meant in papal thinking that all cultures must adapt to a Rome-centered view of the church.[84] Given his emphasis on inculturation, it is not surprising that Francis has reinstated the role of the social sciences as means to better understand the complexity of cultures and how they can assist the process of pastoral discernment.[85] Contrary to Vatican II thinking, Rome had become increasingly suspicious of these sciences.

Dialogue

Francis believes in the importance of dialogue—something that is abhorrent to fundamentalists. He returns to the importance of polar opposites, an integral quality of the Vatican II documents.[86] For example, in his Exhortation, *The Joy of the Gospel,* he uncompromisingly repeats the church's stand against abortion: "This is not something subject to alleged reforms or 'modernization.' It is not 'progressive' to try to resolve problems by eliminating a human life."[87] But immediately he enters a different discourse: the world of human praxis, from which he has repeatedly stressed that doctrinal and moral certainties must never be divorced. He writes,

> On the other hand, it is also true that we have done little to adequately accompany women in very difficult situations, where abortion appears as a quick solution to their profound anguish, especially when the life developing within them is the result of rape or a situation of extreme poverty. Who can remain unmoved before such painful situations?[88]

---

[83] Pope Francis, *The Joy of the Gospel,* par. 122.

[84] See Arbuckle, *Culture, Inculturation,* 138–51.

[85] See Pope Francis, *The Joy of the Gospel,* par. 40.

[86] See Gillian Paterson, "'On the Other Hand . . .' The Catholic Church and Some Discourses on Population," *The Heythrop Journal* 55, no. 6 (2014): 1109.

[87] Pope Francis, *The Joy of the Gospel,* par. 214.

[88] Ibid.

"On the other hand," he writes. And in that lies a profound truth. For Francis is trying to balance two kinds of opposing moral discourse: one that rightly takes an absolute view of human life, and another that rightly shows a compassionate appreciation for vulnerable people in the context of their lived human realities. What that means is that there can be no "monolithic body of doctrine guarded by all and leaving no room for nuance."[89] Four times in the same document he uses the phrase "on the other hand." Likewise, in his Exhortation, *The Joy of Love*, he uses the expression ten times, for example,

> "[P]rincipal tendencies . . . are leading individuals . . . to receive less and less support from social structures than in the past," *but* "[O]n the other hand equal consideration needs to be given to the growing danger represented by an extreme individualism."[90]

> "[T]he supposedly mature believers within the family become unbearably arrogant," *but* "Love, on the other hand, is marked by humility."[91]

> "It needs to be emphasized that biological sex and the sociocultural role of sex (gender) can be distinguished but not separated," *but* "On the other hand, the technological revolution in the field of human procreation has introduced the ability to manipulate the reproductive act."[92]

> "Those who know that their spouse is always suspicious . . . will tend to keep secrets . . . and pretend to be someone other than who they are," *but* "On the other hand, a family marked by loving trust, come what may, helps its members to be themselves and spontaneously to reject deceit."[93]

> "It is a joy and a great consolation to bring delight to others," *but* "On the other hand, joy also grows through pain and sorrow."[94]

---

[89] Ibid., par. 40.
[90] Pope Francis, *The Joy of Love* (*Amoris Laetitia*), pars. 32, 33.
[91] Ibid., par. 98.
[92] Ibid., par. 56.
[93] Ibid., par. 115.
[94] Ibid., pars. 129, 130.

He does not, and cannot, say *how* the polar opposites are to be reconciled in particular situations. This shows how desperately we need appropriate catechesis and dialogue to avoid fundamentalism based on the exclusive emphasis on either one pole or the other in the tension. As Pope Francis writes, "We have been called to form consciences, not to replace them."[95]

Summary Points

1. "Integralism" is a term that describes the fundamentalist attitudes of Catholics who reject the teachings of Vatican II. The documents of the council, if wrongly understood, lend themselves to fundamentalist interpretations.

2. Since the council's documents undermined the existing culture of order and predictability, many in the church experienced cultural trauma.

3. Given the breakdown of the church's existing culture, it is not surprising that Catholic fundamentalist movements resulted, for example, traditionalist/schismatic and conservative/non-separatist. Prior to Pope Francis, the Roman Curia, in an effort to control what was happening sided with conservative fundamentalists.

4. Pope Francis by word and action has declared an unambiguous "no" to fundamentalism in the church. For example, he is firmly behind Vatican II's insistence on the development of dogmas: "The Church . . . she needs to grow in her interpretation of the revealed word and in her understanding of truth. . . . For those who long for a monolithic body of doctrine guarded by all and leaving no room for nuance, this might appear as undesirable and leading to confusion. But in fact such variety serves to bring out and develop facets of the inexhaustible riches of the Gospel."[96]

---

[95] Ibid., par. 37.
[96] Pope Francis, *The Joy of the Gospel*, par. 40.

Discussion Questions

1. Pope Francis writes that "Religious fundamentalism is not religious, because it lacks God. It is idolatry, like idolatry of money." What does he mean?

2. Pope Francis challenges every diocese, parish, school, and individual when he writes, "More than by fear of going astray, my hope is that we will be moved by the fear of remaining shut up within structures which give us a false sense of security, within rules which make us harsh judges, within habits which make us feel safe, while at our door people are starving and Jesus does not tire of saying to us: 'Give them something to eat'(Mark 6:37)."[97] Discuss.

---

[97] Ibid, par. 49.

Chapter 5

Islamic Fundamentalism: Responding to Cultural Trauma

Local Islam is often very different from "Global Islam."[1]

—Raymond Scupin

The truth of the matter is: Islamism, like any other ideology, owes more to the historical conditions in which it was conceived than its advocates would like to admit.[2]

—Hazem Kandil

Key Points

- The historical context for the establishment of Islam by the Prophet Muhammad

- Contemporary types of Islam: traditional, modern, and restorative

- Causes, nature, and types of Islamic fundamentalism

---

[1] Raymond Scupin, "The Anthropology of Islam as 'Applied Anthropology,'" *Reviews in Anthropology* 32 (2003): 157.

[2] Hazem Kandil, *Inside the Brotherhood* (Cambridge: Polity Press, 2015), 177.

Raymond Scupin is right. There are many different local, historical, and cultural expressions of Islam, so that it is impossible to speak of a monolithic global Islam. For example, Muslims in Australia have migrated from fifty-seven different Muslim countries and each community brings with them a unique set of cultural behaviours and attitudes.[3] Nor does there exist a centralized authority to decide what is authentically Islamic. Hazem Kandil is also correct. Islamic fundamentalist movements have emerged over the last two centuries as a response to the cultural trauma caused by Western imperialism, the impact of Western values so contrary to the Islamic religion, and local political dictatorial elites.

In 1916, the British and French governments appointed Sir Mark Sykes and George-Picot, respectively, to decide secretly how to divide the lands of the Ottoman empire for the benefit of the victors at the conclusion of the First World War. At the war's end the borders were drawn so arbitrarily that the multiethnic and multiconfessional states that resulted are now difficult to govern. Sykes-Picot has become a catchphrase for the imperial duplicity by which Western powers have economically and militarily dominated the Arab world. The tragic consequences are particularly evident in the recent turmoil in Syria and Iraq.[4]

The aims of this chapter are to give a short introductory overview, briefly describe the historical emergence of Islam with its key concepts, and describe contemporary Islamic fundamentalist movements. The chapter will examine the way Islamic fundamentalism has been, and continues to be, influenced by political power movements external to and within Muslim countries. However, one chapter cannot do justice to the complexity of the many militant movements among Islamic fundamentalists and the multiple factors involved in their development. It is often assumed that if Islamic militants could be eradicated the problem of fundamentalism would cease. This is dangerously simplistic.[5] But while this chapter focuses on Islamic fundamentalism, we also need to remember that there are many mil-

---

[3] See Mehmet Ozalp, *Islam between Tradition and Modernity: An Australian Perspective* (Canberra: Barton Books, 2012), 144.

[4] See *The Economist* (January 2, 2015): 59.

[5] See Jason Burke, *The New Threat: The Past, Present, and Future of Islamic Militancy* (New York: New Press, 2015), 1–13 and passim.

lions of devoutly compassionate Muslims who earnestly seek to be close to the presence of God. As Pope Francis reminds us,

> We must never forget that [Muslims] profess to hold the faith of Abraham, and together with us they adore the one, merciful God, who will judge humanity on the last day.[6]
>
> They also acknowledge the need to respond to God with an ethical commitment and with mercy towards those most in need. . . . Faced with disconcerting episodes of violent fundamentalism, our respect for true followers of Islam should lead us to avoid hateful generalisations, for authentic Islam and the proper reading of the Koran are opposed to every form of violence.[7]

Overview

Following the conflagrations in New York and Washington on September 11, 2001, there was rejoicing on the West Bank and in Palestinian refugee camps, among the Taliban in Afghanistan, and praise to Allah among fanatical Muslims in Pakistan and northern Nigeria. The celebrations were overwhelmingly among the poor and dispossessed in the Muslim world. Some Westerners find this jubilation difficult to understand.[8] Why was this so?

Muslim peoples have an old and proud culture, but have long felt under attack from the West and this has left many traumatized. Islamic radicalism draws its power from a deep sense of injustice. Since the early nineteenth century scarcely a decade has passed without some Muslim area in Asia or Africa being threatened by Western powers. The Western world came to dominate once-proud Islam in military tactics, politics, trade, education, science, art, architecture, literature, and values.[9] Islamic fundamentalists feel that much has

---

[6] Vatican II, "Dogmatic Constitution on the Church" (*Lumen Gentium*), par. 16.

[7] Pope Francis, *The Joy of the Gospel* (*Evangelii Gaudium*) (Strathfield, Australia: St. Pauls, 2013), pars. 252–53.

[8] See Gerald A. Arbuckle, *Violence, Society, and the Church: A Cultural Approach* (Collegeville, MN: Liturgical Press, 2004), 200–201.

[9] See Vali Reza Nasr, American specialist in Middle East and Islamic affairs, "European Colonialism and the Emergence of Modern Muslim States," in *The*

been destroyed by contact with the West, including Koranic education, a sense of community, social coherence, the old religious legal system, and above all, respect for ancient Muslim culture and values. Globalization has intensified this feeling of loss by propagating pornography on the Internet, atomizing families, and contributing to the neglect of religious values. The West is blamed, but the United States in particular is seen as the "Great Satan" leading the destruction of all that is considered sacred. Political terrorism draws on this bitter resentment, and terrorists have a perverted hope that in the violent downfall of the Great Satan the world will be put right again.

The policies of the United States over the last twenty years have helped to create both Osama bin Laden and the fundamentalist Taliban regime that protected him in Afghanistan.[10] Bin Laden was outraged by the American occupation of the Saudi peninsula during and following the First Gulf War, and at the Saudi royal family for permitting the presence of American troops. For Osama, the killing of Americans and their supporters was the obligation of every Muslim.[11] The idea of jihad, or holy war, had almost stopped in the Islamic world after the tenth century but was revived, with American backing, in order to create a pan-Islamic movement following the Soviet invasion of Afghanistan in 1979. The United States sent billions of dollars' worth of weaponry to groups fighting the Soviets. The aid succeeded and the Soviets were forced to withdraw, but the results are everywhere to be seen: huge supplies of arms, powerful local warlords, and religious zealotry. Now the jihad has been taken into Pakistan, to the unjust kingdoms of the Gulf, the repressive states of the southern Mediterranean, and to the West itself. There are efforts to build states on Islamic foundations—some radical, for example, Iran and ISIS—and some less so, for example, Pakistan, Malaysia, and Indonesia.[12]

Oxford History of Islam, ed. John L. Esposito (Oxford: Oxford University Press, 2000), 549–99.

[10] See Richard MacKenzie, "The United States and the Taliban," in *Fundamentalism Reborn? Afghanistan and the Taliban*, ed. William Maley (London: Hurst, 2001), 90–103.

[11] See James Fergusson, *Taliban* (London: Corgi Books, 2010), 122.

[12] There is a vigorous Islamic revival taking place in Indonesia. Muslims who assert it is the duty of the state to enforce their puritanical style of religious piety are challenging pluralist Muslims who support an open modernistic society. See Merle C. Ricklefs, *Islamisation and Its Opponents in Java: A Political, Social, Cultural*

Today there are thousands of Palestinian exiles in refugee camps in Lebanon, Syria, and Jordan[13] living in poverty and overwhelmed with hopelessness. Frustration and outrage are attracting growing numbers of refugees to Islamic extremist groups. These dispossessed refugees believe violence in defence of their political and religious rights is the only way out of their oppressive conditions.[14] As long as the West continues to contribute to the volatile atmosphere, and unless the injustices are addressed, we can expect more violence and fundamentalist terrorist activity directed not just to fellow Muslims but also to Westerners.[15] The situation has been become more volatile because none of the injustices that drove the Arab Spring uprisings in the Middle East and North Africa have been addressed. In fact they have worsened.[16]

> There can be little doubt that terrorism . . . flourishes in circumstances where the state is perceived as corrupt or alien, ethnically or religiously unrepresentative or otherwise partisan and unrepresentative of the cultural and political aspirations of the population over which it governs, or a significant part thereof.[17]

The American anthropologist Dale Eickelman believes that the politicization of Islam in recent years is due not only to the ready availability and speed provided by contemporary communication technologies, but also to the decline of the influence of traditional religious scholars (*ulama*): "Increasingly the carriers of religious knowledge are those who claim a strong Islamic commitment, as is

---

and Religious History, c.1930 to the Present (Honolulu: University of Hawai'i Press, 2015); Carool Kersten, *Islam in Indonesia: The Contest for Society, Ideas and Values* (New York: Oxford University Press, 2015); Jeremy Menchik, *Islam and Democracy in Indonesia: Tolerance Without Liberalism* (New York: Cambridge University Press, 2016).

[13] As of February, 2016, over four million Syrian refugees are in Turkey, Lebanon, Jordan, Iraq, and Egypt.

[14] See *The Economist* (September 8, 2001): 51.

[15] See Burke, *The New Threat*, 1–13.

[16] See March Lynch, *The New Arab Wars: Uprisings and Anarchy in the Middle East* (New York: Public Affairs, 2016), 253. The apocalyptic civil war in Syria has displaced over ten million people and thousands have fled to Europe.

[17] Malise Ruthven, *A Fury for God: The Islamist Attack on America* (London: Granta Books, 2002), 238.

the case with many educated urban youths. Freed from traditional patterns of learning and scholarship, which have often been compromised by state control, religious knowledge is increasingly interpreted in a directly political fashion."[18]

The Origins of Islam

According to Islamic tradition, the angel Gabriel appeared to the Prophet Muhammad in the seventh-century Arabia, revealing to him, over the course of twenty plus years, messages from God. Muslims accept some earlier Judeo-Christian prophets—including Moses and Jesus Christ—as messengers of the same true God. In Islam, however, Muhammad is the last and the most esteemed prophet, whose revelations alone are authentic.[19] Justice, the love of God and neighbor, and mercy are at the foundational core of Islam. In 622, Muhammad escaped from persecution in Mecca to the city of Medina, accompanied by an army and overcame the city for Islam. The beginnings of Muslim political organization date from this incident. As noted in chapter 2, the greatest schism in the Muslim world appeared between 656 and 661, less than thirty years after the death of Muhammad. The reasons for this were purely political—who was to lead the Muslim community? The greatest schism was between Sunni and Shia. The Sunni, now almost 90 percent of all Muslims, claim that the leader or caliph must be a descendant of Muhammad's Arab tribe of Quraysh; on the other hand, for the Shia, now around 10 percent of Muslims, claim that the leadership must derive from a descendant of the Prophet. Shia are mostly found today in Iran and Iraq and among the Palestinians.

Today, despite the fact that Sunnis vastly outnumber Shia, Sunnis frequently feel marginalized in the Arab heartland—pushed to one side by the Shii majority in Iraq, under brutal assault by the regime of Bashar al-Assad in Syria (dominated by Alawites, an offshoot of Shiism), bullied in Lebanon by Hezbollah (a powerful Shia militia),

---

[18] Dale Eickelman, cited by Malise Ruthven, *Islam: A Very Short Introduction* (Oxford: Oxford University Press, 1997), 132–33. Ruthven is a renowned scholar and commentator on Islam and the Arab world.

[19] See Karen Armstrong, *Islam: A Short History* (London: Weidenfeld and Nicolson, 2001), 3–31.

and scattered and occupied by Israel in Palestine. In Yemen, Sunnis have been ousted by Houthi fighters. "It is often said that Shias cannot believe they have won power and Sunnis cannot accept they have lost it, which perhaps makes the strife more vicious."[20] As we will see both groups have extreme factions.

Five Pillars

Although Islam is a mythological collection of beliefs and rituals, it is also an arrangement of laws and a system of jurisprudence derived from the Koran and from the traditions of the Prophet Muhammad's rulings, as well as the history of social and legal decisions and interpretations. Taken together, all of this is known as *sharia*.[21] For this reason, we can say that "Christianity is primarily religion of love, Islam is above all the religion of justice."[22] The sacred text of Islam, the Koran, was written in Arabic within thirty years of the death of Muhammad and Muslims believe that it contains the literal word of God. For believing Muslims, the Koran is "the speech of God, dictated without human editing . . . to be regarded as 'uncreated,' hence coextensive with God."[23] No Muslim should touch the Koran if they are ritually impure, so sacred is its contents. The text is to be the only source of secular as well as religious law. For many Muslims, Islam is not only a personal faith but also a plan for arranging a perfect society. In other words, this means there can be no division between the secular world and religion. Also important is the tradition of the sayings and actions of Muhammad and companions which are called the Sunnah. The Koran affirms that Islam is a return to the purity of the religion of Abraham, who is neither Jew nor Christian.[24] In Islam, there are to be no appeals to prophets, saints, or any entity other than God.

---

[20] *The Economist* (May 14, 2016): 11.

[21] *Sharia*, strictly speaking, refers to the law that is divine and eternal; *fiqh* refers to pure human knowledge "of something already presumed to exist, the inquiry into how divine law works out in practical terms." Malise Ruthven, *Islam in the World*, 2nd ed. (London: Penguin, 2000), 137.

[22] Ibid., 219.

[23] Ruthven, *Islam: A Very Short*, 21.

[24] See Jacques Jomier, *How to Understand Islam* (London: Spartan Press, 1989), 14.

Islamic religious practice centers on the Five Pillars of Islam. The first pillar is the *shahada*, the profession of faith: "I testify that there is no god but Allah, and I testify that Muhammad is the Messenger of Allah." A conversion is assumed to be authentic when the profession is made in public. The second pillar is *salat*, or, prayer, a fundamental obligation to be performed both individually and publicly. Public prayer is required of men on Fridays and feast-days. *Zakat* is the third pillar, a type of tithe meant to support the poor. It has tended to lapse, except in countries such as Saudi Arabia, but it has been revived in contemporary fundamentalist movements. The fourth pillar is *sawm*, the annual fast of Ramadan during the ninth month in the lunar calendar, in which all food, drink, and sexual activity are not permitted between dawn and dusk. The fifth pillar is the *hajj*, the pilgrimage to Mecca, an obligation of every free male Muslim who has the finances to cover the costs of the journey and to support his family during his absence.

No topic is more contentious today than that of women and Islam.[25] Muhammad's thinking about the role of women in society was, as measured by the time of the seventh century, quite advanced. For example, Islamic law insisted that the education of girls was a sacred obligation and women had the right to own and inherit property. However, he did enshrine women's "inequality in immutable law, passed down as God's commandments and eventually recorded in scripture."[26] Thus, Islam accepts polygamy, teaches that men have a unilateral right to divorce without judicial trial and greater rights of inheritance, while women should be veiled.[27] The Koran (Surah 4:34) says that men have "pre-eminence" over women and that "the husband of an insubordinate wife should first admonish her, then leave her to sleep alone and finally beat her."[28] An Islamic theologian, Mehmet Ozalp, however, argues that puritanical Muslims instead of

[25] Ruthven, *Islam in the World*, 91–115.

[26] Lisa Beyer, "The Women of Islam," *Time* (November 25, 2001), reprint, 1, www.content.time.com/time/printout/0,8816,185647.00.html (accessed March 15, 2016).

[27] For a fuller analysis the role of women in Islamic religion, see Malise Ruthven, *Islam in the World*, 151–65.

[28] Beyer, "The Women of Islam"; see also Malise Ruthven, *Islam: A Very Short*, 91–115.

"looking at the totality of the Qur'an and the prophetic traditions and seeing how Islam and the Prophet empowered women . . . tend to rely on a few weaker traditions and interpret them in a manner that effectively suffocates the hopes and aspirations of Muslim women."[29]

Types of Contemporary Islam

It will be helpful to give a summary of the divisions within the Islamic world in response to the pressures arising both in history and modernity. Despite differences in the Islamic world, it is possible to identify three broad categories of reactions, with fundamentalists belonging to the third category:[30]

Traditional

Traditional forms of Islam combine the Muslim faith with the customs of local cultures in a process of acculturation. Thus, for example, in Indonesia much of the prior Hindu culture can be found in Islamic practices, for example, despite prohibitions about "no other god," Indonesians love stories about the Hindu god Ram.[31]

Modern

This type of Islamic thinking first developed in the eighteenth century and aimed to reform Islam by reviewing the prophet Muhammad's practices in light of contemporary reason. The major eighteenth-century thinkers for this form are Jamal al-Din al-Afghani (1838–1897) and Muhammad 'Abduh (1849–1905). The former argued that those who deny the importance of science and knowledge on the assumption that they are protecting

---

[29] Mehmet Ozalp, *Islam between Tradition and Modernity: An Australian Perspective* (Canberra: Barton Books, 2012), 192.

[30] For the following threefold division I am grateful to Leo D. Lefebure, "Islam and Modernity," *Chicago Studies* 42, no. 3 (2003): 322–33.

[31] See Robert W. Hefner, *Civil Islam: Muslims and Democratization in Indonesia* (Princeton, NJ: Princeton University Press, 2000), 14.

Islamic religion are really enemies of that religion. 'Abduh struggled to reform the major Islamic Egyptian educational institution, the University of al-Azhar. He believed that reason in Islamic religious thought is important and Islam must not be frightened of the consequences of reason.[32] As regards the integration of Muslims in Western countries, Malise Rutven, a well-known commentator on Islam, believes there "are many . . . indications of a positive and fruitful future for Islam in the West . . . where the climate of free association, freedom of expression, and religious freedom fosters the development of the spiritual as distinct from the legalistic Islamic traditions."[33]

Within Muslim countries, however, the interaction between Islamic thinking and modernity continues to be problematic.[34] Nurcholish Madjid (1939–2005) was a prominent Muslim Indonesian academic who argued that for Islam to be victorious in the global struggle for ideas it needs to embrace the concepts of tolerance, democracy, and pluralism. He claimed that the Koran had not demanded an Islamic state and that many Muslims had falsely sacralised a human-created political institution. Muslims, he argued, should secularize the political but retain what is sacred in Islamic tradition. He disagreed with the Western view of secularization that calls for religion to be reduced to something private and marginalized (see chapter 2). He believed that religion is an inevitable force and contended that the Islamic idea of *tawhid*, the conviction that God must be seen as one, involves a commitment to knowledge, reason, and science. His view has not been well received by those Muslims who strongly believe that Western secularization is incompatible with the aims of forming an Islamic state.[35]

[32] See John O. Voll, "Fundamentalism in the Sunni Arab World," in *Fundamentalisms Observed*, ed. Martin E. Martin and R. Scott Appleby (Chicago: University of Chicago Press, 1991), 354–56.

[33] Ruthven, *Islam in the World*, 400.

[34] See Fazlur Rahman, *Islam and Modernity: Transformation of an Intellectual Tradition* (Chicago: University of Chicago Press, 1982); Benazir Bhutto, "Politics and the Muslim Woman," in *Liberal Islam: A Source Book*, ed. Charles Kurzman (Oxford: Oxford University Press, 1998), 107–11.

[35] See Hefner, *Civil Islam*, 116–19.

Restorative

Restorative Muslims severely reprove Muslims for failing to follow strict Islamic doctrine, rituals, and practices, thus condemning traditional and modern types. Restorative Muslims claim that Islamic modernists and traditionalists have relapsed into the corrupt times of *jahiliyya*, that is, the deplorable condition of society prior to the coming of Muhammad. They often believe that Islam's military and political decline is due to the failure to be faithful to original Islamic sources. Present day militant Muslims belong to this group, but not all restorative Muslims are militants. God, according to the militant fundamentalist, and contrary to nonmilitant restoratives, needs human help for good eventually to triumph over evil because "most humans are believed to have only a weak commitment to God." It is the militant's task,[36] as God's helpers, "to serve God's cause by leading the fight against evil and protecting the majority against its natural propensity to sinfulness."[37] Islamic fundamentalist leaders are rarely theologians, rather, they are social thinkers and political activists.[38] For this reason they are particularly prone to choose whatever scriptural text helps their cause.

The Clash of Civilizations [39]

In 1996, the Harvard political scientist, Samuel Huntington, published his controversial book, *The Clash of Civilizations*,[40] in which he

[36] Mehdi Mozaffari, professor of political science at the University of Aarhus, Denmark, believes that *militancy* is the quality that defines every different form of Islamic fundamentalism. "Islam in Algeria and Iran," in *Islamic Fundamentalism*, ed. Abdel Salam Sidahmed and Anoushiravan Ehteshami (Oxford: Westview Press, 1996), 229.

[37] Bhikhu Parekh, *A New Politics of Identity: Political Principles for an Interdependent World* (Basingstoke: Palgrave Macmillan, 2008), 147.

[38] See Abdel Salam Sidahmed and Anoushiravan Ehteshami, eds., "Introduction," *Islamic Fundamentalism*, 3.

[39] See Gerald A. Arbuckle, *Culture, Inculturation, and Theologians: A Postmodern Critique* (Collegeville, MN: Liturgical Press, 2010), 69–70.

[40] See Samuel P. Huntington, *The Clash of Civilizations and the Remaking of World Order* (New York: Simon and Schuster, 1996).

argues that we have reached a phase in history, following the end of the Cold War, when the clash of ideologies has ended. In his view cultural identity would become more important in determining friendships within and conflicts between "civilizations." With the decline in the influence of Western nations, he wrote that the world would be dominated by six "civilizations": the West, Islam, a Confucian bloc, a Hindu bloc, Latin America, and eastern Orthodox Christianity. The "central focus of conflict for the immediate future will be between the West and several Islamic-Confucian states."[41]

Huntington asserts that civilizations represent distinct cultural groupings of people, but this is where the author's thinking is seriously in error. His adoption of the discredited modern definition of culture, which is that cultures are rigidly discrete, homogeneous structures, undermines his thesis. For example, he wrongly assumes that everyone in Islamic countries shares the same values. It is true that religious and ethnic fundamentalism is on the rise, but there is little evidence that conflict is increasingly between blocs of "civilizations." For example, there are serious conflicts between Russia, Ukraine, and Georgia, which happen to belong to the same "civilization" according to Huntington's thesis. Islam, according to the author, is monolithic despite the fact that it consists of factions that are more hostile than mutually friendly. He overlooks the reality that the Chinese business elite is much more interested in the technical skills of Silicon Valley in California than in their Confucian past. In the following, Bhikhu Parekh critiques the author's oversimplifications.

> Huntington's idea . . . is methodologically flawed because it reduces [civilizations] to one of their many strands of thought. It is also biased ideologically, because he chooses the worst strand in other civilizations and the best in his own. For him, Islam is all about fundamentalism, and Western civilization is all about liberalism, and the two are radically different.[42]

In summary, Huntington's theory is fundamentally naïve and potentially dangerous because it is built on a faulty understanding

---

[41] Samuel P. Huntington, "The Clash of Civilizations," in *Foreign Affairs* 72, no. 3 (1993): 48.

[42] See Parekh, *A New Politics*, 152–62, 294–95.

of culture.[43] That cultures are considered to have inflexible structures is essential to his argument: he plays supposedly homogeneous, cultural profiles against one another.[44] His thesis is a deliberate, demagogic combination of security interests and an unscholarly statement of civilizational (cultural) differences. As anthropologist Jan Pieterse concludes, "it merges two existing enemy discourses, the 'fundamentalist threat' of Islam and the 'yellow peril,' and its novelty lies in combining them."[45] A hazardous mix.

Islamic Fundamentalism

Jihad: Mythological Drift

> It is the . . . Islamic fundamentalist movements . . . that seek to essentialize Islam. They envision Islam as a comprehensive and stable set of beliefs and practices that determines social, economic, and political attitudes and behavior. Thus they give the narrowest possible readings to Islamic concepts.[46]
>
> —R. Scott Appleby

> Terrorism everywhere is nourished in injustice and wielded in hatred.[47]
>
> —*New York Times*

It is difficult to speak about Islamic fundamentalism because it differs from country to country depending on "many different internal variables—historical, political, and ethnic—and with such a problematic relation to 'the West.'"[48] Despite these differences it is possible

---

[43] See *The Economist* (January 3, 2009): 29.

[44] See critique by Dieter Senghass, *The Clash within Civilizations: Coming to Terms with Cultural Conflicts* (London: Routledge, 1998), 1 and passim.

[45] Jan N. Pieterse, *Gobalization and Culture* (Lanham: Rowman and Littlefield, 2004), 43–44.

[46] R. Scott Appleby, *The Ambivalence of the Sacred: Religion, Violence, and Reconciliation* (Oxford: Rowman and Littlefield, 2000), 105.

[47] Editorial, *The New York Times* (July 8, 2003), A22

[48] Jack D. Eller, *Introducing Anthropology of Religion* (Abingdon: Routledge, 2015), 295.

to say that Islamic fundamentalism developed within the context of Western colonialism and domination, which had devastating consequences for the Middle East and neighboring Muslim regions. Islam has never accepted a division between religion and the state, from the time of the Prophet they developed together. The efforts to reconcile this with the realities of developing governments and vibrant economies in the postcolonial world has been extremely problematic. Muslim fundamentalists have concluded that modernity evokes the fury of Allah. The situation has intensified when governments are financially corrupt and under the control of despotic elites. Western governmental support, particularly from the United States, of these elites intensifies the ferocity of those who feel alienated. This and economic stagnation have especially affected young people who form the majority of the population in Islamic lands, thus providing an atmosphere for fundamentalist movements which see the need to return to a literalist interpretation of the Koran and *sharia*. The internet provides disaffected youth with ready access to the most extreme preachers rather than their more moderate colleagues in their local mosque.

The Arabic word jihad is frequently translated as "holy war," but more correctly it means "struggle": a twofold struggle, the so-called greater jihad, the inner struggle against one's own evil self, and lesser jihad, the struggle against the enemies of Islamic faith.[49] In the Koran the meaning of jihad differs according to the context, for example, it can mean acknowledging and loving God, striving for religious deeds, having the courage to preach the truths of Islam, freeing people from tyranny, including the removal of perfidious rulers from power. Traditionally, if military jihad is required to protect Islam from others, there must first be diplomatic, economic, legal, or political endeavors to resolve the problems. But "Permission [to fight] is given to those upon whom war is made because they are oppressed, and most surely Allah is well able to assist them" so "slay the idolaters wherever you find them."[50] That is, if there is no peaceful alternative

---

[49] See David Cook, *Understanding Jihad*, 2nd ed. (Oakland: University of California Press, 2015).

[50] Surah 22:39, 9:5, as cited by Eller, *Introducing Anthropology*, 247; see also Abdulaziz A. Sachedina, "Activist Shi'ism in Iran, Iraq and Lebanon," in *Fundamentalisms Observed*, ed. Martin E. Marty and R. Scott Appleby (Chicago: Uni-

the use of force is permitted, but there are rigid moral requirements: innocents, for example, women, children, invalids, must not be harmed, and any peaceful efforts from the enemy must be respected. In case military action is necessary, not everyone can declare jihad; the religious military campaign has to be declared by a proper authority, advised by scholars, who say the religion and people are under threat and violence is imperative to defend them. This emphasis on defence in the Koran does present "a well-developed religious justification for waging war against Islam's enemies."[51] The Koran reads: "Fight those among the People of the Book [Jews and Christians] who do not believe in God and the Last Day."[52] Thus, one of the aims of jihad is to overcome and control non-Muslims, ostensibly in self-defence.

Mark Juergensmeyer comments that this stress on self-defence "is a far cry from justifying acts terrorism, though there were rogue groups of Muslims in the twelfth century . . . who used what might be called terrorism in establishing a small empire based in the north of Persia."[53] However, the concept of jihad has been usurped by many political and religious groups over the centuries in a bid to justify various forms of violence. There is no overall centralized and officially mandated authority in Islam to decide what defending means in specific situations. This is a particular problem among Sunni Islamists. Their ability to pick and choose religious ideas and take them out of context is partly due to the fact that there is no respected religious authority in Sunni Islam, for example, Cairo's al-Azhar University[54] has very limited power. The problem is little less among

---

versity of Chicago Press, 1991), 420–24; Dominic Arcamone, *Religion and Violence: A Dialectical Engagement through the Insights of Bernard Lonergan* (Eugene, OR: Pickwick Publications, 2015), 130–38.

[51] Cook, *Understanding Jihad*, 11.

[52] Surah 9:29. The Koran directs Muslims to respect the beliefs of Jews and Christians: "Do not argue with the followers of earlier revelation otherwise than in the most kindly manner—unless it be such of them as are bent on evil-doing" (Surah 29:46); see also Armstrong, *Islam*, 9.

[53] Mark Juergensmeyer, *The Terror in the Mind of God: The Global Rise of Religious Violence* (Berkeley, CA: University of California Press, 2003), 81.

[54] Al-Azhar Mosque in Cairo was dedicated in 972 and slowly evolved into the foremost institution in the Islamic world for the study of Sunni theology and *sharia*, or Islamic law.

Shia because almost every Shiite respects one of a small group of Grand Ayatollahs.[55]

Jihad against Co-Religionists

In many instances, Islamic splinter groups have used jihad to fight other Islamic peoples.[56] For example, the Egyptian scholar Abdel Salam Faraj (1954–1982) explicitly called for violent jihad against the Muslim ruler who does not implement *sharia* and insisted that it was imperative to establish an Islamic state. Anyone who deviates from the moral and social dictates of Islamic law are legitimate targets for jihad.[57] Today, the worst of the violence perpetrated by jihadists has been against their co-religionists. Thus, most of the victims of resurgent Islamic fundamentalism have been Muslims: apostasy or failure to accept *sharia* is deemed worthy of death.[58] Christians living among Muslims have also become terrorist targets, for example, in Pakistan and in the Islamic State of Iraq (the forerunner of ISIS), focused suicide attacks on Christians increased between 2008 to 2012.[59] Meanwhile, the tension between Sunni and Shia has been increasing. Jason Burke judges that "the new threat" from Islamic militancy is being directed mainly at other Muslims, particularly against the Shia. Tragic though the Islamic terrorist attacks are in the West, the number killed "is only a fraction of the total who have died in the Islamic world from violence related to extremism"[60]

The Indian-Pakistani scholar Abul Ala Maududi (1903–1979) called for a *universal* jihad which he did not see as only a defensive military struggle but a revolutionary battle to grasp power for the welfare of all humanity. Such jihad, he claimed, is the central precept of Islam. Peaceful means of relating to the modern Western way of life have failed. It had never occurred before that jihad should become so central to Islamic thinking. He would have a profound impact on

[55] See *The Economist* (January 17, 2015): 26.
[56] See www.islamcsupremecouncil.org/understading-islam/legal-rulings/5 -jihad-a-misunderstod-concept-from-islam.htmi?start=9 (accessed April 26, 2016).
[57] See Cook, *Understanding Jihad*, 93–127.
[58] See *The Economist* (January 17, 2015): 26.
[59] See Cook, *Understanding Jihad*, 167; Burke, *The New Threat*, 45, 143–44.
[60] Burke, *The New Threat*, 7–8.

others, including the development of Islamic militants and terrorists.[61] In Pakistan the Barelvis are a broad movement within the majority Sunni community that has long been considered to be nonpolitical and nonviolent. However, after the execution in early 2016 of the Punjabi governor, Mumtaz Qadri, for murdering his employer, the once-peaceful Barelvis under the leadership of their mullahs turned violent. The Barelvis wanted to preserve a draconian ban on blasphemy which the governor had seriously criticised. For this reason Qadri has become a hero to be revered because he dared to stand up against someone considered to be anti-Islamic.[62]

The misreading of jihad was to justify the assassination in 1981 of President Anwar Sadat, Egypt's president; it also warrants the killing of Syrian and Iraqi Muslims who overlook the need to pray five times daily, smoke, or disagree with any part of the interpretation of Islamic theology. Ahmed al-Tayeb, the grand imam of Egypt's al-Azhar mosque, declared in early 2016 that extremism was caused by "bad interpretations of the Koran and the Sunnah. . . . There has been a historical accumulation of excessive trends"[63] that have led some people to embrace a misguided form of Islam. He argues that the Koran frequently stipulates that the Prophet Muhammad's teachings do not cancel out the revelations of earlier prophets, such as Abraham, Moses, and Jesus, yet the fundamentalists deny this. For example, the Koran insists that Muslims speak with great respect to "the people of the book—say to them we believe what you believe—your God and our God is One."[64] Al-Tayeb and other mainstream Islamic scholars, who try to set Islamic teachings in their historical or cultural context, increasingly find it difficult to be heard.[65]

[61] See Karen Armstrong, *The Battle for God: Fundamentalism in Judaism, Christianity and Islam* (London: HarperCollins, 2000), 238–39.

[62] See *The Economist* (April 16, 2016): 22.

[63] Ahmed al-Tayeb, www.theguardian.com/world/2015/feb/23/top-muslim -cleric-ahmed-al-tayeb-urges-education-reform-to-counter-extremism (accessed April 28, 2016).

[64] Rohan Gunaratna, *Inside Al Qaeda Global: Network of Terror* (New York: Columbia University Press, 2002), 14.

[65] See *The Economist* (January 17, 2015): 26. Dauda Bello, an imam from Nigeria's northeastern region, where Boko Haram, an violent Islamist fundamentalist insurgent group is active, said, "*Jihad* does not mean holy war but striving to achieve peace and anything good in obedience to Allah." *The Economist* (February 28, 2015): 51.

Sunni and Shia: Different Mythological Memories

For at least a century, between 1830 and 1930, almost the entire Islamic world was overrun by non-Muslim Western forces. This was a completely new experience, especially for the Sunnis. Jason Burke, a foremost commentator on Islamic militancy, tellingly writes, "What today's commentators . . . often forget—the militants repeatedly remind themselves and anyone else prepared to listen—is that the supremacy of the West is a relatively new phenomenon in historical terms. Across much of the world, for two-thirds of the last 1,300 years, the power, the glory and the wealth was, broadly speaking, Islamic."[66] The militants strive to return the world's Muslim community to what they see as its due status: a global superpower.

This reality is deep in the collective mythological memory of Sunnis who acutely resent their downfall. They have known nothing but success for close on twelve centuries, success that comes from God. Their shameful loss of power is the sign that they have deviated from God's rule; God's honor will be restored only when Muslims return to the primitive founding mythology of the Prophet. Ruthven comments, "Sunni Islam, in contrast to Shiism, contains a strand of dogma that is irrational because God's commands are supposed to be accepted without being questioned, while their implementation was based—historically—on a theology of manifest success. The early conquests of Islam, from central France to the borders of China, were seen as proofs of divine favor. . . . [It] worked well during periods of triumph."[67] On the other hand, the Shia did not experience the lengthy success of the Sunni, even their founding figures had suffered martyrdom. Success is not a part of their founding mythology. For this reason Shia, unlike Sunnis, have become more adaptable to modern conditions of political and economic pluralism.[68]

---

[66] Burke, *The New Threat*, 85.

[67] Malise Ruthven, "Inside Obedient Islamic Minds," *Atlantic* (April 7, 2016): 79.

[68] Ibid., 80.

Suicide-Martyrdom

Islamic law unequivocally forbids suicide: as a mark of despair in God, it warrants eternal punishment, but some Islamic groups now approve of it under certain conditions. Shaykh Muhammad Husayn Fadlallah (1935–2010), a religious scholar and a former leader of Hezbollah,[69] wrote, "The self-martyring operation is not permitted unless it can convulse the enemy. The believer cannot blow himself up unless the results will equal or exceed the [loss of the] soul of the believer."[70] Others argue that the act must be assessed according to the intention of the perpetrator: "That is, they focus on the actor's intention to engage in jihad and reject the idea that the intent was to commit suicide. This effectively recasts the act as one of 'legitimite martyrdom' and not as one of suicide."[71] The fact is that suicide attacking has become common only in very recent times.[72] In the Middle East, suicide-martyrdom was first used by the Hezbollah in Lebanon in 1982. Now, particularly under the influence of people such as Sayyid Abu Mawdudi in Pakistan, Hassan al-Banna in Egypt, Sayyid Qutb in Egypt, and Iranian Khomeini, it has become a "normal" militant method. They have distorted the traditional Islamic mythology of suicide and martyrdom. In Khomeini's campaign against the Pahlavi Iranian regime he linked two words—*mostazafin* (oppressed) and *shadid* (martyr)—and thereby reshaped the meaning of martyrdom.[73] The martyr is the person who in battling against the oppressor sacrifices his life. A person who wishes to be a martyr must do so with a pure motive, namely, to act according to God's will and not in self-interest. Those who die in the cause of Islam, including suicide bombers, are believed to go immediately to paradise without having to delay until the resurrection or judgement day,[74] because death in

---

[69] Hezbollah, "Party of Allah," is a Shia Islamic militant group and political party based in Lebanon.

[70] Shaykh Muhammad Husayn Fadlallah, cited by Martin Kramer, "Hizbullah: The Calculus of Jihad," in *Fundamentalisms and the State*, ed. Martin E. Marty and R. Scott Appleby (Chicago: University of Chicago Press, 1993), 550.

[71] Jessica Stern and J. M. Berger, *ISIS: The State of Terror* (London: William Collins, 2016), 277.

[72] See Burke, *The New Threat*, 203–14; Cook, *Understanding Jihad*, 142–47.

[73] See Arcamone, *Religion and Violence*, 174–88.

[74] See Ruthven, *Islam in the World*, 117.

the cause of Allah is "a mark of the elect, a calling, an expression of one's love for him."[75]

Robert Pape, an American specialist in international security, seeks to answer the question: why do Muslim people, many of whom are well-educated, engage in suicide bombing? His answer is brief and alarming. It is due, he concludes, to "deep anger at the presence of Western combat forces in the Persian Gulf region and other predominantly Muslim lands."[76] The tragedy is that for those whose purpose it is to achieve as much destruction as possible, not just maximum publicity, suicide-martyrdom is the natural choice. This is one reason why it has become so popular today among radical Islamists. A spokespeople for Hamas, a Sunni Palestinian fundamentalist organization, justified a suicide bombing in 2002 in which civilians were killed by saying it was a necessary act of self-defence—the only weapon they have to protect Palestinian women and children: "If we should not use [suicide bombing]," Hamas leaders stated, "we shall be back in the situation of the first week of the Intifada when the Israelis killed us with impunity."[77] Al-Qaeda, like Hamas, invest much time and energy in preparing their fighters for death. This is the reason "why an unusually high percentage of al-Qaeda attacks are suicide operations. By condemning the target and reiterating the reward of sacrifice, the ideologues reinforce the appeal of death in war . . . [as well as driving] fear into the enemy."[78]

Particular Islamic Fundamentalists

Malise Ruthven explains the origins of significant contemporary fundamentalist movements.[79] The mythology of Islamic fundamentalists assumes an utopian golden age, the era of the Prophet Muhammad and his immediate successors, in which the evils of

[75] Parekh, *The New Politics of Identity*, 125; see also the analysis by Mark Juergensmeyer, *Terror in the Mind*, 167–89.

[76] Robert Pape and James K. Feldman, *Cutting the Fuse: The Explosion of Global Suicide Terrorism and How to Stop It* (Chicago: University of Chicago Press, 2010), 5.

[77] Quoted by Avishai Margalit, "The Suicide Bombers," *The New York Review of Books* (January 16, 2003): 36.

[78] Rohan Gunaratna, *Inside Al Qaeda Global: Network of Terror* (New York: Columbia University Press, 2002), 91–92.

[79] See Malise Ruthven, *A Fury for God*, and *Fundamentalism: A Very Short*, 24–28.

alcohol abuse, unregulated sex, and criminal behaviour were under firm control, and women knew their place. Fundamentalists look around them and see a world they believe is in total cultural trauma. The authentic Muslim mythology must be restored, even if it means violence. Two influential Muslim figures, Abd al-Rahman al-Jabarti (1754–1822) and Sayyid Qutb (1906–1966), have emphasized this utopian mythology and the need to restore it to its rightful place. Their influence on the emergence of contemporary fundamentalism is profound.

Jabarti was a noted Egyptian historian who described Napoleon's invasion of Egypt in 1798. While he was impressed by the scholars who accompanied Napoleon, he was appalled by evils of the French irreligion. Qutb was particularly influenced by the writings of Hassan al-Banna (1906–1949), the founder of the Egyptian Muslim Brotherhood, who struggled to restore *sharia* and resist British rule. He wrote, "It is the nature of Islam to dominate and not to be dominated, to impose its law in all nations and to extend its power to the entire planet."[80] Banna called for Islam to be rid of evil foreign influences, such as "their half-naked women . . . their liquors, their theaters, their dance halls, their amusements, their stories, their newspapers, their novels, their whims, their silly games, and their vices."[81]

Sayyid Qutb, swayed by writings of this kind and shocked by President Nasser's (1918–1970) suppression of the Muslim Brotherhood, wrote similar condemnatory tracts while imprisoned and tortured by Nasser's police. Qutb, possibly the most persuasive Muslim militant fundamentalist theorist of the last century, reasoned against the "hideous schizophrenia" of contemporary life coming out of the Western world, "that led people to picture God's domain in one place and the ordinary business of daily life in another place."[82] There was, he said, a twofold offensive against religion: externally from the West, the distant enemy, and internally from Muslim secular governments. His answer to these was "an eternal jihad to implement divine

[80] Hasan al-Banna, cited by Fereydoun Hoveyda, *The Broken Crescent: The "Threat" of Militant Islamic Fundamentalism* (Westport, CN: Praeger, 1998), 56.

[81] Hasan al-Banna, cited by Eller, *Introducing Anthropology of Religion*, 296.

[82] Qutb, as quoted by Paul Berman, "Al Qaeda's Philosopher: How an Egyptian Islamist Invented the Terrorist Jihad from His Jail Cell," *New York Times Magazine* (March 23, 2003). See Richard T. Antoun, *Understanding Fundamentalism: Christian, Islamic, and Jewish Movements* (Lanham: Rowman and Littlefield, 2008), 157.

authority on earth and a permanent revolution against internal and external enemies."[83] He preached that because of the lack of *sharia* law, the Muslim world was no longer Muslim, having reverted to the moral corruption and ignorance (*jahiliyya*) that existed prior to the coming of the Prophet Muhammad. To restore Islam, he wrote, a vanguard movement of righteous Muslims was required to build "true Islamic states," enforce *sharia*, and purge the Muslim world of any non-Muslim influences, such as socialist or nationalistic ideas. He was executed in 1966 but his writings gave his followers the encouragement to justify the killing of President Anwar Sadat (1918–1981) in 1981, and "the Islamist attacks on the Egyptian and other nominally Muslim governments, on Western personnel and tourists, and the atrocity that killed nearly 3,000 people in New York and Washington on 11 September 2001."[84] Qutb had equated *jahiliyya* with the Western behaviour of modern governments, including Islamic ones.

> The idolaters of our own time are worse in their idolatry than the ancients because the ancients were worshipping God in times of affliction and associating others with Him in times of prosperity, but the idolaters of our own time are always guilty of associating others with God whether in prosperity or affliction.[85]

Jabarti and Sayyid Qutb were both traumatized by the gap between the Islamic residual founding myth (see chapter 2) and the depravity they perceived in the West and around them. As already explained, the Islamic residual myth is that for centuries following the Prophet Mohammad, Islam knew nothing but success. Islam controlled a major section of the world but now no more. The crisis for them and their militant successors particularly results from "the contradiction between the collective memory of the triumphal progress of Islam under Muhammad and his immediate successors and the experience of recent political failure during the colonial and postcolonial periods when most of the Islamic world came under Western political, cultural, and commercial domination."[86] This memory, together with

---

[83] Ibid.

[84] Ruthven, *Fundamentalism: A Very Short*, 25.

[85] Sayyid Qutb, cited by Malise Ruthven, *Islam in the World*, 267.

[86] Ruthven, *Fundamentalism: A Very Short*, 27.

the division between religion and politics that the West insists is an integral quality of democracy, intensified, and continues to intensify, the fury of Islamic fundamentalists. The behavior of Muslim political and economic reformers, for example, Mustafa Kemal Ataturk (1881–1938) in Turkey, Reza Shah Pahlavi (1878–1944), and his son Muhammad Reza (1919–1980) in Iran, aimed to impose with violence the division between religion and the secular world. This fed the feverish rage of restorative and fundamentalist Muslims (see chapter 1).

Karen Armstrong correctly says, "If some Muslims today fight shy of secularism, it is not because they have been brainwashed by their faith but because they have often experienced efforts at secularisation in a particularly virulent form."[87] This rage led to the fundamentalist revolutionary overthrow of Iran's leaders by Ayatollah Khomeini in 1979 and the establishment of "a theocracy, with all sovereignty and legislative power placed on God, and the Council of Guardians (composed of ayatollahs) to lead the way."[88] Clerics replaced Westernized professionals and secular-oriented technocrats from their once powerful positions. Emancipated women were targeted "as traitors to Islam, or 'Western dolls,' as they were labelled. . . . Harsh criminal penalties were imposed to punish and deter any conduct by females that conservative clerics found indecent or immoral."[89]

In summary, Qutb's writings continue to set the pattern for Islamic radicals among Sunni Muslims in particular and his influence remains profound. Mohammed Jamal Khalifa, a close associate of Osama bin Laden, wrote,

> Islam is different from any other religion; it's a way of life. We [Khalifa and bin Laden] were trying to understand what Islam has to say about how we eat, who we marry, how we talk. We read Sayyid Qutb. He was the one most affected our generation.[90]

[87] Karen Armstrong, "The Myth of Religious Violence," www.theguardia.com /world/2014/sep/25/-sp-karen-armstrong-religious-violence-myth-secular (accessed March 15, 2016); see also her book, *The Battle for God*, 199–277.

[88] Eller, *Introducing Anthropology of Religion*, 297.

[89] Ann E. Mayer, "The Fundamentalist Impact in Iran, Pakistan, and the Sudan," in *Fundamentalisms and the State*, ed. Martin E. Marty and R. Scott Appleby, 116.

[90] Cited by Lawrence Wright, *The Looming Tower: Al-Qaeda and the Road to 9/11* (New York: Knopf, 2006), 79.

Qutb's main contribution to Al-Qaeda and other militant Islamic groups has been to nullify the power of moderate Islamic theologians and provide bin Laden and others with the authority to interpret founding Islamic mythology.[91]

Fundamentalist Movements

Wahhabism

Wahhabism, an Arabian form of Salafism,[92] is a fundamentalist movement within Sunni Islam and with its roots in Saudi Arabia. Its founder Abd al-Wahhab (1703–1792) had an uncompromising opposition to traditionalists who, he claimed, had contaminated Islam with non-Muslim practices taken from Christianity and local sources. He maintained that Islam of his day was more ignorant and corrupt than even before the Prophet Muhammad's time.[93] In 1744, Muhammad bin Saud, the founder of the present royal dynasty in Saudi Arabia, formed an alliance with al-Wahhab, in which the latter provided the decisive religious support for the former's plan to unify and centralize the aggressive tribes of Arabia, thus bringing them under his tutelage. The kingdom embraced the Wahhabi literalist interpretation of Islamic law, including the cutting off of the hands of thieves and the stoning of adulterers.[94] Today Wahhabism continues to provide religious legitimacy to the increasingly corrupt house of al-Saud. Historian John O. Voll writes,

> Wahhabism represents an important type of fundamentalism that continues to operate within the modern world but was not initiated as a result of conflict within the modernizing West. The Wahhabis succeeded in establishing a state which, while imper-

[91] Antoun, *Understanding Fundamentalism*, 157.

[92] Salafism is "a fundamental approach to Islam, emulating the Prophet Muhammad and his earliest followers—al-salaf al-salih, the 'pious forefathers'— right down to their facial hair." *The Economist*, www.economist.com/news /middle-east-and-africa/21656189-islams-most-conservative-adherents-are -fiding-politics-hard-it-beats (accessed May 1, 2016). There are three categories in the movement: the largest group are the purists (or quietists) who avoid politics; the second category are the activists, who involve themselves in politics; the smallest category are the jihadists, who are committed to violence.

[93] See Cook, *Understanding Jihad*, 74–75.

[94] See Armstrong, *The Battle for God*, 222.

fect, has nonetheless been recognized by many in the Islamic world as consonant with the fundamentalist mission to create an Islamic society.[95]

In 1979, the stability of the Saudi monarchy was threatened by three events: local extremists seized the Grand Mosque in Mecca, the Soviet invasion of Afghanistan, and the Iranian Shia revolution against the Pahlavi regime. The extremists, neo-Wahhabis, demanded a return to the revolutionary teachings of Wahhab, challenging the compromises of the Saudi monarchy with Western values. They have not hesitated to attack tobacco smoking, use of telephones, radios, and television as novelties with no scriptural foundation.[96] Surprisingly the support for neo-Wahhabism developed especially among wealthy, educated younger people, including the late Osama bin Laden.[97] The kingdom's masters continue to respond to these threats by ruthlessly suppressing local reforming Wahhabists, but also by extending the intolerant Wahhabi faith around the world. They do this through the use of their vast oil revenues to pay for the building of religious schools, mosques, and Islamic universities in many parts of the world. Their influence impacts on the entire Islamic world, essentially changing "faith, observance and religious identity for hundreds of millions of people," so that there has been a "shift of cultural influence from Egypt, once the unchallenged intellectual centre of the Arab world, to Saudi Arabia, its religious centre."[98]

Wahhabism is thus capturing mainstream Sunni Islam. Its intrinsic intolerance significantly accelerates its global presence; it relegates women to second-class status and brands Shia and Sufi Muslims[99] as

---

[95] John O. Voll, "Fundamentalism in the Sunni Arab World," in *Fundamentalisms Observed*, ed. Martin and Appleby, 361.

[96] See Ruthven, *Islam in the World*, 268.

[97] See Galina Yemelianova, "Explainer: What is Wahhabism in Saudi Arabia?" www.theconversation.com/explainer-what-is-wahhabism-in-saudi-arabia-36693 (accessed March 15, 2016).

[98] Burke, *The New Threat*, 43.

[99] Sufism is defined as the inner spiritual aspect of Islam. Sufis often belong to different congregations that meet around a grand master and they strive for perfection of worship and the desire to come closer to God. Louis Massignon, an authority on Sufism, writes, "The mystic call is as a rule the result of an inner rebellion of the conscience against social injustices, not only those of others but primarily and particularly against one's own faults: with a desire intensified by

heretics and apostates to be persecuted together with Christians and Jews. The beliefs of al-Qaeda and ISIS are built to a noteworthy degree on Wahhabism. For example, the ideology of al-Qaeda-type fundamentalism is similar to Wahhabism but is more extreme; thus militants in Iraq and Syria do not hesitate to enslave women as plunders of war.[100]

Muslim Brotherhood

Brief reference has already been made to this notable fundamentalist group and its origin in Egypt. Its turbulent history follows the pattern: once people become conscious of the cultural trauma they experience, then fundamentalist movements are bound to occur and the failure of one movement to achieve results begets yet more radical successors. Founded in 1928, this movement has had a profound influence around the world with its model of political activism combined with Islamic charity work. It has spread to other Muslim countries, including Syria, Jordan, and Tunisia, as well as countries where Muslims are in the minority.

Foreign imperialism left Egyptians feeling inferior to Westerners. This had to change. Hence, the Muslim Brotherhood's founder, Hassan al-Banna, recognized the desperate need to educate people in Islamic beliefs in the hope that through personal and family transformation they would grow in self-esteem and ultimately change the nation. Radical change, Banna declared, must grow slowly from below. Thus, initially the movement had the simple aim of spreading Islamic morals and good works, but very soon it became involved in political activity, especially in the crusade to remove Egypt from British control and purify it of all Western contamination particularly following World War II. An observer in the 1950s noted that membership had grown and included people from rural and urban lower class backgrounds, but significantly the "membership largely represented an emergent and self-conscious Muslim middle class."[101]

---

inner purification to find God at any price." Cited by Malise Ruthven, *Islam in the World*, 223.

[100] See Patrick Cockburn, *The Jihadis Return: The ISIS and the New Sunni Uprising* (New York: OR Books, 2014), 96.

[101] Richard P. Mitchell, *The Society of the Muslim Brothers* (London: Oxford University Press, 1961), 331; Cook, *Understanding Jihad*, 97–99.

While Banna demanded unquestioning obedience to the aims of the movement, including his insistence on nonviolence, nonetheless, in 1943, a small terrorist group, called "The Secret Apparatus," developed, with the aim to free Egypt from British control. The humiliating loss of Palestine to the new state of Israel and the consequent expulsion of thousands of Palestinians from their homes further traumatized Egyptians. The paramilitary Apparatus refusing Banna's restraints became increasingly violent towards the government which in turn brutally tried to suppress the entire Brotherhood. After an unsuccessful attempt to assassinate President Nasser in 1954, many thousands of followers were again imprisoned and tortured. It was then that the movement, now underground, came under the influence of the writings of the radical Islamic thinker and activist Sayyid Qutb who at the same time influenced the development of other fundamentalist groups in Egypt. One such movement, *takfir*, accused all existing Muslim societies of atheism.[102] In the mid-1960s the government again sought to suppress the Brotherhood and the execution of Qutb in 1966 further enraged supporters of the Brotherhood.

One militant group in the mid-1970s, however, "saw the Brotherhood's gradualism as cowardice, and their reliance on divine intervention as abhorrent fatalism."[103] Following Qutb's teaching, "non-Islamists are, for all practical purposes, infidels . . . [and] they could be killed, their property destroyed, their wealth confiscated, their women enslaved, and so on."[104] The radicals further believed that because sovereignty lies solely with God they cannot accept democracy. God does not share his sovereignty.[105] The moderate Brotherhood's attempt to counter this extreme militancy failed. It did not succeed in 1980 in controlling Muhammad 'Abd al-Salam Farag who openly declared that Muslims had discarded one of Islam's foundational mandates, namely holy war, and in the same year he assassinated President Sadat.[106]

[102] See Ruthven, *Islam in the World*, 307–22.
[103] Hazem Kandil, *Inside the Brotherhood* (Cambridge: Polity Press, 2015), 150.
[104] Ibid.
[105] See Maha Azzam, "Egypt: The Islamists and the State under Mubarak," in *Islamic Fundamentalism*, ed. Abdel Salam Sidahmed and Anoushiravan Ehteshami, 109–22.
[106] See Kandil, *Inside the Brotherhood*, 151.

During the 1980s, the movement tried once more to join the political mainstream. Like all radical and moderate Islamists, the Brotherhood is committed to implementing *sharia*, but, unlike the radicals, the moderate Brotherhood believes that it is preferable to operate wherever possible as a political party. Their political campaigning became so successful that President Hosni Mubarak, feeling threatened, sought to suppress the movement. Mubarak was ousted in 2011 and in the democratic election in 2012, Mohammad Morsi, chairman of the newly formed Freedom and Justice Party, the political wing of the Brotherhood, became president with the additional support of the ultraconservative Salafist Nour party. Secularists and others feared Morsi, despite his protestations to the contrary, would force Egypt to become an Islamic state. But with his overthrow by the military in 2013, the Brotherhood again became the target of persecution. On April 15, 2014, an Egyptian court disqualified current and former members of the Brotherhood from running in the presidential and parliamentary elections.

Al-Qaeda

> We—with God's help—call on every Muslim who believes in God and wishes to be rewarded to comply with God's order to kill the Americans and plunder their money wherever and whenever they find them.[107]
>
> — Osama bin Laden

For the secretive and highly disciplined al-Qaeda the principal aims of jihad are to eradicate injustice and oppression, establish justice, wellbeing and prosperity, and to destroy the barriers to the spread of Islamic truth. Al-Qaeda, founded by Osama bin Laden in 1988 as an international terrorist group, has organised vicious bombing attacks, the most notorious being the assaults in New York and Washington, DC, September 11, 2001. It is also responsible for violence against what it considers to be liberal Muslims, the Shia, Sufis,

---

[107] Osama bin Laden and others (February 23, 1998), cited by Rohan Gunaratna, *Inside Al Qaeda: Global Network of Terror* (New York: Columbia University Press, 2002), 1.

and other sects who are branded as heretics. The movement has particular hatred for the United States, for example, al-Qaeda insists that until American troops are removed from Saudi Arabia and other Muslim lands Muslim society will be "living in sin."[108]

Al-Qaeda inherited a full-fledged training and operational infrastructure funded by the American, European, Saudi Arabian, and other governments for use in the anti-Soviet jihad in Afghanistan.[109] Bin Laden, considered to be a model Islamic fundamentalist leader, was described as possessing "charismatic and authoritarian leadership, [supported by] a disciplined inner core of adherents, [and promoting] a rigorous socio-moral code for his followers."[110] Characteristic signs of al-Qaeda include suicide attacks and the simultaneous bombing of different targets. Ideologically it is committed to a total destruction of all foreign influences in Muslim countries and the formation of a new caliphate state over the entire Muslim world.[111]

Ayman al-Zawahiri (b. 1951), a surgeon from Egypt, succeeded bin Laden in 2011. Earlier he had contemptuously admonished the Muslim Brotherhood for their moderation, claiming that they were also responsible for making God's will dependent on votes and referendums. He says, "Anyone who claims to be a Muslim democrat is an infidel that must be killed. It is as implausible as being a Muslim Christian or a Muslim Jew. . . . We are here—the real Islamic front and the real Islamic opposition [as opposed to the Muslim Brotherhood]."[112] Following the terrorist destruction of New York and Washington, DC, in 2001 he avowed that the terrorists "reflected God's own power . . . [God] has given them knowledge and strength drawn from His own, and turned them from a scattered few into a power that threatens the stability of the new world order."[113] Since bin Laden's death the movement has broken apart into a variety of

---

[108] See Rohan Gunaratna, *Inside Al Qaeda: Global*, 88.

[109] Ibid., 1–53.

[110] Martin E. Marty and R. Scott Appleby, foreword to *Islamic Fundamentalisms and the Gulf Crisis*, ed. James Piscatori (Chicago: University of Chicago Press, 1991), xiii.

[111] See Appleby, *The Ambivalence of the Sacred*, 94–95.

[112] Al-Zawahiri cited by Hazem Kandil, *Inside the Brotherhood*, 151–52.

[113] Ibid., 153.

regional movements that have little connection with one another.[114] Both bid Laden and al-Zawahiri, following the pattern of other Islamic militants, have misrepresented the Prophet's sayings in order to foster support for their political purposes. Marty and Appleby describe the role of these Islamist ideologues:

> By selecting elements of tradition and modernity, fundamentalists seek to remake the world in the service of a dual commitment to the unfolding eschatological drama (by returning all things in submission to the divine) and to self-preservation (by neutralising the threatening Other).[115]

Taliban

To understand the reasons for the rise of the Taliban we must appreciate the impact the Soviet invasion of Afghanistan and its consequences. The pro-Soviet Nur Mohammad Taraki government grasped power in 1978 and began to impose on the population with immense cruelty policies of land redistribution, re-education, and atheistic-inspired secular values. The people traumatized by this massive assault on their lives and religious values openly rebelled. The Soviet army intervened, thus leading to the Soviet-Afghan war that lasted over nine years from 1979 to 1989.[116] In the power vacuum following the forced Soviet withdrawal in 1989 from Afghanistan, the fundamentalist Sunni Taliban took control and immediately introduced draconian restrictions on the population. Unlike al-Qaeda, the Taliban is not interested in creating terrorism outside Afghanistan.[117]

---

[114] See www.wikipedia.org/wiki/Al-Qaeda (accessed March 17, 2016). The main source of financing for Al-Qaeda is Saudi Arabia. See also Patrick Cockburn, *The Jihadis Return: ISIS and the New Sunni Uprising* (New York: OR Books, 2014), 87.

[115] Martin E. Marty and R. Scott Appleby, foreword to *Islamic Fundamentalisms*, ed. James Piscatori, xii.

[116] David Cook notes that the campaign against the Soviets "was the first time in centuries that people from all over the Muslim world had gathered together—irrespective of their ethnic and sometimes doctrinal differences—to fight exclusively *for the sake of Islam*." *Understanding Jihad*, 128. Italics in original.

[117] See Fergusson, *Taliban*, 122.

The Taliban as a fundamentalist movement had its origins at two levels: in the poverty-stricken refugee camps of Pakistan during the jihad against the Soviet occupation and in a system of interconnected rural Muslim religious schools (*madrasas*). Its declared aim is to establish a pure Islamic state cleansed of all the evils enacted by their predecessors. Influenced by Qutb's writings[118] movies, television, music of all kinds, popular kite-flying (considered to be a Hindu custom), pigeon-keeping, smoking, alcohol, and the internet were all forbidden; beards became obligatory for men. There is not much fun in fundamentalism! Women were particularly targeted: among other things, employment outside the home and education was forbidden and the tent-like burqa was required in public.[119] Offenders "suffered the harshest punishments systematically inflicted since the Europe of the Middle Ages and the Inquisition . . . amputations of hands and feet for theft; stoning for adultery; burial alive for sodomy."[120] The Taliban lost power once the United States intervened militarily in Afghanistan after September 11, 2001, but the movement is reestablishing control as Americans and allies withdraw.[121]

ISIS (Islamic State of Iraq and al-Sham)[122]

ISIS is a jihadi fundamentalist militant group, deeply influenced by bin Laden although its radicality owes more to Abu Musa'b al-Zarqawi.[123] The invasion of Iraq led by the United States destroyed the state political structure and created a power vacuum. Nonstate actors, including al-Qaeda, bitterly struggled to gain control in the midst of bloody sectarian chaos. The extremist ISIS, fuelled by Sunni resentment over years of marginalization by the Shia minority, finally achieved power ahead of al-Qaeda. ISIS at the same successfully

[118] See Appleby, *The Ambivalence of the Sacred*, 94–95.

[119] See Nancy Hatch Dupree, "Afghan Women under the Taliban," in *Fundamentalism Reborn?*, ed. Maley, 145–66.

[120] John K. Cooley, *Unholy Wars: Afghanistan, America and International Terrorism* (London: Pluto Press, 2002), 3.

[121] See Ruthven, *Islam in the World*, 393–94; see also William Maley, "Interpreting the Taliban," in *Fundamentalism Reborn?*, ed. Maley, 1–28.

[122] ISIS is also known as ISIL and Daesh.

[123] See Abdel Bari Atwan, *Islamic State: The Digital Caliphate* (London: Saqi Books, 2015), 55–60.

infiltrated Syria, taking advantage of the Sunni hatred of President Bashar al-Assad's dictatorial and increasingly anarchic regime.[124] As the first caliphate for a hundred years, under the leadership of Abu Bakr al-Baghdadi,[125] ISIS claims worldwide religious, political, and military authority over all Muslims. As of December 2015, it controlled extensive territories in Iraq and Syria, with a population estimated to be between three and eight million people, and where it imposes its understanding of *sharia* law ruthlessly.[126] As in the time of the Prophet, the establishment of a caliphate with its territory, is an essential requirement of its identity.

ISIS[127] aims to return civilization to a seventh-century legal environment of the age of the Prophet Muhammad and his earliest followers, and ultimately to bring about the apocalypse;[128] it claims to follow the prophecy and example of Muhammad in meticulous detail. The movement is committed to genocide, that is the killing of all who refuse to accept its teaching, Muslims included.[129] Unless Muslims adhere to its uncompromising teachings, for example, slavery, crucifixion, and beheadings for various "crimes," they are regarded as Islamic apostates. The Shia, the main enemy of ISIS, are branded as heretical because it is believed that some of their practices have no foundation in the Koran. "This means roughly 200 million Shia are marked for death."[130]

---

[124] See Fawaz A. Gerges, "ISIS and the Third Wave of Jihadism," *Current History* (December, 2014): 339–43. Gerges is professor of international relations at the London School of Economics.

[125] Like Osama bin Laden, Abu Bakr al-Baghdadi is highly educated, holding a doctorate in Islamic studies from the University of Baghdad.

[126] As of July 2016, ISIS had lost half the land it had taken in Iraq and 20 percent of its territory in Syria; see *The Economist* (July 9, 2016): 39.

[127] The recruiting power of ISIS is remarkable. From June 2014 to December 2015, ISIS doubled the number of foreign recruits, to a total of 27,000 to 31,000, but border controls by Turkey have reduced the number of new arrivals. But the fact that they have come from at least 86 countries indicates the effectiveness of its propaganda. *The Economist* (December 12, 2015): 41.

[128] See Graeme Wood, "What ISIS Really Wants," www.thealantic.com/features /archive/2015/02/what-isis-really-wants/384980/?utm (accessed March 4, 2016).

[129] See Fawaz A. Gerges, *ISIS: A History* (Princeton, NJ: Princeton University Press, 2016), 32, 252.

[130] Wood, "What ISIS Really Wants," Al-Baghdadi believes that the Koran demands that offensive jihad is an obligation on Muslims at all times: "O,

ISIS differs significantly from al-Qaeda, which it opposes, and other Islamic fundamentalist groups.[131] For example, al-Qaeda operates like a secretive political movement, but ISIS deliberately publicizes its aims and strategies with worldly goals in sight at all times— the expulsion of non-Muslims from the Arabian peninsula, the destruction of the state of Israel, the cessation of support for Muslim dictatorships. Its unique publicity emphasis is the End of Days or apocalyptic thinking; it believes that there will be only twelve caliphs, and the present one is the eighth. Its apocalyptic belief is that there will be a major military clash against non-Islamic forces in northern Syria; Constantinople will be conquered by Muslims; the Antichrist will appear and travel to Jerusalem; a messianic figure will come to earth, kill the Antichrist, and convert the masses to Islam; and the world's non-Muslim infidel countries will be destroyed.[132]

ISIS has a duty to terrorise its enemies by beheading and enslaving even women and children. The spectacular indiscriminate killing of innocent people and bombing of sites within "infidel" territories, such as occurred in Paris in January 2015 (*Charlie Hebdo*) and November the same year, will, it is assumed, hasten Muslim victory by forcing their enemies to mass their forces against the ultimately successful Muslim armies.[133] The greater the hostility toward Muslims in Europe caused by the arbitrary and theatrical brutality and killings and the deeper the West becomes involved in military action in the Middle East, the closer, ISIS believes, it comes to creating and managing apocalyptic chaos.[134] A tract written for ISIS on how to hasten the

---

Muslims, Islam was never for a day the religion of peace. Islam is the religion of war." Baghdadi, cited by Fawaz A. Gerges, *ISIS: A History* (Princeton, NJ: Princeton University Press, 2016), 252.

[131] Members of Hamas, a Palestinian Sunni-Islamic fundamentalist organization, the de facto government of Gaza, subject to Israeli rule, are considered infidels by ISIS because they place the nationalist battle for a Palestine state before the campaign for a caliphate; see Sarah Helm, "ISIS in Gaza," *The New York Review of Books* (January 14, 2016): 18–20.

[132] See Jessica Stern and J. M. Berger, *ISIS: The State of Terror* (London: William Collins, 2016), 221–31.

[133] See David Kilcullen, *Blood Year: Islamic State and the Failures of the War on Terror* (Carlton,Vic: Black, 2016), 114–17.

[134] See Scott Atran and Nafees Hamid, "Paris: The War ISIS Wants," www .nybooks.com/daily/2015/11/16/paris-attacks-isis-strategy-chaos (accessed December 15, 2015).

chaotic trauma states: "Work to expose the weakness of America's centralized power by pushing it to abandon the media psychological war and war by proxy until it fights directly."[135] Continuing to hound Western countries into a definite battle in Syria is a dangerous element in the planning of ISIS. The former director of the Central Intelligence Agency, Leon Panetta, said in 2014, "I think we're looking at kind of a 30-year war, one that will have to extend beyond Islamic State to include emerging threats in Nigeria, Somalia, Yemen, Libya and elsewhere."[136] His insight has proved correct. Fawaz Gerges foresees that "Even if ISIS is pushed back militarily, it will mutate and go underground— as its predecessor, Al Qaeda in Iraq, did from 2007 until 2010—and bide its time until the next round."[137] A most disturbing insight,

---

Persecution and Genocide of Christians

The number of Christians is lessening significantly in the mainly Muslim countries of the Middle East to almost 4 percent of the population. Even though Christianity began in this region, many Christians who see these nations as their homeland are being compelled to leave because of persecution. Worse still, Christians together with other minorities, are being kidnapped and murdered. They are being intentionally targeted by fundamentalist Islamist militants and it is so ruthless in the lands held by ISIS that the US State Department calls it genocide.[138]

---

[135] Quoted by Atran and Nafees Hamid, "Paris: The War ISIS Wants."

[136] Leon Panetta, www.usatoday.com/story/news/politics/214/10/06/leon-panetta-memoir-worthy-fights/16737615/ (accessed May 7, 2016). ISIS has declared that it is establishing a subsidiary caliphate in Mindanao in Southern Philippines; see editorial "Danger on the Doorstep As Islamic State Pushes Closer," *The Australian* (January 12, 2016): 11.

[137] Gerges, *ISIS: A History*, 290.

[138] www.christianitytoday.com/gleanings/2016/march/do-christians-face-genocide-isis-john-kerry-syria-iraq.html (accessed May 28, 2016); Gerges, *ISIS: A History*, 32–33.

Boko Haram

Boko Haram was founded in 1995 in the midst of political and commercial corruption as a nonviolent religious movement in the northern Muslim-dominated states of Nigeria. By 2003, the movement had turned to violence and since then it has been the cause of thousands of deaths. It conducted its first attack against foreign interests in Nigeria in August 2011 when it detonated a vehicle bomb against the United Nations headquarters in Abuja, Federal Capital Territory. Since then Boko Haram has continued to target foreign interests in Nigeria and neighboring countries.[139] Its aim is to impose by force, if necessary, *sharia* law within Nigeria and countries close at hand; unlike al-Qaeda and ISIS, Boko Haram has no globalist ambitions.[140] Despite causing widespread suffering wherever it operates surprisingly little is known of its organization, although Boko Haram has recently publicly aligned itself with ISIS.[141]

Summary Points

1. Islam began in the pagan-dominated town of Mecca with the Prophet Muhammad who peacefully proclaimed (ca. 610) the absolute unity of God.

2. Violence was initially not integral to Islam's founding mythology. The concept of jihad developed as Muhammad and his followers were persecuted.[142] Consequently, according to the Koran, if there is no peaceful alternative to defending Islam, the use of force (jihad) is permitted, but there are rigid moral requirements: innocents, for example, women, children, and invalids, must not be harmed, and any peaceful outreach from the enemy must be respected.

---

[139] As a result of Boko Haram actions in a six-year period over 20,000 people have been killed; in 2014 it was responsible for 6,644 deaths, a 300 percent increase from the previous year. *America* (February 29, 2016).

[140] See Cook, *Understanding Jihad*, 174–77.

[141] See Mike Smith, *Boko Haram: Inside Nigeria's Unholy War* (London: I. B. Tauris, 2015), 1–18; Stern and Berger, *ISIS*, 284–85.

[142] See Cook, *Understanding Jihad*, 5–11.

3. However, the concept of jihad has been commandeered by many political and religious groups over the centuries in a bid to justify various forms of proactive violence. The two main branches of Islam, Sunni and Shia, split during the strife over the succession to Muhammad in the mid-seventh century. Relations between both groups are still conflicted.

4. Contemporary Islamic fundamentalism, for example, the Muslim Brotherhood, al-Qaeda, and ISIS, is rooted in the last hundred years of cultural trauma resulting from the impact of Western values and colonialism in the Middle East and neighboring Muslim regions. "ISIS adheres to a doctrine of total war, with no constraints. It disdains arbitration or compromise even with Sunni Islamist rivals."[143] The Islamic State is not likely to survive as a territory in Syria and Iraq but "the model and the idea it represents will likely continue to metastasize and adapt to survive in new conditions."[144]

5. In the Middle East, suicide-martyrdom was first used by the Hezbollah in Lebanon in 1982. Now it has become a normal militant method for fundamentalist groups. Its devotees have distorted the traditional Islamic mythology of suicide and martyrdom. Many parts of Islam face a major challenge, as described by the Muslim scholar Ziauddin Sardar (b. 1951): "Our recent past, that is, the last four centuries, and our present, I submit, do little credit to the ideals of Islam; still less do they reflect the civilisation that was once the pacesetter of humanity."[145]

Discussion Questions

1. Pope Francis says that "We Christians should embrace with affection and respect Muslim immigrants to our countries in the same way that we hope and ask to be received and respected in countries of Islamic tradition. . . . Faced with disconcerting

---

[143] Gerges, "ISIS and the Third Wave of Jihadism," *Current History*, 340.

[144] Lynch, *The New Arab Wars*, 252.

[145] Ziauddin Sardar, *The Future of Muslim Civilisation* (Beckenham: Croom Helm, 1979), 11.

episodes of violent fundamentalism, our respect for true followers of Islam should lead us to avoid hateful generalizations, for
authentic Islam and the proper reading of the Koran are opposed
to every form of violence."[146] What are the implications of this
statement for ourselves personally, our parish, and our school?

2. Some politicians in the Western world actively campaign to stop
all Muslim immigration, even refugees. What reasons are they
giving? What do you think the Scriptures say about this campaign?

[146] Pope Francis, *The Joy of the Gospel*, par. 253.

Chapter 6

Fundamentalism: Pastoral Responses

All good people agree
And all good people say,
All nice people like Us, are We
And everyone else is They.[1]

— Rudyard Kipling

Fundamentalism is a sickness that is in all religions. . . . Religious fundamentalism is not religious, because it lacks God. It is idolatry, like idolatry of money. . . . We Catholics have some—and not some, many—who believe in the absolute truth and go ahead dirtying the other with calumny, with disinformation, and doing evil.[2]

— Pope Francis

Most Westerners are at least familiar with the main division in Islam, between Sunnis and Shi'ites, but too many know little else and actually suffer from stereotypes and what has been called "Islamopobia" or fear and loathing of Muslims.[3]

— Jack D. Keller

[1] Rudyard Kipling, "We and They," *Debts and Credits* (London: Macmillan, 1926), 327–28.
[2] Pope Francis, comments to journalists on the plane returning from Africa (November 30, 2015), www.lifesitenews.com/news/pope-francis-attacks-funda mentalist-catholics-dismisses-condom-ban-as-unimp (accessed March 26, 2016).
[3] Jack D. Keller, *Introducing Anthropology of Religion*, 2nd ed. (Abingdon: Routledge, 2015), 183.

Paul fought hard at the Council of Jerusalem to stop the early church communities from becoming fundamentalist groups. Jewish Christians were demanding that non-Jews adopt Jewish customs as a condition of being received into the faith. Inspired by faith, Paul responded to the challenge presented by the Jewish Christians with courage, respect, and dialogue. If he had not succeeded, the church would have become a sect, inward-looking and lifeless. "There is no longer Jew or Greek, there is no longer slave or free, there is no longer male or female; for all of you are one in Christ Jesus" (Gal 3:28). "But now that faith has come . . . you are all children of God through faith" (Gal 3:25-26).[4]

Fundamentalism: All-Capable

Response 1

We are all in danger of becoming fundamentalists.

Prejudices are an integral quality of fundamentalists; they are imprisoned in, and blinded by, prejudices against anyone who dares to differ from them. They are firmly convinced that they are right and no one can teach them anything! We need to be alert to the danger that our own prejudices, if left unchecked, can solidify into fundamentalist behavior. "I am," wrote Charles Lamb (1775–1834), "in plain words, a bundle of prejudices—made up of likings and dislikings." And Kipling's comment in the epigraph is right also: We learn that "All nice people like Us . . ." unconsciously absorb the prejudices in our own culture about other people and things. Why? I suggest readers return to axiom 4 in chapter 2. We as humans demand order and predictability; those who are not like us endanger our yearning for order. We fear and resent disorder. And we express this craving for order by boxing outsiders into stereotypes. For example, during the American Civil War Northerners were neatly classified by one religious minister as "atheists, infidels, communists, free-lovers, rationalists, Bible-haters, anti-Christian levellers, and anarchists." Southerners, on the other hand, were "God-fearing and Christ-loving,

---

[4] See Gerald A. Arbuckle, *Laughing with God: Culture, Humor, and Transformation* (Collegeville: Liturgical Press, 2008), 143.

conscientious people . . . that . . . have a zeal for God, and seek his glory and the good of man."[5]

Response 2

Have a sense of humor.

Fundamentalists cannot live with ambiguities because they demand impossible certitudes in life. There is little humor in their lives; they take themselves far too seriously. This is why the gift of authentic humor is necessary. A positive sense of humor is the gift whereby we kindly contemplate the ambiguities or incongruities of life in faith and express this meditative reflection in laughter, smiling, or simply an inner joy or peace. If we contemplate the multitude of incongruities in the Scriptures we cannot take ourselves too seriously but end in trusting God, the source of true joy. Then we can laugh at ourselves—at our own foibles and stupidities. There are incongruities aplenty in the Scriptures. God is born to a peasant girl, not in a palace but in the rough atmosphere of a primitive stable, and redeems the world by dying an ignominious death on the cross and rising from the dead. People with a gift of humor have a healthy scepticism; they are wary of simplistic answers to today's challenges and keep asking the question "Why?" This stops people from cognitive stagnation—the barrier to creativity.[6]

Prejudice

Response 3

We need to be aware of the dynamics of prejudice and discrimination.[7]

Prejudice, the jumping to conclusions without wanting to consider the facts, has two dimensions: the meaning and feeling aspects.

---

[5] David Goldfield, *America Aflame: How the Civil War Created a Nation* (New York: Bloomsbury Press, 2011), 173. Goldfield is quoting from C. C. Goen, "Broken Churches, Broken Nation: Regional Religion and North-South Alienation in Antebellum America," *Church History* 52 (March, 1983): 33.

[6] See Arbuckle, *Laughing with God*, 27–41.

[7] See Gerald A. Arbuckle, *Earthing the Gospel: An Inculturation Handbook for Pastoral Workers* (New York: Orbis Books, 1990), 147–66.

Meaning aspect: This is commonly referred to as a stereotype, that is, a preformed image or picture that we have of things or people; it is a shorthand, but faulty method of handling a complex world. By placing things and people into preformed categories, I feel I am controlling a world that threatens my sense of order or meaning. The stereotype may not be entirely false; it may rest on a grain of truth. For example, concert pianists are said to be temperamental. By and large, they are forced to practise a highly sensitive craft in a setting, such as a draughty hall, where there are many possibilities of interference in the intensity of the concentration that the artistry requires. No wonder it is said that pianists can be temperamental! But the error is in expecting *all* concert pianists to act in this way. The stereotype is a *pre*-judgement. It is the judgement that I make without first checking the facts about things or people.

Feeling aspect: Prejudices are not just about stereotypes; they are stereotypes motivated by strong, and often powerful, feeling impulses. The feeling aspect is the "blinding power" in prejudice, that is, it obstructs objectivity and the openness of dialogue; it forces the prejudiced person to see *only* what he or she wants to see, even to see things that are not there at all.

Example

On one occasion Jesus spoke about how the people received John the Baptist and himself, "For John came neither eating nor drinking, and they say: 'He has a demon'; the Son of Man came eating and drinking, and they say, 'Look, a glutton and a drunkard, a friend of tax collectors and sinners!'" (Matt 11:18-19). No matter what Jesus does, his enemies will only see evil in him!

Prejudice takes many forms, for example, cultural, racial, sexual, religious, and an awareness of social status. Prejudice can quickly lead to action and then we have discrimination. For example, sexism is the *prejudice* that someone is inferior in some way or other as a human person because they belong to a certain biological category. Sexist *discrimination*, like racism, assumes that members of a particular sex are objects to be freely used for the pleasure and the preservation of the dominant position of the other gender.

Ethnic/Gender Jokes: Veto

Ethnic/gender jokes are common in most cultures. Are they really funny? Reflect on the following: "How do you make an Irishman laugh on Monday? Tell him a joke on Friday!" On careful examination it will be seen that the object of an ethnic or gender joke is to put down members of other cultures. At the same time, one's own group is presented as normal and superior. Sometimes one hears the defensive comment: "I know members of minority groups who really enjoy the jokes and they even retell them to one another. So why all the fuss about the jokes?" When minority members retell ethnic or gender jokes about themselves, it is frequently to deprive the jokes of their emotional power. By retelling jokes, they hope to build up an immunity to the prejudices inherent in them, thus curbing their anger and aggressive instincts towards members of the dominant culture. The practical conclusion is not retell ethnic or gender jokes. They can be unjust and deeply offensive. Moreover, they help to further divide cultures and can facilitate fundamentalist attitudes.[8]

Response 4

Be alert: Receive without prejudice migrants and parishioners from cultures different from our own as Christ would wish.

> You shall allot it [land] as an inheritance for yourselves and for the aliens who reside among you . . . They shall be to you as citizens of Israel. (Ezek 47:22)

USA: Hispanic Threat Narrative

The United States House of Representatives passed an anti-immigration law in 2005 aimed at Mexican Hispanics. The widespread prejudice, vigorously encouraged by alarmist media, is

---

[8] See Arbuckle, *Laughing with God*, 17–18.

that contemporary Hispanic immigrants are not like former migrants who ultimately integrated into the American way of life. Now they are stereotyped as "unwilling or incapable of integrating, of becoming part of the national community . . . [and] bent on reconquering land that was formerly theirs."[9] This prejudice is evident in survey reports. The Pew Research Center (USA) disturbingly reported in late 2015 "that 41 percent of all Americans see immigrants as a 'burden' on our society, but 55 percent of white (i.e., non-Hispanic) Catholics do. More than a third of white Catholics do not think undocumented immigrants should be permitted to stay, even when the strict conditions included in immigration reform proposals are met."[10]

Many immigrants to Western countries, particularly Hispanic and Muslim peoples, encounter xenophobia and discrimination, sometimes made worse by racist politicians and populist speakers.[11] They tend to come from poor rural areas, most are not well educated, and many are brown. They speak the language of the wider society either poorly or not at all, so they find it difficult to get employment and their children struggle at school. They congregate in poor districts, often in state-owned housing. They desperately need to be welcomed and assisted to integrate into the wider society. Host Western nations understandably urge immigrants to integrate, but there is often confusion about what "integration" means. Too often in practice it is synonymous with assimilation, that is, immigrants are expected to acquire quickly the symbols, mythologies, and rituals of the dominant culture, so that *all* their distinguishing cultural qualities disappear. This is a form of violence, because only from a position of cultural

[9] Leo R. Chavez, *The Latino Threat: Constructing Immigrants, Citizens, and the Nation* (Stanford, CA: Stanford University Press, 2008), 2.

[10] Brett C. Hoover, "Blaming the Stranger: Parishes Must Resist the Myth of the 'Latino Threat,'" *America* (May 16, 2016): 24.

[11] In the days following the successful referendum to exit the European Union the reports of hate crime increased by 57 percent in Britain, compared with the same period four weeks earlier. Polish and other minorities were targeted. Cardinal Vincent Nichols expressed concern, "This upsurge of racism, of hatred towards others is something we must not tolerate." www.thetablet.co.uk/news/5770/0/cardinal-nichols-condemns-upsurge-in-racisst-attacks-post-brexit (accessed July 11, 2016).

strength and identity will migrant peoples be able to move out to contact other cultures, with a sense of self-respect and confidence.[12]

Authentic integration is a very slow, painful, and uncertain process involving for immigrants a journey through three stages: economic, social, and identity integration. In *economic* integration immigrants struggle to survive and to find employment; *social* integration begins when immigrants feel confident enough to begin to relate to people other than their own ethnic group; in *identity* integration immigrants are recognized as members of the wider cultural society but at the same time with roots in their own ethnic group. This is a lengthy process. It requires not just efforts by immigrant peoples themselves, but more importantly the goodwill of the host society and its willingness to eliminate institutional prejudice/discrimination and to guarantee legal and civil rights to immigrants. Where there is identity integration there is authentic multiculturalism.[13] Pope Francis exhorts us,

> Migrants present a particular challenge for me, since I am the pastor of a Church without frontiers. . . . For this reason, I exhort all countries to a generous openness which, rather than fearing the loss of local identity, will prove capable of creating new forms of cultural synthesis. How beautiful are those cities which overcome paralysing mistrust, integrate those who are different and make this very integration a new factor of development! . . . We Christians should embrace with affection and respect Muslim immigrants to our countries in the same way that we hope and ask to be received and respected in countries of Islamic tradition.[14]

---

[12] See Arbuckle, *Earthing the Gospel*, 179–85.

[13] See Mehmet Ozalp, *Islam between Tradition and Modernity: An Australian Perspective* (Canberra: ACT: Barton Books, 2012), 49. "Multiculturalism" is a highly disputed term. For clarification, see Arbuckle, *Culture, Inculturation, and Theologians: A Postmodern Critique* (Collegeville, MN: Liturgical Press, 2010), 99–120. There must be a balance between fostering minority cultural identities and the need to ensure that minorities respect fundamental mainstream values of the dominant culture, which is a difficult challenge. See the insightful comments of Anthony J. Gittins, *Living Mission Interculturally: Faith, Culture, and the Renewal of Praxis* (Collegeville, MN: Liturgical Press, 2015), 18–21.

[14] Pope Francis, Encyclical *The Joy of the Gospel* (*Evangelii Gaudium*) (Strathfield, Australia: St. Pauls, 2013), pars. 210 and 253.

In April, 2016, Cardinal Rainer Maria Woelki, Archbishop of Cologne, publicly criticized leaders of the right-wing Alternative for Germany (AFD) political party for their statements against Islam, insisting "whoever says 'yes' to church towers must also say 'yes' to minarets."[15]

Ideology

Response 5

Be alert: Ideology is a prejudice that is integral to all fundamentalist movements.

"Ideology" is a highly contested word.[16] However, in the context of fundamentalism ideology is an action-oriented, rigid, and dramatic understanding of the person and the world. It is "the distortion of truth for the sake of collective interests."[17] A person or culture is emotionally and entirely controlled by an ideology, and it becomes for the people involved a dogmatic faith which can in no way be questioned. Ideologists *pre*-judge everything according to this dogmatic assertion and they will not listen to any argument that in any way throws doubt on the truth of the pre-judgement. For example, a religious fundamentalist will see evil in every person or group that does not think or believe as they do. Pontius Pilate claimed to be an open Roman ruler, a so-called liberal thinker, but he was in fact also a vigorous ideologist. "Pilate asked him, 'What is truth?' After he had said this, he went out to the Jews again" (John 18:38). He was so committed to the view that no objective, unchanging truth can exist that he refused to listen to any opinion to the contrary. He asked his question of Jesus, but immediately rushed off to avoid hearing the answer.[18] The truth Pilate did not want to hear was the revelation

[15] Rainer Maria Woelki, www.cruxnow.com/church/2016/05/10/two-germans-two-takes-on-islam-and-d (accessed May 8, 2016).

[16] See Lewis S. Feuer, *Ideology and the Ideologists* (Oxford: Oxford University Press, 1975); Clifford Geertz, *The Interpretation of Cultures* (New York: Basic Books, 1975), 193–233.

[17] Gregory Baum, *The Twentieth Century: A Theological Overview* (Maryknoll, NY: Orbis Books, 1999), 244.

[18] See T. E. Clarke, "Fundamentalism and Prejudice," *The Way* (January 1987): 33–41.

that Christ brings from the Father, the revelation that God loves us and that we are called to love our neighbours as ourselves.

Open to Learning

Response 6

Recognize that the Holy Spirit is the source of all truth, no matter where it is found; hence, even in the midst of the negativities of fundamentalist movements the Holy Spirit may be sending us important messages.

Despite the fact that at times Christ criticizes Pharisees, nonetheless, he reminds the disciples that there are positive points in their behavior towards himself: they caution Jesus that Herod endangers his life (Luke 13:31); they invite him for meals (Luke 7:36-50; 14:1); Jesus admires their zeal (Matt 23:15) and their concern for perfection and purity (Matt 5:20); and they shelter early Christians (Acts 5:34; 23:6-9). Certain church Fathers, such as Justin, Irenaeus, and Clement of Alexandria, either explicitly or in an equivalent manner, speak about the "seeds" sown by the Word of God in cultures.[19] Justin claims, "Everything good that has been said, no matter by whom, is Christian."[20] The Word of God is actively present, although in an incomplete way, in all cultures. This presence or glimmer of the transcendence is the foreshadowing of the fuller revelation of Jesus Christ in the Scriptures and tradition. Whatever is good, however small it may be, in cultures comes from the Spirit.[21] As Karl Rahner writes, "the very commonness of everyday things harbors the eternal marvel and silent mystery of God and [God's] grace."[22] St. John Paul II describes this mystery in these inspiring words, "Lying deep in every culture, there appears this impulse towards a fulfillment. We may

[19] See Arbuckle, *Culture, Inculturation, and Thelogians: A Postmodern Critique* (Collegeville, MN: Liturgical Press, 2010), 169; Pontifical Council for Inter-Religious Dialogue and the Congregation for the Evangelization of Peoples, *Dialogue and Proclamation*, Origins 21, no. 8 (July 4, 1991): 125.

[20] Justin the Martyr, cited by Leonardo Boff, *Church, Charism and Power: Liberation Theology and the Institutional Church* (London: SCM Press, 1985), 94.

[21] For a fuller description of this mystery, see Arbuckle, *Laughing with God*, 111–13.

[22] Karl Rahner, *Belief Today* (London: Sheed and Ward, 1973), 4.

say, then, that culture itself has an intrinsic capacity to receive divine Revelation."[23]

Responding through Dialogue

Response 7

Cultivate the difficult art of dialogue, which is the antidote to fundamentalism.

> Today, we adults need you to teach us how to live in diversity, in dialogue, to experience multiculturalism not as a threat but an opportunity.[24]

— Pope Francis

Dialogue is an "address and response between persons in which there is a flow of meaning between them in spite of all the obstacles that normally would block the relationship."[25] It is that interaction between people in which each aims to give themselves as they are and seeks also to know the other as the other is. Dialogue is authentic, therefore, if three conditions are met: people feel they understand the position of others; they also feel that others understand their points of view; and there is a readiness on the part of all to accept what is decided because it was reached openly and fairly. The capacity to listen places people in contact with the wider dimensions of the world in which they live. Authentic listening is able to break through the rigid borders that imprison fundamentalist thinking; this allows people to engage with the world beyond. In most attempted dialogues "we don't listen; we just reload."[26] In his encyclical *Laudato si'*, Pope Francis used the word "dialogue" twenty-five times.[27]

---

[23] John Paul II, Encyclical Letter *Fides et Ratio* (Faith and Reason 1998), (Vatican: Vatican Press, 1998), par. 71.

[24] Pope Francis, Address to World Youth Day (July 30, 2016), www.ncronline. org/news/vatican/francis-makes-rousing-call-millennials-get-couch-and-fix -world (accessed July 31, 2016).

[25] Reuel L. Howe, *The Miracle of Dialogue* (New York: Seabury Press, 1963), 37.

[26] William Isaacs, *Dialogue: And the Art of Thinking Together* (New York: Double-day, 1999), 87.

[27] See Frances Forde Plude, "A Listening Church," *America* (April 4–11, 2016): 22–23.

Admittedly, dialogue with fundamentalists of any type is always to be a challenging task, particularly because fundamentalists see no need of it. Patience and creativity are required in large measure to win through the walls of intolerance.

Response 8

Recall the example of Jesus Christ; he challenged fundamentalism in word and action.

Jesus Christ, sensitively aware of prejudice and discrimination among fundamentalists of his time, deliberately challenges these crippling realities in various ways.[28]

(1) By accepting Samaritans: Jews looked on Samaritans in a fundamentalist and racist manner; they were pictured as stupid, lazy, and heretical. And the Samaritans had similar stereotypes of their Jewish neighbors. Scripture scholar John McKenzie writes, "there was no deeper break of human relations in the contemporary world than the feud of Jews and Samaritans, and the breadth and depth of Jesus' doctrine of love could demand no greater act of a Jew than to accept a Samaritan as a brother."[29] Hence, when Jesus told the story of the Good Samaritan, his listeners would have been left in no doubt about its meaning for them (Luke 10:29-37). A man is left to die on the roadside. Some very important people in the Jewish hierarchical social-status system see him dying, but excuse themselves from any obligation to do anything because they are too busy. But the one considered by the Jewish people to be stupid and uncouth—a Samaritan—sees the dying Jew and immediately goes to his aid. Jesus' listeners must have been stunned to hear him say: "Go and do likewise" (Luke 10: 37). They could no longer live as Christians and at the same time hold on to fundamentalist ethnic or racist prejudices. The choice is spectacularly clear.[30]

(2) By associating with the marginalized: Contrary to the behavior of the Pharisees, Jesus associates with sinners, that is, with those who

---

[28] See Arbuckle, *Earthing the Gospel*, 158–59.

[29] John McKenzie, *Dictionary of the Bible* (London: Geoffrey Chapman, 1968), 766.

[30] See Gerald A. Arbuckle, *Catholic Identity or Identities? Refounding Ministries in Chaotic Times* (Collegeville, MN: Liturgical Press, 2013), 182–98.

are publicly known to be violators of the Jewish fundamentalist moral and ritual code: "Now all the tax collectors and sinners were coming near to listen to him. And the Pharisees and the scribes were grumbling and saying 'This fellow welcomes sinners and eats with them'" (Luke 15: 1-2).

(3) By dialoguing: While strongly disagreeing theologically with the fundamentalist scribes and Pharisees, Jesus remains friendly, open to them, or unprejudiced towards them. We even see him dining with a Pharisee, overlooking at first the fact that his host had given him no special welcome. Jesus uses the occasion to point out gently what true conversion means; he reflects on the deep repentance and love of the woman who washed his feet with her tears and "to dry them with her hair" (Luke 7:38).

The Woman at the Well (John 4:1-42): Dialogue in Action

The description of Jesus speaking to the Samaritan woman at a well is a particularly rich example of a dialogue across fundamentalist boundaries.[31] It illustrates how with the building of trust dialogue can be the catalyst for the transformation not just of the woman but also Jesus. Here they both represent the two antagonistic fundamentalist cultures: Jewish and Samaritan. The drama begins with a simple appeal to a stranger for water. Jesus is journeying through a part of Samaria with his disciples. Weary from his ministry he pauses to rest beside a famous Samaritan pilgrimage site, Jacob's Well (John 4:4-6). While the disciples are absent buying food a Samaritan woman of doubtful morality appears and she and Jesus meet alone, with Jesus taking the initiative in asking for a drink of water.

This surprises the woman for two reasons. It is a dishonorable thing for Jews to greet women in public and, secondly, "Jews do not share things in common with Samaritans" (John 4:9). Samaritan women had the additional stigma of being regarded as menstruants from birth, that is, inherently unclean.[32] By custom a Samaritan village should refuse to give Jesus and his

---

[31] See Arbuckle, *Culture, Inculturation*, 159–60.

[32] See Teresa Okure, "John," *International Bible Commentary*, ed. William R. Framer (Collegeville, MN: Liturgical Press, 1998), 1468.

disciples hospitality on their way from Galilee to Jerusalem (Luke 9:52). So, in this chance meeting between Jesus and a woman of such stigmatized cultural and personal origins, the questions are—how is Jesus to handle the situation? Will he or she end the process of dialogue that has just begun? Will Jesus continue to act dishonorably, contrary to the norms of Jewish culture? In fact they will proceed both showing extraordinary storytelling skills.[33]

Jesus fosters an atmosphere of trust between the woman and himself, which is a fundamental requirement of dialogue, by letting her know he is aware of her private life (vv.16-19). With confidence established there are two key issues that Jesus wishes to explain to the woman that knowledge of God is a gift of "living water" (v. 11), and the discovery of the true identity of Jesus himself (v. 14). Pleased with her trust in him, Jesus leads her to grasp these two realities through a conversational dialogue that is deeply respectful of her and of her ancestral and religious traditions, but at the same time plainly pointing out that worship will not be confined to a definite place either in Jerusalem or on the sacred Samaritan mountain, but within Christ himself (vv. 20-26).

The incident moves forward. At this point the woman is so transformed and energized by her conversion to Christ that she leaves behind her water jug, a symbol of human thirst and affections that can never be satisfied without Jesus Christ, and hastens to share her faith with her kinsfolk. (vv. 2-30, 39-42). There is a quite humorous touch to this incident because Jesus incongruously uses as his messenger to these Samaritan people a woman whose marital history is well known to them. However, there is another drama that has yet to begin and it focuses on the disciples. When they return with food they react as Jewish men are culturally expected to behave. They are startled, even annoyed and ashamed, that Jesus is speaking to a woman and a Samaritan one at that (v. 27). This should not be! Sharing the racist and fundamentalist prejudices of their own culture, they press him to eat, but he replies in a puzzling way by saying that his "food is to do the will of him who sent me and to complete

---

[33] See J. Martin C. Scott, "John," *Eerdmanns Commentary on the Bible*, ed. James D. Dunn and John W. Rogerson (Grand Rapids: Eerdmans, 2003), 1171.

his work" (v. 34). By contrast with the enthusiastic Samaritan woman who has gained so much through her dialogue with Jesus, the disciples ironically give the impression of being uninterested in the dramatic nature of his words and do not seem to want to learn from the incident.

The events at the well reveal two important themes of the evangelist St. John: his particular theological emphasis and the evangelizing method of Jesus. Jesus shows respect for people and their mythologies or traditions. Even when he disagrees with them, as in the case of the Samaritan belief where true worship is to take place (John 4:20-24), he does so in a culturally respectful manner. At the same time evangelization calls us to struggle against the entrenched obstacles of fundamentalist prejudice and discrimination that degrade people.[34]

(4) By respecting the dignity of women: According to Jewish culture at the time of Jesus, as in the case just described, women were considered inferior to men. However, in his daily life, Jesus expresses concern for the welfare of women, but in ways that are not condescending or prejudiced; he heals sick women and forgives sinners among them. And he appears to Mary Magdalene before he reveals himself to the apostles; she is charged to carry the news of his resurrection to the disciples (John 20:11-18).[35]

Response 9

Therefore, following Christ's example, approach other cultures and also fundamentalists with patience, respect, and a willingness to listen and dialogue.

Prejudice in all its forms is a highly emotional topic because people's identity or security can be dependent on the maintenance of their prejudices. Therefore, it is recommended not to confront large groups of people directly with what you know, or feel to be, *their* prejudices. There may well be emotional and hostile reactions, thus further

[34] See Okure, "John," 1469.
[35] See G. Soares-Prabhu, "The Unprejudiced Jesus and the Prejudiced Church," *The Way* (January 1987): 4–13.

reinforcing their prejudices. Work instead in small groups, where people feel less threatened and thus more open to listening and dialogue. The advice Pope Francis offers is highly relevant in relating to any religion or culture, even if they are not fundamentalist.

> In order to sustain dialogue with Islam, suitable training is essential for all involved, not only so that they can be solidly and joyfully grounded in their own identity, but so that they can also acknowledge the values of others, appreciate the concerns underlying their demands and shed light on shared beliefs.[36]

Fundamentalism and Violence

Response 10

Remember, violence in all its forms, for example, terrorism and bullying, is contrary to the Gospel.[37]

During his life on earth Jesus was surrounded by terror. When he was born Herod hoped to kill him along with other innocent children (Matt 2:16-18); in his crucifixion he shared the fate of doomed slaves and the powerless poor.[38] Yet Jesus Christ by word and action condemns violence as a way to achieve power over others or even in defence of one's rights. In his vision Jesus goes beyond the dreams of the Israelite prophets and declares that the fullness of the reign of God means the end of all suffering, violence, and injustice, the coming of a new community of perfect love and justice (Rev 21:1, 4). His mission from the Father is to proclaim in speech and action what must be done to realize this vision (Luke 4:18). In the Old Testament times, God was one of those who suffered,[39] but in Christ there is total identification with the violated. Jesus himself was a poor one,

---

[36] Pope Francis, *The Joy of the Gospel*, par. 253.

[37] See Gerald A. Arbuckle, *Violence, Society, and the Church: A Cultural Approach* (Collegeville, MN: Liturgical Press, 2004), 230–34.

[38] See Lee Griffith, *The War on Terrorism and the Terror God* (Grand Rapids: Eerdmans, 2002), 278.

[39] Abraham Heschel movingly speaks of the divine pathos in the Old Testament, the capacity of God to suffer because God has entered through the covenant into a personal relationship with Israelites. As they suffered, so God suffers. *The Prophets: An Introduction* (New York: Harper and Row, 1969), 24.

born in a stable (Luke 2:7) because the structures of poverty con-demned him to no better. He, the Poor One, accepts death that others might live (Luke 27:35).

The universal guideline in relating to others is: "So always treat others as you would like them to treat you" (Matt 7:12). And love must be the motivating force: "But I say this to you, love your ene-mies and pray for those who persecute you. . . . For if you love those who love you, what reward will you get? (Matt 5:44, 46). Love for one's persecutors, not the "eye for an eye" directive of some terror-ists, is to be the principle of action: "You have heard it said: 'Eye for eye and tooth for tooth.' But I say this to you: offer no resistance to the wicked" (Matt 5:38).

But Jesus is quick to explain that "no resistance" is not synonymous with accepting powerlessness. The violator wants the violated pre-cisely to agree that they are powerless, insignificant, less than human. To be in control of one's life, even under violence, is a fundamental right of every person, for it is the source of one's self-esteem and the foundation of the belief that one has significance.[40] Jesus is so insistent on this point that he uses several concrete colorful examples.[41] For example, Roman soldiers could by law bully people to carry their baggage a limited distance only and if a person offered to carry the burden an extra mile, this placed the soldier in the embarrassing situation of violating Roman practice. So, Jesus says to victims of bullying: "And if anyone requires you to go one mile, go two miles with him" (Matt 5:41).

The ministry of Jesus consists of nonviolent public protests against the violence of fundamentalists. For example, he challenges oppres-sive ritual regulations that forbid healing on the Sabbath (Luke 14:3); associates with the ritually impure, e.g., tax collectors and prostitutes (Luke 15:1-3); associates publicly with women, who were considered inferior to men (Luke 23:55); speaks with Samaritans, who were thought to be racially and religious impure (John 4); and heals people marginalized because of disease (Mark 10:46-52).

Out of love he seeks to dialogue with his enemies. As explained, while Jesus strongly disagrees theologically with the scribes and

[40] See Rollo May, *Power and Innocence: A Search for the Sources of Violence* (New York: Norton, 1988), 243.

[41] See Walter Wink, *Engaging the Powers: Discernment and Resistance in a World of Domination* (Minneapolis: Fortress Press, 1992), 175–84.

Pharisees, for example, by denouncing their many formalistic rules and regulations, he nonetheless seeks to remain friendly and unprejudiced towards them. Finally, by forgiving his executioners, he confronts violence with love. The cross, the most powerful Jewish symbol of violence and death, becomes instead a symbol of peaceful, active protest against everything that seeks to degrade and subjugate humankind and the universe. And the Resurrection is the hope that ultimately the violated "shall have the earth as inheritance" (Matt 5:4). For St. Paul nonviolence is central to Christ's teaching. To the Corinthians he writes, "I am glad of weaknesses, insults, constraints . . . for Christ's sake. For it is when I am weak that I am strong" (2 Cor 12:10). Without inner conversion and the power of Christ within oneself nonviolence is impossible (Eph 6:12-13). History shows us that wherever and whenever the call to conversion by Jesus is not remembered, those who claim the name of Christian have shown a special tendency to give loyalty to violence in its many forms: "All violence by Christians is also an attack upon the memory of Jesus."[42]

Mass Media

Response 11

Beware of moral panics fuelled by the media.

> Outbursts of rage [in the west and in Islamic countries] can . . . be stirred by political grandstanding and mischievous politicians preying on an ill-informed and aggrieved populace.[43]
>
> — *The Economist*

"Moral panics" refers to the way parts of the mass media exaggerate and over report an event by unpopular individuals and subgroups, including actual or potential fundamentalist subcultures, which then provides the foundation for a backlash by the public and officials who then label their behavior as deviant, dangerous, and likely to recur.[44] For example, in the lead up to the tragic episode of

---

[42] Griffith, *The War on Terrorism*, 48.

[43] *The Economist* (September 15, 2012): 44.

[44] See chapter 2, n. 60; Stanley Cohen, *Folk Devils and Moral Panics* (Oxford: Martin Robertson, 1972), 22–23.

the deadly interaction in 1993 at Waco, Texas, between Branch Davidians and military officials, media representatives were very willing
to work closely with government officials to describe the movement
in excessive negative light. The result was the burning of the Branch's
compound where dozens of women and children were killed.[45]

Countering Islamophobia

Response 12

*Critically assess the biases against Islam projected by politicians
and the mass media.*

> The narrative in general regarding Islam in the United States and
> Europe has been set for quite a while. For all of our sakes, it is time
> to begin writing a more nuanced story.[46]
>
> — Bill McGarvey

All cultures and religions have a capacity for fundamentalism.
Well before the current tension between the West and Islam, Edward
Said, a Palestinian-American literary theoretician, argued "that the
western media represented Islamic peoples as irrational fanatics led
by messianic and authoritarian leaders."[47] In recent years the negative
image presented by the media has intensified. It is common for
Muslims to be branded with derogatory stereotypes. Hence, the term
"Islamophobia," that is, fear and loathing of Muslims, a reality sadly
reinforced by behavior of people such as Donald Trump. Arun
Kundnani, professor at New York University, describes Islamophobia
as "a form of structural racism directed at Muslims and the ways in
which it is sustained through a symbiotic relationship with the official
thinking and practices of the war on terror."[48] The consequence of

[45] See James A. Beckford and James T. Richardson, "Religion and Regulation,"
in *Sociology of Religion*, ed. James A. Beckford and N.J. Demerath (London: Sage,
2007), 408.

[46] Bill McGarvey, "Misinformation Age," *America* (May 16, 2016): 32.

[47] See ibid.; Edward Said, *Covering Islam* (London: Routledge, 1981).

[48] Arun Kundnani, *The Muslims are Coming: Islamophobia, Extremism, and the
Domestic War on Terror* (London: Verso, 2014), 10–11.

Islamophobia is a "dread and hatred of Islam—and, therefore, a fear and dislike of all or most Muslims."[49]

The following facts are not presented to defend Islamic atrocities, but only to draw attention to the point that there is a certain dispiriting negative imbalance in media reporting. Chris Barker says, "In other words, most western politicians and media have adopted the somewhat implausible view that we in the west are angelic and that Islam is the Devil incarnate."[50] On this matter, you might recall axiom 4 in chapter 2: *Groups see their cultures as "clean" or "pure" and others as "dirty" or "impure," and therefore dangerous— to be avoided, changed, or eliminated.*

Research of approximately a million stories from "United States and European media outlets between 2001 and 2011 discovered that in 2001, 2 percent of all those stories presented images of Muslim militants, while just over 0.5 percent presented stories of ordinary Muslims. By 2011, 25 percent of the stories dealt with militancy, while images of ordinary Muslims remained at 0.5 percent. The negative coverage has only increased since then."[51] The fact is that Muslim terrorists form only a tiny fraction of 1 percent of the world's 1.6 billion people.[52] In 2006, a study of all British newspapers found that 91 percent contained destructive accounts of Islam and Muslims and approximately 50 percent spoke of Islam and Muslims as a "threat" to social order and national safety.[53] Moreover, while the media highlights the fact that forty-five people have been killed by Muslim terrorists in the United States since the attacks on New York and Washington, DC, the same media has failed to emphasize that in the same period forty-eight were murdered by right-wing terrorists.[54] Arun Kundnani also highlights the fact that the media emphasizes jihadist violence but neglects to give the same coverage to racist murders by non-Muslims.

---

[49] Chris Allen, *Islamophobia* (Burlington: Ashgate, 2010), 54.

[50] Barker, *Cultural Studies: Theory and Practice*, 4th ed. (London: SAGE, 2012), 274.

[51] McGarvey, "Misinformation," 32.

[52] Ibid.

[53] See Allen, *Islamophobia*, 96–99; Mehmet Ozalp, *Islam between Tradition and Modernity: An Australian Perspective* (Canberra: Barton Books, 2012), 244–61.

[54] See www.vice.com/read/an-interview-with-arun-kundnani (accessed May 8, 2016).

Like the violent acts we normally think of as terrorism, racist violence not only takes the lives of its immediate victims, but also sends a larger message of fear to the wider population. Yet terrorism and racist violence are not considered to be equally significant threats by governments and the establishment media. . . . [R]acist murders are rarely reported beyond the local newspaper. . . . In Europe, the violence carried out by far Right groups, which have racism as a central part of their ideology, is of a similar magnitude to that of jihadist violence.[55]

Two further significant media distortions are (1) blame for the violent struggle between the United States and Iraq was directly assigned to Saddam Hussein. Yet in 1988, after he had murdered more than 180,000 Kurds, the United States still went ahead and doubled their financial aid to Iraq and Britain underwrote a massive loan. This was rarely referred to by the media as Saddam was then seen as a crucial ally.[56] By 2002, the United States no longer needed its former ally. Iraq was named as a member of the "axis of evil" along with North Korea and Iran and incorrectly blamed for the tragic attacks on New York and Washington.[57]

(2) The Taliban are the object of negative reporting by the media, but it is rarely mentioned that during the Soviet military occupation of Afghanistan (1979–1989), the United States joined its allies in aiding the Taliban movement in its effort to force the Soviets out of the country, despite the fact that the Taliban were known for their cruelty to the country's citizens. Rarely reported is the fact that bin Laden strongly resented the stationing of US troops in Saudi Arabia believing this to be a "violation of sacred Islamic ground."[58] In 1996, Bin Laden also attacked the United States for committing "acts that are extremely unjust, hideous, and criminal whether directly or through its support of the Israeli occupation of [Palestine]."[59]

[55] Kundnani, *The Muslims are Coming*, 22.

[56] See Abdel Bari Atwan, *Islamic State: The Digital Caliphate* (London: Saqi Books, 2015), 29.

[57] See George W. Bush, "President delivers State of Union Address" (January 29, 2002), www.whitehouse.gov/newes/releases/2002/01/20020129-11.html (accessed May 8, 2016); see also Stuart Croft, *Culture, Crisis and America's War on Terror* (Cambridge: Cambridge University Press, 2006), 265–86.

[58] Barker, *Cultural Studies*, 274

[59] Interview between bin Laden and Robert Fisk for *The Independent*, www .robert-fisk.com/fisk_inerview3.htm (accessed May 8, 2016).

Response 13

Be mindful of the complex causes of Islamic terrorism.

Two theories are commonly and exclusively given for the radicalization of young Muslims that provide governments with foundations for policies in their "war on terror." The first theory is that terrorism is caused by the failure of Islamic cultures to adapt to the realities of modernity and the demands of globalization. The second theory focuses not on Islamic cultures but on the fact that dangerous people such as bin Laden have distorted the founding mythology of Islam. There is significant truth in both assumptions as this book shows. But, as this book also illustrates, we must emphasize that Muslim peoples and countries have in the past, and in recent times, been subjected to grave injustices by Western imperial governments. The poverty of Muslim migrants in Western countries is another important factor influencing the rise of terrorism. These factors, plus the Islamophobia that innocent Muslim peoples are subjected to, creates a dangerous mix, especially for young Muslims.[60]

Response 14

Understand that the vast majority of Muslims in the West are model citizens even in the face of racism.

> Faced with disconcerting episodes of violent fundamentalism, our respect for true followers of Islam should lead us to avoid hateful generalisations, for authentic Islam and the proper reading of the Koran are opposed to every form of violence.[61]
>
> — Pope Francis

Millions of Muslims live in the West—close to two million in Britain, four million in Germany, and five million in France. Islam is the fastest growing religion in the United States. The great majority live peacefully beside their neighbors and do not threaten democratic values. Governments must be proactive in assisting immigrants to integrate but in ways that respect as far as possible their cultures. For example, in France, the policy that immigrants should abandon all

---

[60] See Arun Kundnani, *The Muslims are Coming*, 10.
[61] Pope Francis, *The Joy of the Gospel*, par. 253.

cultural characteristics of their native cultures has been very slow to change. To be forced to give up one's cultural roots only leads to social and political disaster.[62]

Response 15

Be aware of the good example set by many Muslims.

Pope Francis reminds Christians that the "sacred writings of Islam have retained some Christian teachings; Jesus and Mary receive profound veneration and it is admirable to see how Muslims both young and old, men and women, make time for daily prayer and faithfully take part in religious services. Many of them have a deep conviction that their life, in its entirety, is from God and for God. They also acknowledge the need to respond to God with an ethical commitment and with mercy towards those most in need."[63]

Response 16

Remember that a simple greeting to a stranger can change hearts.

Dialogue with Muslims is exceedingly difficult, however, "we cannot leave the dialogue with Islam, but we must deepen it."[64] But how? Timothy Garton Ash, professor of European Studies at Oxford University, offers an answer. It is the personal views and behaviour of non-Muslim Europeans, *"in countless small, everyday interactions,"* that will decide whether their Muslim fellow citizens begin to feel at home in Europe or not. Of course individual preferences of individual Muslims and the leadership they receive from their spiritual and political leaders is equally important. However, Ash continues,

> if the message they hear from us is that the necessary condition for being European is to abandon their religion, then they will choose not to be European. For secular Europeans to demand that Muslims adopt their faith—secular humanism would be

[62] See Arbuckle, *Earthing the Gospel*, 167–85; *The Economist* (August 10, 2002): 9–10, 19–21.

[63] Pope Francis, *The Joy of the Gospel*, par. 252; see also Garry Wills, "My Koran Problem," *The New York Review of Books* (March 24, 2016), 16–19.

[64] Cardinal Kurt Koch, Vatican's head of ecumenical relations, reported in *The Tablet* (May 28, 2016): 5.

almost as intolerant as the Islamist jihadist demand that we should adopt theirs. But, the Enlightenment fundamentalist will protest, our faith is based on reason! Well, they reply, ours is based on truth![65]

The Power of a Greeting (Mark 10:46-52):

Bartimaeus, a blind beggar, is "sitting on the roadside" (Mark 10:46). This phrase suggests that because of his blindness and poverty he has become a social outcast. (Poor people, especially those who were ritually unclean, had to remain silent and accept their fate—which, as it was falsely believed, was God's punishment for their sins.) Even for his family and friends Bartimaeus has socially ceased to exist. Hearing Jesus approaching, Bartimaeus cries out for healing, but the crowd condemns the arrogance of someone who was supposed to remain silent (Mark 10:48). The crowd has followed Jesus and listened to his words on compassion and justice, but they remain blinded by their prejudice against people like Bartimaeus.

Jesus will have none of this fundamentalist and violent nonsense. He calls Bartimaeus to his side. Bartimaeus detaches himself from his past identity as a beggar by throwing off his cloak and running to Jesus, an act that signifies the chaos stage for Bartimaeus. The cloak is his only symbol of official identity; it is the equivalent of a license to beg. Without it he is bereft of any identity that could give him some minimum of protection: "So throwing off his cloak, he sprang up and came to Jesus" (Mark 10: 50). Jesus, the ritual leader, asks what Bartimaeus needs: "My teacher, let me see again" (Mark 10:51). Jesus heals him. "Immediately he regained his sight and followed him on the way"(Mark 10:52). The words "on the road," in contrast to the opening verse where Bartimaeus "was sitting by the road-side," symbolically mean that he joins the community that had rejected him. His social exclusion has ceased. All because someone listened and greeted him.

---

[65] Timothy Garton Ash, "Islam in Europe," *New York Review of Books* (October 5, 2006): 34. Italics mine.

Index

www.ingramcontent.com/pod-product-compliance
Lightning Source LLC
Chambersburg PA
CBHW060039030426
42334CB00019B/2394